Stories from Wisconsin's World War II Veterans

THE HERO
NEXT DOOR

Kristin Gilpatrick

Badger Books Inc.
Oregon, WI

DEDICATION

To my forever friend, my sister Shelly, who lost her battle against Cystic Fibrosis in 1997. I know this book would be so much better if she were here to edit it.

To the 'Heroes Next Door' in my family:

Grandfather John Steinman, Navy, W.W. II
Grandfather Ray Nichols, Merchant Marines, W.W. II
Stepfather Craig Nichols, Air Force, Vietnam
Uncle Paul Gilpatrick, Navy, Vietnam
Uncle Bruce Lasecki, Navy, Vietnam
Father-in-law Carl Halverson, Navy, Korea
Grandmother Lou Nichols, WAVES, W.W.II

To the Heroes Next Door who answered the call to share their stories with me, and you.

And, to the men and women of every American family who have gallantly and quietly served this country during its great times of turmoil and served their communities and families well in every moment since.

Thank you for your sacrifices.
Thank you for my freedom.

ACKNOWLEDGMENTS

There are so many who have helped and pushed me along the way to bringing this book to press. Among those to thank are:

• My parents Robert Gilpatrick and Barbara and Craig Nichols who encouraged my love of writing and history and who taught me that there is nothing I cannot do or be.

• Ann Christianson, my graphic designer for this book, who created the inspired cover and made my words look good.

• Mary Arnold, Fred Johnson and all those at the Credit Union Executives Society who afforded me the time to chase the dream of writing this book.

• Sara Cox Landolt, Renee Halverson, Barb and Craig Nichols, Dee and Carl Halverson and Steve and Susan Gordon, who helped edit this book.

• Rev. Bruce and Cindy Burnside of St. Stephen's Lutheran Church whose enthusiasm over this book is contagious and whose spiritual support has helped sustain me.

• My Little Sisters Kristy and Breona for the humor and friendship they've brought to my life, especially when I've needed it most.

• The Wisconsin Veterans Museum and countless librarians and veteran historians who've assisted me in my research.

• The 14 veterans featured in this book who I am especially honored to have come to know. They were by and large recommended to me for this book by their family or friends because they exemplify the spirit of the Hero Next Door — men and women who humbly served their country well in war and peace. They are a small sampling of the scared but determined young men fighting for their lives and for their buddies, while fighting for their country, in a place so far from home that mere mention of home hurt. I am grateful that these veterans were willing to share the often painful memories of their war experiences so the next generation will have them to learn from. I have always called these veterans heroes and feel deeply privileged to call them friends as well.

• And, my husband Steve. I never would have had the courage to see this book through without you to support, encourage — and even push — me to keep at it. I have always felt blessed that I am able to do what I love for a living. But I am more truly blessed to share that passion with a man who can be my most honest critic, my loudest cheerleader, the love of my life and my best friend.

TABLE OF CONTENTS

INTRODUCTION

Every time I've interviewed a war veteran in my work as a journalist during the past 10 years I've had the idea for this book. I lamented often to my husband how I wished there had been more room in that day's paper to "really tell the story," how some-one should write a book about this veteran or that battle. And he would quietly, and not so quietly, say, "yeah. It's too bad we don't know any writers ... ."

But I didn't get pushed far enough to actually sit down and write veteran stories until the original "Heroes Next Door" of my life — my stepgrandfathers — died within a few years of each other.

Both were World War II veterans, one a destroyer lieu-tenant with the Navy, the other a Merchant Marine. As a reporter I had always wanted to talk to them about their war experiences, to record the when and where they fought for our family's future generations. It was one of those things we talked of doing, one of those things we just never got around to doing. And then it was too late.

Their deaths before I had the privilege to know their sacrifices for our country inspired my desire to docu-ment the stories of Wisconsin's other W.W. II heroes.

This book is not the complete history of World War II, nor even of Wisconsin's part in it. You will not find the strategic details of battle here. This isn't the story of so-called great men, of generals and such.

This is the story of the every day G.I., of the small part in a massive war that individual Wisconsinites fought and survived in — that tiny area around a soldier that W.W. II veteran James Church calls his "worms-eye view of the war."

There were more than 300,000 *(Wisconsin Veterans Museum)* Wisconsin men and women, who saw that view of World War II overseas and stateside in all of Americas' Armed Forces. More than 8,300 of them were killed in action.

The 14 men in this book do not dare to represent the sacrifices and stories of all those Wisconsin veterans. They are simply, and heroically, 14 examples of the Wisconsinites who served in combat and behind the lines, of the Wisconsinites who suffered the horror, hurt and homesickness of war.

These are the recollections of life and battle from 14 who answered their country's call to arms and served their country well. These are their stories, told from what they recall of their small parts in the most far-reaching war in American history. More than 55 years have past since these Wisconsin veterans were "over there." Some memories are foggy; others crystal clear; others too painful to remember yet still vivid enough to have happened yesterday. The veterans in this book each chose which of their tales of war to tell, what pictures to show, how much to tell.

In most cases, the recollections they offer here are stories that were not often told. These veterans came home and largely tucked their memories away and got on with their lives as best they could, starting families and businesses and giving their time to helping their neighbors when they could.

In many cases those neighbors — we neighbors — still have no idea about the sacrifices the resident living next door, or down the street, made half a century ago. We do not know the Hero Next Door.

Let me introduce you to some of them.

THE WAR
IN EUROPE

THE WAR IN EUROPE

In this chapter you'll come to know a few of the Wisconsinites who fought with hundreds of thousands of Allied units to free the continent of Europe from Nazi Germany's deadly grasp. These Heroes Next Door include:

• **James Geach,** a paratrooper with the 82nd Airborne who began his combat service as the Nazis were fleeing Africa and saw his first combat as the Allies pushed into Italy;

• **Carlyle Van Selus,** a ball turret gunner in the 92nd bomb group out of England who was shot down over Nazi-occupied France and made a harrowing journey back to England through the French Underground;

• **James Church,** an infantryman engineer with Gen. Simpson's 9th Army who first saw combat in the hedgerows of France and survived the Battle of the Bulge;

• **Brothers Archie Sanderson**, who slugged his way across the battlefields of Europe as part of the 294th Combat Engineers, and **Gerald Sanderson** who flew in the flak-torn skies above as a gunner for the 815th Bomb Squadron out of Italy;

• **Joe Reilly,** a paratrooper with the 101st Airborne who saw his first combat in the D-Day invasion of France and was among those nicknamed The Battered Bastards of Bastogne for their defense of the surrounded city in the Battle of the Bulge; and

• **Ernie Tresch,** a bomber pilot with the 320 Bomb Group out of Africa and later Italy who returned stateside to become a pilot for the highest ranking military official of the war-and future president of the United States — General Dwight D. Eisenhower.

DISTINGUISHED TROOPER
James L. Geach
Island Lake
Hurley, Wis.

Life was a struggle for James L. Geach of Hurley, Wis., long before it was battle in World War II. He was born in 1922 into a mining family of four brothers and sisters in Hurley. Geach's father died when Geach was 12 of lung cancer contracted while working in iron ore mines. His mother and siblings subsisted as best they could and Geach took a assistant janitor's job at Hurley High School to help make ends meet, graduating from there in 1942.

Geach pursued a career in tool and die as an apprentice in Milwaukee before he was drafted into the Army in December, 1942, and sent to basic training in Camp Walters, Texas.

It was there that he volunteered for the 82nd Airborne's newest pathfinders platoon, as part of the equally unique 325th Glider Infantry. The Glider pathfinders would ride in and land silently in WACO CG-4A canvas gliders — or parachute like other troopers from C-47s — and hit the ground running to tackle the special and

dangerous assignments of combat, jumping in behind enemy lines and sneaking ahead to set up observation points and patrols for others to follow.

It was a job Geach performed heroically through some of the European Theater's biggest battles and in the greatest invasion ever waged, the D-Day Invasion at Normandy, France. It was there that Geach was awarded the Distinguished Service Cross, the second highest award for bravery. He was subsequently inducted into the Fort Bragg, N.C., Hall of Heroes for his D-Day valor.

Geach was assigned to the S-2 Intelligence Section of Headquarters Company with the 1ˢᵗ Battalion throughout the war and had parachuted with them into St. Mére-Eglise on the Cherbourg Peninsula for 33 days of intense fighting beginning in the early morning hours of D-Day, June 6, 1944.

About 29 days later, the headquarters company Geach was with received a field phone call from a nearby 1ˢᵗ Battalion company taking heavy fire from a German tank and infantry. The company had dwindled from some 250 down to 15 men and had lost all its officers and noncoms. They were getting disorganized and demoralized. It was an especially precarious situation since most infantry units didn't have their own tank support and only their service weapons, hand grenades and occasional rocket launchers to fight German tanks. The company needed help and a Lt. Col. Teddy Sanford sent in Capt. Knuckles, who asked Geach to come along. The two responded rapidly and heroically.

"The first thing we had to do was stop that tank. Capt. Knuckles asked for someone to take the bazooka (rocket launcher) and go up a hedgerow and try to knock out the tank. Nobody wanted to go and I could understand that because they were so demoralized. So I volunteered, though I had never fired a bazooka before.

"I ran across an open field with German infantry shooting at me to get to a hedgerow on the other side of the road. I found a farm equipment entrance with a big

15

wooden gate and hid behind it.

"The tank was almost up to me, though the road by the gate was deeper than the field so I couldn't see it. I knew it was coming closer because I could hear and feel it rumbling. It was so close that I thought that if I hit the side of the tank I'd have to worry about shrapnel coming back at me.

"The tank almost came up to my position where I could have gotten a great shot but then it stopped just short and all I could see of it was a few feet of its barrel. Then it fired and the ground around me just shook. I thought, I can't let it fire at those guys again!

"So, I aimed as best as I could and shot at the barrel. Now, if we were in a movie, that would have gone right down the barrel and the tank would have blown up. But that's not how things work in real combat.

"Instead the shot missed and hit the bank behind it. So I fired another couple of rounds and that scared them good! They pulled back so fast they were running into ditches and everything! I think the tank thought our artillery was zeroing in."

The problem was there were six infantry with the tank. The infantry had sought shelter in a hedgerow. Alone, Geach attacked the enemy infantry and quickly killed four with his rifle as the other two retreated.

Though they never saw the tank again, Capt. Knuckles and Geach realized the company would still need help to take out some Nazi pillboxes and a building up ahead. They remembered that a company close by had tank support. As the rest of the company moved up the hedgerow, Geach ran to get those tanks in on the fight.

He got to them and the tank drivers offered him a ride into position. "I said 'no thanks. I'm going to take my chances on the ground. I didn't want to get blown up in one of those things. The ground had kept me alive just fine so far, thank you.'

"So, I ran all the way from there to where I had shot the tank and then led our tanks into a field and into

position. By this time the enemy had launched a strong counter attack. There was plenty of machine gun and small arms fire at us, especially when we hit the field, but I just kept running. And, our tanks took out the pill-boxes and the building."

Geach made that dangerous dash without much thought to his own safety and more thought on keeping the company going and winning the fight. "The job had to be done and you just assume you're going to stay alive. You don't have any idea how you're going to stay alive but you really don't have time to think much about it anyway."

Geach and Capt. Knuckles were soon relieved by fresh troops and sent back to their headquarters unit where they continued to push their way into France. He recalls that after 33 days of fighting in Operation Overlord, Geach's division continued on with just 41 of its 113 officers and 956 of its 2,281 soldiers.

It would be five months before Geach would learn he was to win the Distinguished Service Cross for his effort that day, with a citation that read, "for extraordinary heroism in action against the enemy on 5 July, 1944, in France ... the personal bravery, initiative and gallantry exhibited by PFC Geach reflects great credit on himself and the Armed Forces."

In fact, Geach's actions that day made such an impression that he is included in the Department of the Army, 82nd Airborne's annual training guidance manual. His actions are cited as why it's important for every trooper to be trained to use every weapon, because in combat, you never know what you may be called upon to do.

ITALIAN SEASONING

It was a lesson Geach learned well during the fierce fighting he'd endured in Italy long before the D-Day invasion.

Geach first arrived in World War II in North Africa then with the regimental "comando platoon." He came

to North Africa just as the fighting there was dwindling and just in time for the first invasions of Italy, the invasion of Sicily.

Geach's glider company faced strong resistance from both the Nazi and Italian enemy as he and his other rookies in combat struggled to secure the airport at Gela, where about 15 of his company were killed.

More tragically, Geach recalls many of the paratroopers and glider units flying in to fight that day never even made it out of their planes because of a friendly fire incident involving the U.S. Navy. At first, the War Department denied it until veterans went home and started talking to newspapers but eventually the Navy admitted to shooting down 27 Allied aircraft on their way into Sicily. With 27 troopers in every plane and 15 soldiers in every glider, it was a tremendous loss of life.

"The explanation the Navy gave was that there were German planes flying above us and we got caught in the middle. But I'm inclined to think someone was trigger-happy and mistook us for German planes."

It wouldn't be the last time Geach would witness tremendous

James Geach, right, sat for a formal photo with other GIs in 1944.

loss of life, though from then on it was mostly the enemy's doing.

Geach's division was back in North Africa in reserve as the 1st, 3rd and 36th division headed into the Salerno Invasion Sept. 15, 1943. Those divisions were struggling to establish a beachhead against heavy resistance.

Just 15 days after Sicily, Geach and company got an urgent call back into battle.

"After a dinner of C-Rations we were just sitting around and all of a sudden the whistles started blowing and we knew we were going back in," he recalls.

His company was put into Salerno by LCIs, infantry landing craft, behind the German's position to divert the enemy's attention from the beach since they would now have to fight on two fronts.

Though they were seasoned veterans, Geach says they were still scared. "I was scared like everybody else. But the difference going in now is we were experienced. We were a little more confident and knew what to expect."

But that doesn't mean there still weren't lessons to learn.

After Salerno, Geach and other Pathfinders had to establish an observation point on Mount San Angelo. By this time they were used as regular ground infantry having landed days before and now working as Pathfinders on the ground.

"We set up an OP on Mt. San Angelo just south of Naples so we could observe the Germans. The OP was between the two artilleries — there's and ours. They were lobbing shells over our position and, to get to the other side they had to get as close to the top of the mountain — and us — as possible.

He remembers the feeling of a big bomb hitting near his position — a frequent occurrence. "The dirt would roll down on you inside and the ground would tremor. We would often hear them whistling which sounds bad but that's what you want to hear because they generally would be past you before you could hear them whis-

tling, especially the German 88s. If you heard the whistle, you were safe."

The Pathfinders made their OP in a big bomb crater the Germans had occupied until Geach's unit kicked them out.

It was in the struggle for the bunker that Geach learned a valuable combat lesson. "I had already learned the importance of cover and staying concealed and about not being grouped up together so the Nazis could pick you off easy with a mortar shell," he explains. "That night I learned not to trust things I see and hear blindly. They are not always as they appear.

"When we were going up the side of the mountain the Italians had a lot of goats on the side. And all these goats wore bells. You could hear those bells ringing constantly. So after we kicked the Germans out, that next night we could hear those bells and just assumed they were the goats.

"What we didn't know was that the Germans had taken the bells off the goats and were wearing them to camouflage their own sounds as they launched a counterattack against us. They were in our lines, right among us, before we even knew it.

"That was really scary; it just happened so fast. We were taken completely by surprise," Geach recalls.

It took Geach and the Pathfinders three to four hours to end the assault in mostly hand to hand and close fighting, a horrific fight he prefers not to recall. "We killed most of them but a few got away."

The unit stayed on top of the mountain for six days with little water or rations.

After watching the Nazis pull out of Naples for those six days, Geach and a few others formed a patrol to go into Naples and check for snipers and remaining troops. "We never saw any Germans and never fired a shot."

They did, however, have an unexpected and pleasant encounter with one of the Allies' top brass, General Mark Clark.

"We were coming out of Naples and were sitting on

the curb taking a break. We saw a Jeep coming down the road and could see the flags on the front so we knew it was a general. Then as it got closer we saw the three stars and knew the only three-star in the area was Gen. Clark.

"We got up quick to stand at attention and he stopped in front of us and said 'Hey. You're in combat; forget the salute.' Then he saw our 82nd Airborne patches and said, 'You guys are doing one hell of a job. I want to shake your hands.' And then he did, and he had a photographer from *Life* magazine with him. I thought we'd be in the magazine; I even wrote my mom to have her watch for the picture but we were never in there."

After their brush with military fame, Geach and the other Pathfinders moved into a little damaged former hospital in Naples. The two-story building proved comfortable enough despite the lack of beds or heat.

Geach remembers noting how Mt. Vesuvious, the active volcano there, really did glow red like a ruby at night, something their own bombers had used as a guide for their runs when bombing the Naples harbor. That night, the Germans did the same.

"We had an unbelievable air raid that night. Oh, Geez! Did they bomb us."

The next morning as the troops emerged to survey the damage they noticed an excited group of Italians on the sidewalk across from the hospital. "They were yelling and pointing at the building and we thought they were excited about the air raid."

However, an Italian American who spoke the language quickly deduced the real reason for the excitement. There was an unexploded bomb on top of the hospital, a fact quickly confirmed after some scouts sent up to investigate came "flying off of the roof!"

The company called for an Army demolition crew and an American trio was sent in, which — after further investigation — determined the bomb was actually a torpedo on a parachute that had not yet gone off. So, they called in a Navy demolition crew but there weren't any

close by, so a British crew was sent instead.

"The three of them went up there and started disarming it. And, it went off and just blew all three of them into little pieces!"

The damage to the building was actually minimal since the torpedo blew up instead of blowing forward on impact like it would usually do if it hit a ship.

Geach was in Naples for two more weeks before they headed back to base camp in England to wait for and train for the next spring's invasion-for D-Day.

HOLLAND INJURIES

After his D-Day heroics, the seasoned and as yet uninjured PFC Geach would run short on luck during his glider trips into fighting in Holland as the Allies continued to run the Germans home in the fall of 1944. It was in Holland that his division took out the bridge at Nijmegen, Holland, Sept. 23, 1944, as part of the Market Garden operation.

It was on that mission that Geach's Waco CG-4A glider crashed into some trees Sept. 23, 1944.

"The problem is the glider pilots can't see below their glider too good and since they're loaded so heavy they can't gain altitude to pick a different landing location once they lose altitude. When you drop down off the plane, you've got to go down and land.

"That's what happened to us. Our pilot had to land and there was a glider below us so all he could do was go down a different direction and try to put the body of the glider between two trees, knowing that coming in at 70 miles per hour, the trees would sheer off the wings but hoping the men in the body of the glider would be spared.

Sitting toward the front, Geach had a good view of the crash as the canvas and aluminum glider split apart on impact. "We went plunging to the ground when the wings came off and we were tumbling and rolling and breaking apart. There was only fabric over hollow aluminum tubing and our safety harness was attached to

James Geach with his best friend and future brother-in-law, Harry Machie, in Naples, Italy.

the tubing so they easily came undone and we were thrown all over. The glider was loaded with grenades and mortar ammunition and everything was strewn across the field.

"I got knocked out and when I woke up I had my head resting against the landing gear. I was black and blue from the top of my head to my toes. We had lost six guys and one guy had a broken back.

"To make it worse, we were in combat so the Germans were shooting at us the whole time. Even as hurt as we were you find you can do a lot when you're getting shot at and we were able to move to cover and keep fighting."

The Hero Next Door

And, keep fighting he did, battling his way to his second medal of valor, the Silver Star. As part of the intelligence section, Geach often led night patrols behind enemy lines to ascertain enemy positions. On Sept. 25-26, Geach led a 48-hour patrol as much as five miles behind German lines, about one-quarter mile from Germany's Reichwald.

As General Gavin wrote in Geach's Silver Star citation:

PFC Geach, a scout, ... led a reconnaissance patrol deep into territory closely guarded by an alert and active enemy. Operating over unfamiliar ground, and often under attack from machine gun fire, he skillfully utilized minor terrain features in country lacking natural cover to evade the enemy and execute his mission. PFC Geach guided his patrol through streams, canals and mine fields, by roads under constant enemy patrol and through the outer defenses of the Germans up to their main defenses near the boundary of the Reich. His diligence, coolness, courage and leadership during a period of 48 hours, resulted in the acquisition of valuable information concerning German strength and dispositions and movement in the area.

Geach recalls those "spooky" reconnaissance missions well. "The first night we came to a canal in No Man's Land, between the two armies, and we were wading down the middle of it. It wasn't deep, just about chest high. All of a sudden this dog came up and started barking at us. Well, we couldn't have that; it would give away our position. We had two of the Dutch underground with us and one of the boys grabbed the dog and drowned it before he could give us away."

Geach came even closer to being discovered that night. "We had a German combat patrol go right by us in the dark. We were going uphill and they were going along the crest of the hill above us. We laid behind a wooden gate on the ground, trying to make ourselves part of the ground, and they went right through that gate and never saw us!"

The War in Europe

After surviving combat in Europe's bloodiest battles to date, across Italy and into the Normandy invasion, Geach's luck was about to run out.

The night he returned from that patrol, Geach was wounded in the left shoulder Sept. 26, 1944, while in the Kiekberg Woods, near the Reichswald Forest on the German border.

Geach was in a foxhole during heavy combat when he was struck in the back by a piece of shrapnel, about the size of his thumb.

"The Germans had dug foxholes for years in advance in the woods and there were ferns growing out of them, which often hid machine guns. Capt. William Ausenbaum, Cpl. Sparks and Col. Teddy Sanford and I were near some of those foxholes we'd taken over when the colonel asked me to go back to headquarters and get some rations.

"All of a sudden they started shelling us. I was outside of the hole and they were in it so I started to jump into the hole. As I did, a burst of artillery hit the tree above the hole and I took shrapnel in the shoulder.

"Capt. Ausenbaum always swore that I saved his life that day because I jumped on top of him like that; but I wasn't jumping on him to save his life, I was doing it to get out of the way of the shelling and try and save mine."

Geach survived the shelling and the wound he sustained though it was a serious and painful injury.

"Some guys talk about not realizing they're wounded until they look down and see the blood. But I knew I was hit the instant I was hit! It felt like someone hit me with a fist as hard as they could and then it really started burning. I mean burning! After all, this was hot metal going into my body. It went through my airborne pack, my jacket and into my left shoulder and it's still there today.

"I was laying there and could feel the blood running down my back and they were shelling so constantly that I couldn't even move for about 20 minutes. I just laid there wondering if I was bleeding to death."

Buddies, from left, somewhere in Holland: (Front row) unknown private, Darcy Kaminski of Chicago, Harry Mackie; (back row) Private Anderson of Des Plaines, Ill. and Geach.

Geach believed, however, that he would survive. He had a strong faith that carried him and he knew that "my father was watching over me" over there and always.

Fortunately, help was soon sent. Since Geach worked with the command post and knew Col. Sanford well, when word reached him that Geach was wounded, the colonel called on doctor Capt. Bassett to take a Jeep and go and get him.

"He and an aide came. But the aid was so scared and shaking so badly that when they removed the packet strapped to my leg (which paratroopers carried for medical emergencies) he messed up giving me my shot of morphine. He didn't realize he had to take the protective cover off the syringe first. So I thought I'd gotten a shot but I never did. Boy, did it sting!"

They sent Geach by ambulance to Brussels, Belgium but the bombed out road was quite a bumpy ride. From there they evacuated him back to England thinking the shrapnel may have punctured a lung.

Luckily, Geach had no such injury. The piece of shrapnel just lodged under his shoulder blade that x-rays revealed. "It was a big enough piece that the doctor said he could take it out or just leave it in and I could always have it removed later if it bothered me. That was a week after being wounded and I felt pretty good so I just left it in. It's still there."

Geach briefly returned to the 325th Glider Infantry at Sissone. Soon after his arrival, Geach was told he would be sent home to the states on leave. He was one of about 40 such men from all different units assigned to go back to the states on a public relations tour as a reward for exceptional service.

His first stop was home, in Chicago where his mother was living during the winter with her new husband. While there Geach had agreed to stop and visit the parents of his best friend in his unit, Harry Mackie. Harry had given him a ring to give his sister Margie Mackie when Geach arrived.

"I said, 'why, do you want me to marry her?'" Geach notes, never imagining he would do just that.

"I lost the ring on the way home but still stopped to visit. We got engaged the first night we met. We just knew it was meant to be right away. And it was; we've been happily married almost 55 years!"

Though they wanted to be married right away, both families talked the couple into waiting until Geach was out of the service. When Harry Mackie heard the news, shortly after winning his own Silver Star, he was not surprised. "He said he figured the two of us seemed pretty compatible and he kind of thought something like that might happen. So my best friend would be my brother-in-law."

After just a few short weeks together, Geach was back in combat — heading for the Battle of the Bulge in late December, 1944. The wedding had to wait.

"I had heard about the fighting and demanded to be taken back to my company," says Geach who could have elected to be assigned to a stateside unit. "We

27

had started the war together and we would end it together."

GERMAN ATROCITIES

Geach rejoined his company in January, 1945, for the final days of fighting in the Battle of the Bulge and the chase across Germany to the Nazi's surrender.

Near the end of the war, the company reached Ludwiglust, Germany, where they liberated a concentration camp — with dirt floors and no heat — the sights and smells from which not even combat had prepared them for.

"When we went in, there were still people in there. They were walking skeletons at least those that could walk. Many were so weak they couldn't even lift their heads and just laid in this building with a dirt floor. You could see the trenches where they'd buried so many of them.

"You could see that some who get around were feeding off the dead ones, eating the fleshy parts of those who'd died so that they could stay alive.

"I just couldn't stand the smell; I started to get a weak stomach and my stomach was pretty strong after all we'd been through."

Luckily, Geach says, that was the only concentration camp they liberated. Shortly thereafter as the Americans moved in from the west and the Russians from the east, the entire 21st German Army surrendered to Geach's division, rushing to surrender to Americans before the Russians reached them, on May 3, 1945.

"For 24 hours a day, over three days, they kept coming through to us. We took everything and had fields lined up with half-tracks tanks, weapons of all sorts and equipment. They were badly beaten and showed it. It looked as though they had wanted the war to end, knew it would end, long before it did."

It was not the mighty German army the Americans had once feared. "Towards the end there were lots of kids and old men fighting. They were only 12 or 13 years

old some of them but you didn't realize it until you saw them up close. All you saw was a German shooting at you. You had no idea."

Geach's service ended Sept. 24, 1945. He shipped home and was married Oct. 13, and founded a sporting goods store in Hurley with his brother. The Geachs had three sons, Robert, Barry and James Jr., and a daughter, Cathy. However a mine strike forced them out of business so he finished his tool and dye apprenticeship and with his in-laws help got a job in Chicago.

After two and a half years, he became a salesman and eventual branch sales manager in Milwaukee for Salada-Sheriff & Horsey Food. When they turned to brokering and he was out of a job. He applied at Caterpillar where he worked in maintenance for 21 years, working first, second and third shift and forming two bowling leagues.

He retired back to Hurley in 1984, where he is a life member of the VFW Post 1580 and served as vice president of the Island Lake Property Owners Association. He also volunteers in the community for cleaning culverts and cutting trees down for the town. He worked so hard he's trying to enjoy retirement with snowmobiling, ATVs, his pontoon boat and a collection of pistols many of which he got while fighting in World War II, including a handmade, pre-1942 German Luger.

Geach's hard fought victories live on in his memories and in the love of country and the 82nd airborne he's instilled in the next generation. Two sons and a grandson have served their country well too.

In fact, it was his grandson Matthew Decker, an 82nd paratrooper, that would bring Geach's World War II heroics to the forefront of the peers who never knew about his combat duty.

"Matthew was in Fort Bragg and went to the Hall of Heroes where they had all the Congressional Medal of Honor and Distinguished Service Cross winners. He knew I won it but couldn't find me. His mom, our daughter Cathy, called Fort Bragg, and eventually Congressman Tom Petri, to get them to recheck the records.

James and Margie Geach on their 50th wedding anniversary in October 1995.

"It turned out that when they entered everything into the computer they missed mine, but they had kept the paper records and that proved it. They were in the process of building a new Hall of Heroes and were embarrassed about missing me. They invited me to take part in the dedication; it was a tremendous honor."

When word of the long-ago honor spread, many of Geach's neighbors and fellow Caterpillar workers were stunned. They knew nothing about Geach's gallant service.

"When I came home from the war all I wanted was to

be a civilian. I kind of divorced myself from the military and didn't keep in contact. I didn't even talk about it to people I worked with for 21 years at Caterpillar so people were kind of surprised."

Surprised and proud. Since, Geach has become some-what of a Hurley hometown hero. He was the marshall of Hurley's Heritage Parade in 1995, the year of the Hall of Heroes rededication.

But for all the accolades, Geach is most thankful for just surviving the war and having the opportunity to live a good and happy life.

"Not a day goes by that I don't feel guilty for being one of the lucky ones that made it home to enjoy this life with my wife, four wonderful children, grandchildren and great-grandchildren."

UNDERGROUND GUNNER

Carlyle Van Selus
Portage, Wis./Highlands Ranch, Colo.

arlyle Van Selus returned home to Portage April 21, 1944, after being missing in action for nearly two months. He said then that he had "no story to tell" about being shot down over Nazi-occupied France in February and spending 40 days walking and hiding, while attempting to escape — with the help of the French Underground — back to the safety of England.

"At the time, the military told me I couldn't say anything. We were still at war," explains Van Selus. But today, he has no such restriction. And, he has quite the story to tell.

Van Selus, was born Jan. 15, 1923, in Vesta Township, Minn., and was raised by his maternal grandparents in Belview, Minn. after his mother died when he was one. He stayed until after his sophomore year in high school when he moved in with his father in Portage, Wis. He graduated there in 1941 and briefly attended the Milwaukee School of Engineering and worked as a welder before enlisting in the Army Air Corps Nov. 17, 1942.

He admits he had no real idea of what he was in for

when he volunteered to be an aerial gunner.

"I was offered my grandparents' farm so I wouldn't have to go into the service but, to me, that was not an option. I felt it was an opportunity to serve my country and flying appealed to me."

Van Selus especially liked the thought of being a gunner, so he volunteered. "It's like flying my own plane. In the ball, all by myself underneath, it turned 180 degrees in elevation, 360 degrees in azimuth. You get an odd sensation operating it with the movement of the plane." *(Memories are based on Van Selus' interviews for the Wisconsin Veterans Museum and with this author.)*

After five weeks of challenging, strict, cadet-style training at Tyndall Field in Florida, he finished bombardment training at Buckley Field in Denver and Salt Lake Army Air Base. He was shipped to Ephrata, Wash. where his 10-man crew was formed. It included: pilot 1st Lt. M.V. Shevchik of Ambridge, Penn., co-pilot Lt. James Thorson of New Haven, Fla., navigator Lt. James Williams of Jasper, Ala., bombardier Lt. Donald Periolat of Chicago, radio operator Sgt. Robert Sidders of Giltner, Neb., two waist gunners Sgt. Max Craig of Anderson, Ind. (later killed in a mission over Bremen, Germany and replaced by Sgt. William Scanlon of Chicago) and Sgt. Francis Wall of Coal Hill, Ark., tail gunner Sgt. Francis Higgins of Bangor, Maine and Van Selus as the ball turret gunner. Their engineer was Sgt. Everett Stump of Kanova, W.V.

After four months of training, Van Selus and crew went to a Topeka, Kan. staging area before they were sent to England as replacements for crews lost in combat. They were among 18,000 men who left Camp Kilmer, N.J., on a troop train to Brooklynn, N.Y., aboard the Queen Mary to Glasgow, Scotland.

By the fall of 1943 the Portage High School graduate was operating a ball turret beneath a B-17 bomber and gunning down fighters in bombing runs over France and Germany, assigned to the 92nd bomb group, 326th bomb squadron under Colonel Reed's direction at Podington,

33

The Hero Next Door

England, 80 miles northwest of London.

Riding at the bottom of a bomber was an especially dangerous occupation. "You couldn't wear a parachute in the ball turret so if you're in trouble, you've got to get out of the ball and get a parachute on before you could even bail out. But it's so easy to understand now why young people fly. I don't know if it's guts or if you just don't know any better, but it was exciting."

HANGING ON

Van Selus was no stranger to such excitement — to the dangers of war — by the time he hit the ground running in occupied France Feb. 8, 1944.

He came to know danger on his first mission when Van Selus flew with a different, veteran crew (as did all new replacements), for experience. That's when Van Selus watched as Ed Smith, riding as co-pilot in another plane, was killed. Smith and his wife had just had a baby when he and Van Selus were training together in the states.

"I'll never forget it. He was off our left wing and the plane took a direct hit. It just left formation and was flying away from us. All of a sudden, one big explosion. There goes 10 men. It's a blob in your mind."

The next 11 missions Van Selus flew were riddled with Nazi fighters and anti-aircraft fire (flak). There were no real milk runs — a term airmen used to define "easy" runs over areas of little resistance.

"When you're fighting, it didn't bother you as much if you were firing at the enemy; you knew they were firing at you. The worst thing was flak (anti-aircraft fire). You just had to sit there and take it.

"There were two kinds of flak. I remember when we went to Bremen it was like a solid black wall and you had to fly through it. It was terrible to look at but it was not nearly as dangerous as concentrated flak, where there were only four bursts. Whomever saw the first one, called in its position, say 'flak at 2:00 level, high or low.' Then the next one's gonna be closer, then the third

34

one's going to be real close and the fourth one would be a direct hit. So pilots would take evasive action and that was dangerous. Of course we all knew that and that scares you. You're getting shot at and there isn't a thing you can do about it except evasive action."

It was amazing how well the planes — and the men inside — could take such heavy bombardment.

"I saw some planes come back with holes so big you could drive a Jeep in, and they still flew. In fact on all our missions, planes came back with holes or some kind of damage."

Van Selus' plane was among those that almost didn't make it back from a run to Bordeaux, France, on New Year's Eve, 1943.

"The Germans had laid a perfect smokescreen over the city so we had to go to a secondary target, which was an airbase."

It was on the Boredeaux mission that Van Selus got an upclose view of a ME 109. "He came through our formation several times before we got him. He was alone. We'd pick him up about 1,500 yards and start firing. As he came closer he would start rolling so when he went by, the bottom of the plane — which was heavily armored — was facing us. They were great pilots, they had good planes and I had to admire them for that."

"The problem was we didn't have enough fuel to get home. When we got back to England, there was really thick fog which was an every day experience. When you have 20 bombers flying almost wingtip to wingtip, you're not going to fly in formation in that weather, so the formation breaks up. Then, everyone stands by with their parachutes on ready to bail out because, if you felt the propwash from another plane, you knew you were too close.

"Meanwhile, the pilot would be looking for a hole. On that mission, he found one, went down and we landed. That plane must have bounced 50 feet in the air!"

Though every mission could have been a gunner's

last, Van Selus came as close to dying as he ever has on a Dec. 1, 1943 mission over Germany when the turret door was shot off from underneath him.

Van Selus hung in what was left of the ball by his safety belt with little protection from the 55-below-zero temperatures for 8 and ½ hours.

"The pilot told me to get out of the ball since I would have no protection from the cold. I asked for permission to stay in the ball so we wouldn't lose the use (protection) of the two machine guns (in the ball turret).

"And, I wasn't about to sit and do nothing on that plane. That would drive me absolutely berserk.

"I shot down a German fighter plane that day and stayed in the turret until we reached the English Channel. Then other crewmen pulled me out because I was unconscious."

The pilot left formation to get Van Selus to the nearest possible medical aid, landing at a P-47 fighter base where Van Selus spent many days in the hospital.

Though frostbitten on his hands, face and feet, Van Selus' courageous efforts earned him both the Distinguished Flying Cross and the Purple Heart.

NO. 13 LIVES UP TO SUPERSTITON

However hard that mission was, Van Selus was about to face a longer challenge, staying alive in Nazi territory.

A short time after he recovered, on Feb. 8, 1944, Van Selus and his crewmates took off on their ill-fated 13th mission, with little foreshadowing that they might soon be parachuting out of their burning plane somewhere over occupied France.

"Things went wrong right from the start. We had a problem because the other squadrons didn't form the way they should. You have a specific time you have to leave the coast, formation or not. We had our squadron together but other squadrons weren't there. So, we were actually flying alone that day.

"We had gotten a new gunner by then, Francis Wall

from Arkansas. He was a real good guy to fly with, a good gunner. Maxie Crabe had been killed and we got a waist gunner by the name of William Scanlon, the best I ever flew with. He had a lot of missions, he was flying his 24th or 25th mission with us and you only had to fly 25. When I say only, very few of them got 25. But he left the United States, went to Canada and joined the RCAF. When they went to England he joined the RAF and he had been to Berlin three times at night as a tail gunner. Then he came over to the U.S. Air Corps and we got him.

"That morning Scanlon got hit with flak in the cheek. It went right through his cheek, took his jawbone, teeth, the whole works; he was bleeding profusely. We never could turn back for an injured man, so we still had to continue the mission.

In an attempt to get Scanlon medical attention, Wall prepared to parachute him out, in hopes the French would find and treat him.

"The pilot called the other waist gunner and told him to open Scanlon's chute and stuff it under his arm. However, Scanlon wanted to open his own chute because we were at about 30,000 feet and he would not have had enough oxygen to last until he got to a low altitude.

"Then, just when he was ready to bail out, we had a fighter attack. Scanlon got hit again and it actually knocked him out of the plane. I watched from the ball turret and never saw his parachute open."

And, the already horrific 13th mission was not yet over.

"Later in the afternoon, we were hit by FW190s. It was the same old story, he came out of the sun.

"Our plane took a hit in its No. 2 engine.

"Fire just wrapped right around the ball turret. I was sitting in the middle of flames, so I rolled up the ball and went to get out. I knew I had to hurry because we were sitting there with a full bomb load, 100-octane gas filling the wings, all our oxygen equipment (which is explosive) and all our ammunition. We saw too many

37

take a direct hit and blow up.

"I had heavy boots on and my foot was caught in the stirrup. When I finally got free, I fell outside the turret into the plane. The gunner, Wall, saw me, got over there, plugged me in on the main system and flipped it over to pure oxygen.

"When I came to and realized what was going on, I plugged into another system and grabbed the other waist gun because Wall was the only one we had left. I started firing. Then, I remember Wall tapped me on the shoulder and we saw the control cables were hanging down in the plane, so we had no contact with the front. We decided to bail out.

"The radio operator went berserk, so it ended up we had to throw him out. Then Wall bailed out. When I was ready to bail I went to another door right back by the tail where my close friend Higgins was. I stopped and saw that his leg straps were hanging down. I pointed to them and he grabbed them and hooked them back up. If he'd have opened his chute like that he'd have gone right through it."

Bailing out was not a much safer option, especially since Van Selus and crew had no training about how to parachute.

"They'd always tell us there's no reason to practice something that has to be perfect the first time. Well it was simply because they didn't have anything to train us with.

"I was wearing a chest pack and remember thinking you'd just fall straight down. Well, you don't fall straight down. When you hit that prop wash, you swing up and you're spinning and turning. When I started slowing down and opened the parachute, man was I surprised! Bang! I'd hit that hard (when the chute opened), a real jolt! Then, everything was peaceful, away from the noise. I actually saw our plane blow up. That I'll always remember.

"While I was coming down I was circled by two German fighters. They didn't try to shoot me; they could

have very easily but didn't. I also took the oxygen mask off and just threw it away. Why that's important I don't know, but it was. Then, when I got down to low altitude it was really windy on the ground and I drifted for miles. There was a water tower I was afraid I was going to hit but I missed and landed probably 10 miles away."

It was not the easy, feet first landing of training films.

"I came into this field surrounded by a hedge. When I hit, the shroud lines were in front of my face from the chest pack. I went over backwards, hit the back of my head and it knocked me out and also hurt my back. When I came to, I was at the other end of the field. It was a good thing I was wearing a chest pack because the parachute was dragging me on the ground from the shroud lines in front of my face. I was wearing a Mae West and that inflated, which protected me."

THE FRENCH UNDERGROUND

His first moments in enemy territory, in the Beauvais Region of France, started badly and then seemingly got worse.

Soon after he landed, Van Selus was picked up by two German soldiers. But for some unknown reason, the Germans were not overly excited to take him prisoner.

"They searched me but I think they actually just let me go. I was in their truck and they stopped and left. So, I just jumped out of the truck, kept it between me and where they were and just kept going. (Perhaps) I was a nuisance and they were probably looking for guns that I was carrying. I didn't have any. I had eight compasses hidden on me and one was a big pocket watch and they got that. I had another in my knee pocket, but they overlooked it."

Van Selus knew he was not out of danger, not by hundreds of miles.

The crew had been on their way to bomb Frankfurt, so Van Selus knew he was deep in France. His training had taught him that if you bail out inland to try and head south across the Pyrenees Mountains and into

The Hero Next Door

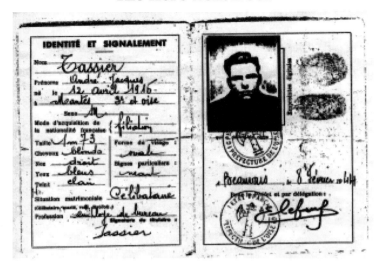

This is a fake passport the French Underground gave to Carlyle Van Selus to use as he made his harrowing journey across Nazi-occupied France to England.

Spain.

"Though Spain is neutral supposedly, the American counsel would check the jails every week. But there was less problem getting you out of Spain than an occupied country. And, there was no way to tell us how to get in touch with the French Underground. If you're shot down in Northern Germany up in the North Sea area, that was a different story, you were supposed to look for boats that had laundry out, red, white and blue, they were the people that would help you."

Given his location, Van Selus headed south. Since he spoke neither French nor German and was wearing his American uniform, he traveled by night and hid by day.

"One morning I was sitting in a hedge at the bottom of a bank. The bank was covered with brush, and I had this hedge spread out so that the sun was shining in on me. I looked up the hedgerow and there was this guy walking toward me. Quietly, I turned around, got on my hands and knees, went up through the brush. When I got to the top there was a guy right in front of me. I

surprised him as much as he surprised me. I just put my hands up and surrendered.

"He turned out to be a Frenchman. He put his hand up and leaned toward me and said 'comrade.' He kissed me on both cheeks. He and his son were going down to cut wood. They took me down there and the boy left and went back up into the village. He came back again and soon a girl came with black bread with meat, either wild boar or rabbit, and wine. Man, I was hungry and I had a feast.

"They couldn't speak English and I couldn't speak French, but it's surprising how you can understand one another. The point was that I was supposed to sleep and, when the sun went down, they'd come back to get me. I was tired after I ate all that and crawled into the brush and slept.

"That night they came back out, got me, took me up into their home with a wooden fence all around it. My back was so sore I can remember this man rubbing my back with some kind of grease — probably wild boar grease — that was warm. The other thing I remember was there was one big pillow that covered the whole bed. I was there for I think five days, and they had a French-English dictionary. I looked up 'toilet,' and they took me out the back door. The toilet was the whole backyard!

"Then, one day, a man came to see me who couldn't speak English either but he wanted my dogtags. We were always told to never argue with the Underground and, to me, this guy was supposed to be the Underground. I realized when he left, that was a mistake. Now, without dogtags, I'm a spy if I'm captured. So I got the message to these people I was with that I had to get these dogtags back and they got one of them for me. Turns out that — and I didn't know it for some time after — but everyone that helped you along the way got compensated by the American government, that's why everyone wanted a souvenir. They had to have some proof.

The Hero Next Door

"A little while later, a guy came in an old truck and we drove to an unknown town some distance away. When we arrived we went into a home. Those people were scared to death, but I stayed there until dark. Then we went across the street to a big framed house.

"Everything was rushed. When we got there they took me upstairs to a room on the second floor. Then they explained to me, that a French Gendarme (policeman), who collaborated with the Germans, lived right below. So they hung a bell on the gate. If he was coming [it would ring] and I had to stay there and just lay on the bed; if he was leaving, I could move around.

"There was an old lady there who spoke broken English. She would take me for a walk at night. The streets were cobblestone and you could hear the Germans' boots on it. When we met them, she'd grip my arm real tight and be talking a blue streak. Of course, I didn't understand a word but neither did the Germans.

"Incidentally, one day the old lady said, 'comrade come, comrade come' and my pilot Shevchik came! He could speak perfect French so he wasn't having a problem. They had him living right next door to a German officer, because the French felt the closer you are to your enemy, the safer you are and that's why they did the things they did. They also said things like 'Germany could not win the war because they had no sense of humor.' The French did."

Later, the Underground moved Van Selus to a new location. This time he was living in a straw cowshed out on a farm.

"Every night the teenage son would come and get me and take me up to the house and I'd have a real good meal. The first thing we'd have was potato soup and I love potato soup."

Then, one afternoon, two men came to visit Van Selus.

"One was a great big bruiser. He had a Mackinaw jacket on and the other was well dressed, derby hat, silk scarf, gloves — the whole works — and he could speak English, no problem. He talked about several different things and all of a sudden said "Who plays with Bob Hope in movies?" I knew then that I was being interrogated by the Underground. I said 'Bing Crosby.' He wanted to know how many bases on a baseball diamond and I said, "three bases and homeplate.' He asked me a whole bunch of stupid questions like that, but they were things that every American would know and the Germans wouldn't. He eventually asked me about all my military, all the crews, my home base and that type of thing and then he even got to my family in Wisconsin.

"When he finished talking, he pulled his hands out of his pocket and had a gun in each hand. He smiled and put the guns away, but I didn't think that was funny! That shook me up a little bit but there was a reason for that as well; I may have been a spy. In fact, he explained that they couldn't take me with them because it was just too dangerous and someone would come and get me the next day."

The next day came but no one returned to get him and Van Selus grew worried, concerned he had trusted someone he shouldn't.

"When I was up to the farm house that night I was really concerned, wondering, 'I don't know if those were Germans or who they were.' So I was going to start walking again. And these people had a fit. They wanted me to stay one more day. So I did.

"That next day this great big bruiser came, he was driving a car with the steering wheel on the wrong side and drove like a maniac into Beauvais. We went into a church, went up in the steeple and here's this Jack, the well-dressed guy. He said this big bruiser wanted to apologize for not coming the day before. What happened was he went to an apartment house to see a girl that lived on the 2nd floor. When he knocked, a man came and invited him in. He said 'no,' he just had a message for her. Talking to this guy, the bruiser noticed a slight German accent, so he hit the guy, knocked him back into the room, ran down the hall. When he grabbed

43

the banister, the guy shot his little finger off. That's why he didn't come to get me."

Van Selus hid in the steeple while the Underground tried to teach him how to act like a Frenchman. Jack gave Van Selus the crucial documents he would need to even attempt to travel through France to England — a forged passport and travel papers, no matter that his name on one was Tassier and on the other it was Kerharo.

They told him he would take the train to Paris by himself, a scary proposition for someone who didn't speak French.

It was unsettling too since Van Selus, a devout Lutheran, would be making the trip with his faith in the Lord to see him through, but without the symbol of his faith he had so far carried into battle.

"My faith in God was strong throughout, evidenced by the fact that I carried a small pocket Testament on all my missions. When I was in the French Underground, they thought it was too dangerous for me to carry (anything written in English) so I gave it to a French woman whose brother was a priest in Switzerland and she wanted to present it to him."

But the Underground prepared him well for the dangerous journey, drilling him on everything he would need to know to travel alone on the train. "The biggest danger was that someone would talk to me. I was to pretend to be asleep or read."

"I was going to follow several steps behind a guy to the train station. When we got to the station this was going to be the hairy part because when you go in the train station and then you leave to go out to the train, at that door, that's where they check your papers. There were two Gendarmes but one of them was a German. And, they told me not to trust them. At one time early in the war, they collaborated with the Underground until the Germans found out about it. Then they put a German with each Frenchman.

"I had my papers checked. You always went through

the gate with a line of people, handed one of them your papers and they would hand them back and you kept going. The fear was someone would speak to me so I had to be sure I was in a line of people. I just handed them my papers and they'd just hand them back. The Germans probably didn't speak French either.

Remembering not to talk and managing to keep his emotions in check was exhausting work, but "when your life is at stake you can do amazing things."

Van Selus made it safely on the train but that night the trip got even more dangerous. Passengers were told that English Mosquitos had bombed the tracks and they would have to walk.

"I didn't know what was going on. There was a lot of commotion so I followed the crowd to a small train station. It was dimly lit and the crowd was all standing around waiting for something. But, I noticed there was one guy walking around in a Mackinaw jacket and a derby hat. He always knew where I was and it made me nervous. I was trying to stay out of sight and here this guy was watching me."

Soon Van Selus and the mysterious man boarded a train for Paris, arriving at the station after curfew.

"I was supposed to go to the waiting room and signal the Underground person waiting for me by removing my beret with one hand and brushing my hair with the other. When someone else did the same, I was to follow that person.

"But people stayed on the train because it was after curfew so I did too. It was the next morning before I was in the waiting room."

Moments like that with the Underground were the most stressful of Van Selus' escape. "They were the most stressful because I never knew what was going on. I always had to be ready to leave on a minute's notice and never knew where I was going. The Underground didn't trust anyone and families didn't trust their next door neighbors because they didn't know who they were collaborating with."

45

The Hero Next Door

Fortunately, Van Selus' worries could ebb for a time the next morning when he spotted his contact.

"In the morning I went into this waiting room and I'm brushing my hair like crazy. I didn't know if it would be a man or woman. I was supposed to remove my beret and brush my hair twice and replace the beret. If someone did the same that was the signal."

A teenage boy, named Renee', gave him the signal.

"We got on the subway, rode for quite a while, got off, walked for several blocks, went into the courtyard of a large apartment building and walked up six or seven stories. Then, he knocked on the door and this woman came in her housecoat. He said something to her and she was petrified. We went in and what had happened was the night before the Germans raided the place where the Underground was and Renee was down waiting for me and so then he didn't know where to take me that next morning. This woman was a friend of his and that's why he took me there. Her name was Margo. But I didn't stay there because she had a sick daughter and they introduced me to her and said 'no fear, no fear' but on the bottle it said something about typhoid and 'no fear,' yeah."

Instead, Van Selus stayed with a friend of the woman who lived across the hall.

"The next day, Renee came back and had this Jack with him, the well-dressed guy. Jack was very perturbed because he didn't know these people, but he talked with them and was satisfied. I remember this woman, the lady where I was staying in that apartment, because she worked in an aircraft parts factory and had a map and showed me exactly where it was. She wanted us to come over and bomb it and she worked there, but they hated the Germans that much.

"Jack came back every day to try to teach me how to act like a Frenchman. He wouldn't tell me when we were going to leave or how, or anything else."

AN ARRANGED 'MARRIAGE' TO FREEDOM

In order to get out of France, Van Selus would have to travel into the tightly secured area within 25 miles of the French coast.

"I needed a special passport for that area and so I needed another picture taken, but the Nazis staked out all the photo shops and camera stores." To avoid detection, the Underground sent Van Selus with an old woman to a store's photo booth. "I stepped in and out quickly and we then hurried away. The Underground members did the rest."

Getting out of Paris was a little less complicated. Van Selus only had to get married.

"We sneaked out by drawing a lot of attention to ourselves. This very pretty French girl — a regular member of the Underground — posed as my bride and we pretended we were newlyweds off on a honeymoon to the coast. The Underground people crowded the train station like our relatives, waving us off."

The happy couple rode the train overnight to St. Brieuc over on the Normandy Peninsula — a place crawling with Gestapo.

"If it hadn't been for her, I'd have been found out. If anyone had spoken to me, we would have been caught and her life would be in danger, not mine. I'd be a prisoner of war most likely."

After changing trains to "a puddle jumper that had anti-aircraft guns on top of each car," they arrived somewhere along the coast.

They didn't check papers there and the two just walked down the path and met up with the last person Van Selus was expecting.

"We were walking down a little path and came around the corner and a man said 'pick up the suitcase follow the man on the bicycle.' I looked up and realized the man talking was the same man that I was worried about at the dimly lit train station while riding the train to Paris! And the girl was still with me until we got up

around the bend and he caught up with me and said, 'this is as far as she goes.' She had tears in her eyes when she kissed me on both cheeks. That was the last I saw of her."

Van Selus followed the man on the bicycle to a church basement where a priest brought him wine, meat and bread.

"This guy told me to make myself comfortable; he had no idea how long we were going to be there. He wouldn't tell me where we were going or anything but there was an old car in there so I crawled in it and went to sleep. The man returned later that day and offered me a Camel cigarette. I almost took his arm off — Man! A Camel cigarette! For all intents and purposes, I was home!"

Van Selus and the man were sitting talking on two stumps that night when he suddenly told Van Selus to get his coat on, they were leaving. They walked only a couple miles in the pitch black night until they reached a crossroads where there was a store and a truck.

"He said get into the back and there were other people in there. We drove into a wooded area and, after some confusion, I went with two Frenchmen, still lugging the Gladstone suitcase which they told me to guard with my life."

After splitting up, Van Selus' group walked along a path to a board fence where they went into a farmhouse. To his pleasant surprise, there were 13 other Americans inside, eating as much potato soup as they could since they didn't know when they might eat again, and waiting with Van Selus until it was time to go.

The Underground led the men to the steep cliffs along the French coast.

"We split up again and crossed some streams up to our armpits and I still had this suitcase and I remember carrying it over my head. There was just moonlight as we descended the cliffs and one of the Frenchmen took my suitcase. We were all wet and cold and laid in these rocks along the beach. I had my suitcase back and we were watching for a sign. I saw just a flash; it was an

English PT boat and those sailors rowed in to pick us up.

"I was cold, wet and tired but happy to be on the road to freedom!

"I remember, the PT boat left real slow and then all of a sudden they opened up and we took off. I have no idea to this day what city we came to in England. That's because the escape route we took was one they only used a few weeks out of the year because the moon there had to be just right — enough so you could see to descend this cliff, but not when that PT boat was out there. That was planning ahead; they knew what they were doing.

"I also remember the first thing they gave us when we got aboard the big ship, a half a glass of rum, a shower and English uniforms with the suspenders and the works.

After arriving in the unknown English port, Van Selus and the others boarded a train that was all shaded so no one could see its contents and they couldn't see out.

Van Selus was soon in London; his Underground ordeal was over. But, he was still a long way from going home and, with just one dogtag, fake papers and a suitcase, he still had to prove who he was.

"I was taken in a staff car to a secret address, 66 Brooks Street. The place was actually guarded because they didn't know who I was — I could have been a German spy — until they brought someone from my homebase to identify me."

Because Van Selus had been shot down and returned to England with information, he was not to fly in combat again as the Germans would immediately take him for a spy if he was shot down. He was to be sent back to the U.S., but first, he was further interrogated and debriefed at the United States Army Strategic Headquarters in London where he was issued new identification papers, a new uniform and money, as well as confidential papers of explanation.

He had strict orders not to talk to anyone about what

happened. "That paper had 'confidential' in big read letters across the top. They told me to go out, do anything I wanted but never to talk about this thing. If I got picked up by MPs for any reason, just show them the heading of this, 'Confidential, Headquarters European Theatre of Operations, United States Army Office of the A.C. of S., G-2.' on it; that's all they had to see."

HOMETIME

Van Selus was soon winging it back to the states, recalling one stop in Newfoundland, Canada, "was the first place I could spend American money again." He flew over New York City at night and remembers noting the contrast between it and the blacked-out city of London an ocean away.

Van Selus' orders were to go to Fort Sheridan, Ill., with a 23-day delay enroute. "It was on a Sunday and I went to a movie. I was going to surprise my parents because they had gotten a telegram that I was missing in action. But at the theater, I ran into a guy from my home town and that blew that story so I called home and my half brother and sister were the only ones home. They were young. When the folks got home they told my father and stepmother I had called and I was at some fort but they didn't know where. My dad knew right away and drove to Fort Sheridan.

"On Monday morning, about April 10, I was getting new orders cut and this Captain said 'I gotta tell you, your father's been down at the main gate since 6:00 this morning!' The captain had a driver take me in a Jeep down to the gate. There, we had a very emotional but happy meeting. It was also the first opportunity I had to completely relax after a period of several months."

Finally coming home was a great relief but also a difficult time. "Everybody wanted to be so nice but I couldn't pick up a glass of water without spilling it; my nerves were just shot. I talked to schools and the Kiwanis club and places like that but, after I was home

20 days, I left. I just wanted to be by myself."

After two weeks in Atlantic City, Van Selus was sent to a St. Petersburg, Fla., military hospital where he could talk to doctors and rest.

"They didn't want you to worry about anything; they had all kinds of entertainment, deep sea fishing, you name it. If you wanted to take a nap, who cares. That was the attitude of the whole thing. When you wanted to talk there was a doctor. I finally got so sick and tired of that place that I asked to be shipped out and that's exactly what they wanted. They sent me to the Good Hotel in Miami Beach for two weeks and then I was sent to Laredo, Texas from there."

Just before he left, while getting his final medical clearance at the hospital, Van Selus is still amazed at the walking miracle he ran into.

"I was walking down the hall, I had just gotten my clearance and a ward boy called me back. And, there was ... Scanlon ... the guy who was shot up! They had wired up his jaw, he was pale, thin and sick. It was Scanlon though. He was tougher than nails and that just made my day! He said he pulled a delayed jump (waiting to open his chute) to a low altitude in order to conserve oxygen and that's why we did not see his parachute."

Soon after, Van Selus graduated from instructor school at Laredo and eventually made his way to the Army Airbase at Bedford, Mass., where he was one of only five chosen to attend MIT to learn about the new gunnery radar equipment for the tail of the B-29. He then moved to the secret proving ground at Eglin Field in Florida to test it. "I shot down 20 OQ and PQ fighters with it, which were remote controlled aircraft and I thought, 'Man this thing is great!'"

So great Van Selus volunteered three times to go to the Pacific with a B29 but he was never allowed to return to combat. Instead, he returned to Laredo.

"They didn't know what to do with me, there weren't any ex-combat men back at that time so I was at this

51

permanent part of the barracks and got to be friends with some guys who worked in the time section of post-operations. Every night we'd go up there and play cards. An assistant operations officer, Captain Fields, asked if I wanted to come work in the time section, saying 'Sgt. Madrid is the only GI there with all these girls and he can never go anywhere. All you have to do is answer the phone.' It sounded good and I was assigned to them. A week later they shipped Madrid out and I was chief clerk in the time section post-operations.

"I read regulations and found out that you're not automatically taken off flying status upon arrival back in the states. I took it in and showed it to Captain Lackness. He said, 'don't tell anyone but find yourself a pilot and go out and fly.' I had to have 12 hours to collect three months back pay. When I went down to collect my money, they had a fit down in finance and said not to let anybody else know about this.

"That year was wonderful because I was on flying status making good money and every weekend I would fly with Captain Fields in an AT-6 and we'd go out and buzz cattle and bounce the thing off clouds. We had a good time, so when I was ready to go home on furlough, all I'd have to do was find a pilot and have him fly me home."

Despite the tough times, Van Selus loved his time in the military. "My military career was the highlight of my life, secondary only to getting married and having four wonderful children and five active grandchildren."

Van Selus gave up those times when he was discharged Oct. 27, 1945.

After that, he studied business administration at the University of Wisconsin-Madison until his father approached him one day with some bad news.

"He and my stepmother were getting a divorce. He had a business of funeral supplies and said 'you're my only son and he'd like to have me take it over.' I didn't know anything about selling; I didn't have any money. He said that's all right the whole thing will be taken

care of. So, I left the university and moved to Pardeeville.

"The first thing that I ever learned to sell was folding chairs and got a franchise from Bentwood Products company of Louisville, Ky., and sold several car loads of chairs because right after the war everybody needed chairs — funeral homes, churches, you name it.

Van Selus gradually worked into the funeral supply business. His father left and married a girl from Denmark, Wis., and moved there leaving a young Van Selus with the business he didn't care much for.

"Finally, I had enough and sold out the merchandise. I put everything that I owned in my car and headed west, about 1953.

Van Selus went to his uncle's ranch near Casper, Wyo., spending a few weeks there before going to work for Northwest Schools.

A REAL MARRIAGE, A GREAT LIFE

Seven years after "marrying" the French girl who saved his life, Van Selus married for real. He met Lois Heaps in Pardeeville, Wis., in 1951, when she was working in the bank there. He married her in Casper in 1956.

The Van Seluses raised four children, living in Salt Lake City and then Denver where he worked as the personnel director for Patricia Stevens Career College for several years. He then went into the industrial chemical business for 10 years with Certified Laboratories out of Irving, Texas, before starting his own chemical business.

After his uncle received a patent on a hoist for hauling long farm machinery, Van Selus struck a deal with him to manufacture the hoist in Grand Junction, Colo., until his partner died. "That took care of that business."

He then went into the communication business with American Cable and eventually United Artists. He retired from there in 1988.

In his spare time, over the years, Van Selus was an American Legion and Masonic Lodge member, taught

The Hero Next Door

Sunday school and served as head umpire in little league, senior league and big league for all of Colorado for six years. He finds more time now to enjoy his favorite hobbies of golf and fishing and spends plenty of time with his five grandchildren and plans to again join the Legion and now the Veterans of Foreign Wars.

"Once you're in the military you're never going to forget the experience. I have a lot of respect for the military, especially the Air Corps. There's something about being a foreign war veteran; I'm closer knit with someone who's been in combat. A lot of guys have been in service but it isn't everyone who's ever been in actual combat and that's different."

It's a pride he believes must be shared with the younger generations. "This country was and is the greatest country in the world. I just hope the younger generation realizes what a privilege it is to live in this great country.

"World War II brought about many changes that affect the way we live today. For example, **Carlyle and Lois Van Selus** before the war there was little air travel but today it is a major means of transportation. That is just one good example of the many good things that came out of the war. We must never forget that there were many good young men and women who paid the price for what we have today!

"I'm very proud of my service and I wouldn't give any amount of money for the experience I had in flying combat missions. I wouldn't want to relive it but thank goodness I went through it."

Van Selus will never forget his service, those he served with and those who risked their lives to see that he survived that service.

"I would like very much to return to France and find the places I was at and to thank the people who saved my life and the lives of so many of us. Though there probably aren't words in either language to say thank you enough."

SOLDIER ENGINEER
Jim Church
Elk River, Minn./Portage, Wis.

Jim Church, born March 1, 1925, has served his country well from the Battle of the Bulge to the Race to the Moon.

Since his sophomore year at Portage High School in Portage, Wis., when his teacher Julia Rusch encouraged his mathematical talents and interests, Church knew he wanted to be an engineer. He was determined to let nothing get in the way of the education he needed to realize his dreams. Not even the Germans' Nazi army would block Church's destiny to serve his country in its greatest war so he could become the engineer that would one day help that country gain one of its greatest achievements, landing on the moon.

Church began his quest for an engineering degree at the College of Engineering at the University of Wisconsin-Madison in September, 1942, after his Portage High School graduation.

After one semester, Church was old enough to answer the call to duty he'd heard since the Japanese bombed Pearl Harbor Dec. 7, 1941. He enlisted in the U.S. Army and was inducted at Camp Grant, Rockford, Ill., and sent to Camp McCoy (now Fort McCoy) near

The War in Europe

Tomah, Wis., for basic training in May, 1943.

There Church earned an Expert-M-1 Rifle medal despite using his left eye and shooting right handed as a way to compensate for a childhood injury to his right eye, an unusual shooting technique he perfected squirrel hunting around Portage.

"When I first went to basic training, my gunnery sergeant screamed at me when he saw how I fired my rifle. He said I would knock my face off firing that way. So a beer bet ensued which I won, along with the expert qualifying score, and I never got any more lip from gunnery sergeants."

After basic and additional training, Church participated in the Army's education program (Army Specialized Training Program) and continued his engineering studies at the University of Illinois, Champaign. The program entered 150,000 of the brightest draftees into college, offering to pay them Army wages to advance their education and benefit the war effort.

By Christmas 1943, the Army's need for Normandy Invasion troops outweighed its ASTP program and college soldiers like Church were reassigned to units preparing for the invasion.

Church retrained in Camp Ellis, Ill., to recover and salvage battlefield equipment, which might be in short supply.

His unit was one of three quartermaster companies initially attached to Gen. Omar Bradley's First Army headquarters in Normandy and at one time or another assigned to its various divisions. They were transferred to Gen. Simpson's 9th Army when it formed in the fall of 1944.

Church's unit performed few of the tasks it was specially trained for and spent most of the time doing what the soldiers learned in basic training — fighting for their country.

"Because there was a plethora of all kinds of Army equipment flowing from England to Europe, we rarely performed the work we were trained to do. We were

The Hero Next Door

James Church, top left, and his buddies capture their first Nazi flag in France in 1944.

mostly used as a back-up rifle company and even left our two, 5-ton tank-recovery wreckers in England when we crossed the English Channel. Except for our personal equipment, the field packs and rifles we took aboard, we never saw our wreckers and other working equipment again."

Church had been one of the hundreds of thousands of troops that sailed to Europe aboard the Queen Elizabeth, converted from a pleasure to a military troop ship. "22,000 of us crossed the Atlantic without any escort in seven days. My unit was berthed in the tourist swimming pool on E-deck and I perspired a lot at night anticipating a torpedo."

They landed in Scotland and moved to southern England for training.

About 20 days after D-day, then private first class Church landed in an LCT (landing-craft-tank) on Omaha Beach a few weeks after the initial bloody landing. Still, the landing was not without peril.

"Our LCT off-loaded us on a galloping pier of huge floating steel boxes that were lashed together. Somehow the 6-by-6, two and a half-ton truck I was driving, and I, withstood the pier's attempt to buck us off."

By then the beach had been policed of bodies and roads cleared through the beach wreckage so troops

58

could advance several miles inland to bivouac at the village of Sees.

It was within the 80-square miles around that town that the 1st Army had been pinned by the Germans since landing, and Church along with it.

"As support troops our task was mostly to hunker down and survive except for occasionally probing German lines with patrols to extend that hedgerow line. As equipment and supplies were pouring up from the beach in a never-ending stream, the need for retrieving equipment — the task we trained for — was almost non-existent.

"As many guys experienced, my first 'pants-wetting' combat event was a German artillery barrage in Normandy. The concussion of exploding shells shocks your brain and body into numbness and you are sure that you are going to die. No hole or slit trench you are in is ever deep enough and you just hunker down, hope and pray a lot."

In all the war, Church recalls that "less than a dozen of the guys in my 674th QM unit were killed, mostly from stepping on land mines."

Of all that the 18-year-old first saw of the remnants of combat, Church has two distinct lighter memories of his "first day in that place."

"First I can still almost taste the delicious coffee we boiled in a helmet which revived us after sleeping on the cold docks of Southampton, England, and the rough Channel crossing.

"Second, I remember the laugh we had at the shock a fellow soldier named Brownfield had when we told him he had unnecessarily broken off a relationship with an English girl after she told him she was 'knocked up.' She had only meant to tell him she was tired. It was a language problem."

And Church remembers how he and other troops spent the Fourth of July, 1944. "I remember the unique celebration on the coast of Normandy about one month after D-Day. To celebrate the Fourth, at about noon,

most American artillery pieces fired one round — only one — at the Germans. It apparently confused the hell out of them."

BREAKING THROUGH THE HEDGEROWS

Thereafter the memories are mostly battle scars of trudging through hedgerow country, pushing the Germans back through France and into Holland.

"There were a million of us surrounded and pinned down by the German Army in 80 square miles of Normandy real estate. The town of St. Lo was the command center of the German resistance, which prevented our advance deeper into France."

Then, in mid-July, a massive American Army offensive launched, preceded by a tremendous bombardment by Army artillery and the Army Air Force, which included 1,800 planes of all types — heavy bombers, dive bombers and fighter aircraft — Church recalls. This breakthrough became known as the St. Lo Breakout and started pushing the Germans into a running retreat across France.

That breakout was not easy. Church especially recalls witnessing the air war losses in the fight from the ground perspective.

As they slugged their way from Normandy, Church was with a buddy Kenny Halterman from San Luis Obispo, Calif., who had a brother that flew P-47s.

"One day, the unit was at the Meuse River and that pilot came in low and rocked his wing in a greeting to his brother. Just then an ME109 came out of the sun and got him. As we all watched, he exploded. The next day, Kenny volunteered to transfer to an infantry unit."

FINDING REST, RELIEVING BOREDOM

The tragedies of the Normandy battles were replaced by quick steps of mass movement as Church spent almost a year in the field, moving from Normandy through central and northern France, Belgium and Holland.

It was a journey spent largely in the open, in all

weather and conditions.

"As we moved west, and then north, nipping at the retreating Germans' heels, we sometimes found shelter in barns or public buildings; we didn't kick civilians out of houses to occupy them until after we crossed the German border. In friendly countries we usually camped out, or dug-in in fields and forests, through all kinds of weather.

"Sometimes when we liberated a village (outside of Germany) and were going to remain for a few days, and there was little danger of Germans, townspeople would invite us into their homes. One such village was Freeren, Belgium (now called Vreren) where my squad spent about one week in the home of an old bachelor farmer. He mothered us with cow's milk and dried our wet, muddy shoes when we came in from patrol. I took a picture of him with a camera — which I had previously liberated from a German soldier — the day we moved out.

"I can recall the inside of that house as if it were yesterday. My wife and I returned to that town 50 years later for the D-Day celebration and the town literally

James Church stands in a destroyed German town in February 1945.

shut down and threw a parade in honor of the town's liberators as I was the first one to ever return. They rededicated the town's war memorial with speeches and honored us with a banquet. It was truly a humbling experience."

Vreren wasn't the only place Church and his comrades found a little shelter and great hospitality.

"A buddy of mine, Arnaldo Saenz, from a tiny Tex-Mex border town called Los Saenz, single-handedly liberated an unattended winery in northern France. Arnaldo and I checked out of the war for the remainder of the day as we quaffed what tasted like wine from a spigot in a high, large-diameter vat, daring each other to climb up and see what might be floating in the vat until, eventually, we didn't care. After filling our canteens with that uncertain liquid, we returned to soldiering."

They found rest and relaxation of a less inebriating kind along the road as well.

"Several times, before the weather turned cold, we were trucked to Rest Centers for very brief showers in portable, outdoor Army facilities and were reissued clothes washed in mobile Army laundries.

"During cold weather, getting occasional showers was a problem, but once we got showers in an underground coal mine in Heerlen, Holland. Another time, after we penetrated Germany, we were taken to a German health spa for baths and clean clothes. This spa, which was operated by tame Germans (who claimed they never supported Hitler) had wonderful, private, deep tiled bathtubs and we luxuriously soaked up to our necks in hot water."

But, rest periods aside, Church and his unit were trucked around a lot. And, time spent in transit and waiting for orders was mostly filled with boredom. To pass the time, soldiers tried everything from singing to cards and other "games."

"At those times when we were out of danger, well fed, rested and in good spirits, we sometimes sang while

62

being trucked about. Several songs we invariably sung were British tunes "I've Got Sixpence" and the ever-popular "Roll Me Over (in the clover)" and "Knees Up Mother Brown." We tended to avoid singing the sentimental American songs for obvious reasons.

"Music was important to us. Songs from our Big Band high school days and early war years played on the BBC and Armed Forces Radio were bittersweet lifelines between our thoughts of home and the misery and brutality that consumed our lives. It was often the glue that held us together.

"During daylight, if someone had a deck of cards and weather permitted, we'd play non-stop Blackjack. Pre-agreed-upon Army rules for the games were strictly enforced by all the weapons lying around.

"Or, sometimes, we competed in target practice at trees with pick-mattocks. They were part of the Pioneer Set, which most trucks and Jeeps had on their sides. This was a frame with a shovel and a pick-mattock (a two-foot long wooden handle with a steel head, a sharp pick on one end of the head and a flat adz on the other). We would compete in accurately throwing that thing and sticking the pick in a tree, from distances up to about 30 feet. We became so deadly accurate with those things that they might have been our weapons of choice if we ever engaged Germans in hand-to-hand combat.

"These tools were also extremely useful for digging foxholes, especially in forested areas laced with tree roots. Of course, when we needed one, they could never be found and we had to resort to using our entrenching tools (folding shovels). When sufficiently frightened, bayonets and helmets were exquisitely efficient for this too.

Nonetheless, as soon as Church got a foxhole finished he was back on the road and marching toward the inevitability of digging another one.

"Fixing up a cozy foxhole was tantamount to immediately being ordered to move out — which provided op-

James Church on Victory in Europe Day, May 8, 1945, in front of a building in Hamm, Germany.

portunity to dig another hole, a forerunner of Murphy's Law."

Given the short time one spent in a foxhole, Church says many would be amazed at "how comfortable a foxhole can be made — with little shelves scooped into its walls for knickknacks and some branches and straw at the bottom to keep from getting too muddy when it rained. And, if you could cover it with your shelter-half (half a pup-tent), you might risk the light from a wee candle for letter writing — that's of course provided you had a scrap of paper, an envelope and something to write with."

Sometimes, as Church learned in Belgium, you could make those foxholes too comfortable.

"I had traded some cigarettes for a small, two-part carbide lamp...and some carbide rocks. When water drips on those rocks, they release acetylene gas, which burns and lights the lamp. The upper part of the lamp is filled with water and screwed into the lower part in which the rocks were placed. The rate the water dripped was controlled by a screw and the gas coming out the tube at the top was lit — just the thing for a cozy foxhole nightlight, right?

"Not exactly. One night a buddy came looking for me and dragged me unconscious out of my covered hole because the lamp had burned up all the oxygen! I never used it again!"

Next to home, the buddies that looked out for you were everything to soldiers like Church. "Most of them were guys you bonded with because you were dependent upon each other to stay alive and that develops a special kind of relationship. Though I remember most the names of the guys in my company, three of us were particularly 'tight,' Gene McKeel from Oregon, Paul Herman from Kalamazoo, Mich., and I. We watched each other's backs with great care.

"Patriotism tends to fade in combat zones in favor of self-imposed peer pressure, i.e.: you and your buddies are bonded and you never let your buddies down. That's your primary motivation."

But while most men Church served with could tell similar non-combat-time stories, Church is sure few relieved the boredom the same way he did much of the time.

He spent it reading, not reading letters from a girlfriend nor other literature that might appeal to young men far from home, but doing math problems from his engineering textbook.

"Some people have trouble believing this, but in my combat pack I carried my Math 51 textbook from the University of Wisconsin-Madison, from the semester I attended there, throughout the war. When appropriate, I studied this book and made notations in its margins as to where I was at that time, if I knew.

"I guess that was extreme dedication (and life expectancy optimism) to achieve a goal of earning a post-war engineering degree. This treasured book survived the war and almost 50 years but was accidentally discarded during our move to our new home in September 1993."

Despite the notations in his book Church is relatively sure that neither he nor most privates really knew where they were most the time. "As a private, we never

65

knew where we were so we were never lost. Oh, we knew the direction we were going but as a private you had a sort of worm's eye view of the war."

A WORM'S EYE VIEW OF THE BULGE

That was a closer view than Church wanted when he became embroiled in the Battle of the Bulge. Church had been in a 1st Army hospital near Liege, Belgium, being treated for trench foot (a condition where wet, frozen feet eventually turned black) for several weeks when the Germans attacked and broke through the lines in the Ardennes Forest of Belgium, just 15 miles away on Dec. 15, 1944. As the Germans' advance threatened to overrun the hospital, Church joined the fighting wounded and cooks and barbers helping to turn back the German breakthrough.

"We almost-ambulatory patients were quickly suited up, given the few rifles around and trucked out to meet the Germans. We filled in as replacements in the patchwork defense that was mustered. Things were messy."

Anyone who could operate a weapon — and could find one — formed the ad hoc squads and companies thrown at the Germans in the Bulge. Church himself picked up a MP-38 off a dead German soldier. "I fought with that machine pistol a long time, until I ran out of ammunition and found a more familiar American M-1. I loved the M-1 rifle because I was good with it and it kept bad guys from getting too near. At those times when I got clean shots at the bad guys and they disappeared, I usually did not know if I hit or missed and I didn't care too much as long as they didn't reappear."

Fighting alongside strangers with unknown capabilities made everyone nervous and trigger-happy. "You were fighting with guys you didn't know and often were surrounded by enemy troops and armor."

Soldier-to-soldier recognition problems were extra difficult, compounded by specially trained squads of Germans which infiltrated the lines dressed in American uniforms, driving American vehicles and speaking

excellent English.

"We invented all kinds of wonderful test questions to challenge suspicious GIs, like 'what kind of musical instrument did Harry James play? (trumpet),' 'what were the names of the Andrew Sisters? (Patty, Laverne and Maxine),' and 'who won the 1944 World Series (I forget.)' American casualties in the Bulge were undoubtedly greatly inflated by GIs who were not hip to the music or baseball of that era."

It was the music of the era — and the hell of the moment — that combined for a hauntingly memorable Christmas as weary troops battled the Nazis and the cold to survive the Battle of the Bulge.

"We were just scared kids sleeping in the cold and snow and fighting to survive any way we could. It was so cold and miserable that you sometimes didn't think dying would be so bad. I once read 'it's not hard to be cold for a day but to know you will be cold for the next day, the next week, the next month, can be very hard' and I found that to be true. We had nothing to look forward to. But it made good soldiers out of us."

And it made thoughts of home that much warmer and Christmas 1944 that much harder, Church recalls.

"It was Christmas Eve 1944 and my squad had found shelter from the Belgian snow and bitter winds in a stone barn that was missing most of its walls and roof. Our leather shoes and clothes were wet and frozen, and we were exhausted.

"As darkness fell, we shared our food and sought safe holes in the rubble to curl up in a blanket, if we were fortunate to have one. Someone must have scrounged a battery-operated radio because, from out of the darkness, came the strains of American music from Armed Forces Radio ... Softly, so as to not give away our location, it played Frank Sinatra's *I'll Walk Alone.*

"As I went into the half sleep/half alert we all became accustomed to, that idiot radio played *White Christmas* of all songs. I could hear sobs coming from several directions. We were no longer the rough, tough 19-year-old veteran soldiers. We were just tired, scared kids who wanted to go home.

There was thankfully little time for such longings for home, however, when just the effort of trying to eat cold food — when you could find it — and sleep and stay warm with a wet, frozen blanket exhausted you as the combat numbed you more.

Just trying to keep warm nearly cost Church his life. He had traded some cigarettes for a sleeping bag and had snuggled in for a warm nap. One night he was sound asleep in his foxhole when the shelling started. He leapt up but could not get his sleeping bag unzipped. "I don't recall if I ripped or cut my way out but I got out of there. To this day, I have to go to sleep with one foot outside of the covers."

Generally though, Church prefers not to recall specific situations of the battles he fought, especially in The Bulge, "because it takes me several days to shake them off," but he recalls one Bulge nightmare all too well.

"Lordy! It was cold. We were frozen. I believe that, the nicer the weather, the more traumatic the thought of being killed in combat. During that time in the Bulge I was so frozen that getting killed was not too unpleasant a thought.

"One night, when we were dug in on a rise (tough digging in the frozen snow and ground) with several other squads, we had a few mortar rounds thrown at us and some rifle fire, so the bad guys knew we were there.

"To make matters worse, there was bright moonlight on the snow which didn't help us hide our movements. During that night, after a couple of mortar rounds came in, we began to hear some guy moaning and calling for help from somewhere out in the darkness.

"We had all heard about units of English-speaking Germans who were infiltrating our lines dressed in American uniforms and we were all pretty nervous about that. So, was this really the voice of a wounded

James Church (center), Kenny Halterman (left) and Charlie Perry (right) in Belgium or Holland in 1944.

GI or a German trick?

"The voice seemed to be coming from at least 50 yards away from the nearest one of us. Whoever it was, he was crying that he was bleeding badly. To get to him would probably have cost someone his life, so nobody tried.

"So, we listened to his voice long into the night. Then it quit.

"The next day, when we moved down off the rise we'd been on, we found his body. He was obviously an American GI."

Yet, for all the horrors and misery of that time, Church recalls the funny moments, and the friendships, in

greater detail.

"It's wonderful how the human mind can remember the funny things so much easier and yet must struggle to recall the pain and misery of the time. For example, I vividly recall the irony of getting our Army Sno-Packs (winter gear) in April. I often wonder if anyone got them any sooner than that?"

And Church remembers the sight of fresh tanks and troops rolling in to relieve the battle-weary troops of the Bulge. "It was purely American innovation that had kept us alive and the Germans off our backs. It was brutally cold and it was even more dangerous than usual because everyone was a stranger and everything was wildly disorganized. There was wrecked equipment, German trucks that had run out of gas and frozen bodies ... in both kinds of uniforms ... everywhere. We were pretty exhausted, drained and miserable by the time organized infantry units replaced us by mid-January, 1945."

It was times like this that Church leaned on his faith to sustain him.

"I had and have a deep belief in God and the hereafter. I feel sorry for people without such faith and don't know how they cope. My grandmother Church gave me a shirt-pocket Bible, with a steel cover, when I left for overseas. I always, almost superstitiously, carried it in my left side shirt pocket during the war. Its last few chapters fell off somewhere along the way and the plating on its steel cover wore off but it and I both survived.

"During such desperate times in combat, you tend to make bargains with God like, 'if you get me through this I promise, ...' We GIs used to talk a lot about the 'one that has your number on it.' It really was a discussion of 'fatalism.' Some guys argued that if someone really believed in that concept, we'd strap them on the muzzle of one of those 155-mm howitzers and see if it misfires; I don't recall anyone ever agreeing to test their theory."

Thanks to his faith, his buddies and some luck, Church found his way safely through the Battle of the Bulge, but he still needed some literal direction to find his way back to his unit.

"After we were relieved, we huddled together to talk about what to do next and how to get back to our assigned Army units" — units they had not seen since long before forming ad hoc units in the hospital nearly one month before.

"Actually, the Army had no idea where we were so some guys decided to head for Paris or Brussels to live it up for a while until the MPs would eventually pick them up and could locate their units and transport them. Most of us though just hitched rides on Army supply trucks, the Red Ball Express, in the general direction of where we thought our units might be."

After a week, Church found his unit in Venlo, Holland, preparing to cross the German border.

LIBERATION & CELEBRATION

"My unit did not liberate any German extermination camps but we did release prisoners from several slave labor camps where prisoners — mostly Russians — were often brutally worked to death."

They were so grateful for their release that some of the prisoners insisted on showing their appreciation by sharing the only thing they had of "value" with the Americans. It was the kind of gesture that upset even a hardened veteran's stomach, literally.

"Some prisoners had secretly constructed stills and were distilling vodka from potato peelings. These tough survivors, both men and women, would become severely offended if you refused to join them in at least a sip of that rotgut. It could rust glass."

Church and company found liquor a little more to their liking when they discovered a number of underground liquor warehouses as they advanced up the Rhur River Valley in Germany. "These were warehouses where the Germans stored a lot of booze that they had 'liberated' from countries they had occupied. So, we 'liberated' it from them!"

The Hero Next Door

James Church (left) and friends Gene McKeel and Paul Herman board the Marine Panther at LaHavre, France to return home from the war on July 11, 1945.

By April, Church had tucked away one of those "liberated" bottles — a vintage bottle of champagne — for the German surrender they knew was fast approaching.

But, his little celebration plans really backfired.

"When we were sent on patrol or on work details and had to leave some of our gear in the German houses we commandeered, I would hide my precious bottle from my buddies — boys, will be boys, you know. One night this almost got me killed.

"I had been sleeping on a bed (a REAL bed) in a stone-walled basement of a German house for several nights and had hidden my bottle in the bed springs. One night, there was a loud explosion and the sound of hissing filled the air. I sprang up, immediately grabbed my rifle — which I slept with — and began firing off rounds. I guess there must have been three or four shots ricocheting off the walls of my room before I stopped and realized what happened. (The champagne bottle had fallen out of the springs and smashed on the concrete floor.)

The War in Europe

"I often wondered what the cause of my death might have been determined to be. But, during those days, the Army didn't spend too much time determining such things. Incidentally, I later found another bottle which made it to the celebration."

Church was in Hamm, Germany, when that May 8 celebration finally came, a celebration of the German surrender that remains vivid, to a point. "We drank everything in sight and the men filled the sky with tracers."

Shortly after, Church packed up to be shipped to the Pacific. The convoys headed to the harbor of LeHavre, France to board ships for home.

There were few dry eyes when Church's liberty ship sailed past the Statue of Liberty and into New York harbor on July 27, 1945. "I cried with joy again when I found out I had picked the exact date and hour of our ship's docking and had won the ship's pool!"

Church's unit was lucky to get a 30-day furlough in the states before being shipped to San Francisco and the Pacific.

While Church was happy to be going home to the states, he was uncertain about what awaited him there. "Home was everything to us. 'Where are you from?' was always the first question GIs asked each other. So, when I received a letter while I was overseas from my sister that told me my parents were divorced, I no longer had a home and I almost came apart.

"I didn't but I was quite confused as to where 'home' was. My mother and sister were living in Peoria, Ill. So, that's where I chose to spend my furlough."

Still Church says the luckiest thing that happened to him in the military happened on that 30-day furlough he spent in Peoria, Ill. That's where Church met his future wife on a blind date with the then student nurse named Donna Kirkpatrick, fixed up by his sister.

Church fell in love, as he learned the war in the Pacific too had ended. He married Donna 68 days after their blind date. Church was discharged Jan. 25, 1946, from Camp Grant in Rockford, Ill, with "five medals for

where I was rather than for what I did during the war. The most significant of which to me is my European Theater of Operations medal with bronze battle stars for Normandy, Central Europe, Ardennes and the Rhineland. I am also proud of the Battle of Normandy medal the French Government awarded me and others at Caen, Normandy on June 5, 1994, when we returned there for the 50th anniversary of D-Day."

WINNING THE MOON

In spring of 1946, he and Donna moved to Madison where Church finally realized the dream that he carried with him in that Math 51 textbook through combat. He finished his electrical engineering degree under the GI Bill in June, 1949.

Little did he know that 20 years and one month later, that engineering degree would help Church propel Neil Armstrong, Buzz Aldrin and Michael Collins to the moon. In May, 1961, then President John F. Kennedy challenged America to land on the moon before 1970.

At the time Church had left a job at Collins Radio in Cedar Rapids, Iowa and was helping to develop a "hush-hush" Air Force's satellite program to monitor Russian deep space nuclear testing. It was Project Vela (nicknamed Eye in the Sky) and was being developed and directed by the Aerospace Corporation, a spin-off of Ramo-Wooldridge in Los Angeles.

As one of the few engineers working in the infant aerospace industry, Church was one of the engineers sought out by the newly formed National Aeronautics and Space Administration in the early 1960s. He began work as a GS-15 at the Manned Spacecraft Center in Houston Sept. 10, 1962, working exclusively on the Apollo program until shortly before Apollo 11's historic moon landing in 1969.

In the early years, Church was Apollo's project officer for guidance and navigation systems of the Apollo spacecraft and later managed the overall planning in that program. It was his job to organize the disciplines

74

between the engineers brainstorming ideas — for everything from new lighter metals, like titanium, to ways to create electricity in space by combining liquid hydrogen and liquid oxygen — to the contractors who had to bring those ideas to life.

"We constantly used failure analysis in the development of the spacecraft and its subsystems. We called it the 'what if game' and we tried to envision and plan for every type of failure."

During his years at NASA, Church worked with many of the early astronauts on a daily basis including John Glenn, Neil Armstrong and fellow Wisconsinite Jim Lovell. Sometimes working 80 hours a week and flying hundreds of thousands of miles a year — after just five years United Airlines gave him a "2 million mile" plaque for the miles he'd flown just on their airline — left little time for family life.

In an interview with the *Daily Register* in Portage April 13, 1996, one of the early astronauts Church worked with, Commander James Lovell, who piloted Apollo 8 as the first man to orbit the moon and who was commander of the ill-fated Apollo 13, commended Church for his work at NASA.

"I worked with so many people in the early years and crossed paths with Mr. Church many times in meetings. We made it to the moon for the very reason that we had people like Jim Church so dedicated to finding solutions to impossible problems. They worked with whatever they had; they invented and created and recreated what could not have been imagined just decades, years or even days before."

While most of the "daring stuff" was left to those astronauts, even NASA engineers would go for a thrill ride once in a while, Church adds, explaining he was known to drag race his Triumph TR3 against fellow Wisconsinite and World War II veteran Deke Slayton's Grand Prix on the occasional Friday night trip to happy hour at Ellington Air Force Base.

But most of the time, Church was hard at work help-

James and Donna Church

ing America realize the ultimate dream of walking on the moon.

As Church learned in World War II, no goal is reached without sacrifice. For NASA, that sacrifice was the lives of astronauts Virgil "Gus" Grissom, Ed White and Roger Chaffee in a 1967 launch pad accident. "I was at NASA when we lost the three guys in fire at the Cape. I knew them all.

"As an engineer who designed that stuff, you always thought maybe we forgot one of the 'what ifs'. And, even after I left NASA, what we designed kept running through my mind, especially when I was watching the Apollo 13 trip unfold. I even had all the old manuals out on the living room floor going over everything, trying to see what may have gone wrong."

Church's concern was part engineering problem solving and mostly personal. "You knew the guys going through it up there, so it wasn't just somebody up there doing that and risking their life, it was your friends up there doing that and risking their lives. So, while everyone else was sweating that the mission was a success, once you know the people involved, you sweat for the people."

Shortly before Neil Armstrong made his "one small step for man and one giant leap for mankind," Church left NASA to work for Honeywell in Minnesota, helping the Japanese develop their space satellite program. Church later took his skills from the skies above the earth to the soil below it— becoming an underground pioneer in ergonomics for the mining industry with the U.S. Bureau of Mines' Research Center at Ft. Snelling near Minneapolis.

The War in Europe

During those years, Church and his wife Donna raised two daughters and two sons.

They retired in 1985, Donna as a head nurse at Minneapolis' Abbott-Northwestern Hospital and Church as manager of ergonomics research in the Bureau of Mines' research center. They settled in Elk River, Minn., where Church is a member of the Elk River American Legion Post and Donna a member of their auxiliary. He remains a member of the Portage VFW. They've been active in Elk River's Union Congregational Church, where Church is a trustee. He and Donna enjoy traveling, especially to the British Isles where they work on tracing their genealogy. Church is also an avid explorer of the Boundary Waters Canoe Area in northern Minnesota and likes to surf the Internet.

Church belongs to Elk River's Retired Seniors Volunteer Program and he often asked to speak at area schools about his Apollo career and World War II. He's been a guest lecturer in English literature classes at Elk River Senior High School on the true story of Britain's King Arthur, a subject he's spent years researching.

For all his many contributions to his community and country, Church remains proudest of his family and their accomplishments.

"I'm proud of my wife Donna who quit nursing for many years to raise our children, which, while I was in Houston with NASA, she did mostly by herself. Then, in 1971, she reentered nursing and retired in 1985 as a head nurse. Each of our kids is uniquely different, each bright, interesting and intelligent and manage their lives with a good value system and national patriotism. The loss of our youngest in 1988 continues to be a source of sorrow.

"I am also proud of serving my country as part of its two most massive goals and victories, one military, one civilian. One, the defeat of the military machine of the Nazi despot Adolph Hitler, and the other, breaching a space frontier that earthlings had only dreamed about since the dawn of time."

FIGHTING BROTHERS
Archie & Gerald Sanderson
Elroy, Wis.

When America went to war, many families went with it, sending their sons into combat. So it was for Carl and Ekaterina Sanderson of Elroy, Wis. Parents who had fought their own battle in the First World War, sent both their sons into the second.

Their eldest, Gerald W., born June 5, 1921, flew as a gunner in the skies above Europe; their youngest Archie L., born Feb. 20, 1923, battled in the European soil beneath him. They both returned home with stories they preferred not to tell and a desire to do something with the second chance at life that surviving World War II afforded them.

In the spring of 1942, Gerald enlisted in the Army Air Corps; his younger brother was drafted into the Army shortly after high school graduation in the fall of that same year. In the next three years, the two close brothers saw each other just once when they met in Austin, Texas, for a day while Archie was at Camp Swift with the 294th Combat Engineers and Gerald was at Fort Sam Houston, with the 95th Division Artillery Band.

The next time they would see each other was when a weary Archie finally made it home to his bed in Elroy, after serving in post-war Berlin, and found his older brother already home, asleep in their room.

Much terror, loneliness, boredom, fighting and a few laughs lay between those two distant days.

The Sanderson brothers, Gerald (left) and Archie, when they were growing up near Elroy, Wis.

BROTHER ENGINEER

For Archie Sanderson, who died in 1997, the fighting in W.W. II began before he even got to France.

Archie shipped out June 5, 1943, to Cardiff, Wales, for further training as a combat engineer assigned to build pontoon bridges and clear mine fields ahead of infantry. As he boarded a ship bound for the Normandy Invasion along the northern French coast nearly one year later, Archie knew his mission would be dangerous. He was to join up with the 82nd Airborne, lay mine fields and fight as infantry.

As they neared the French coast, and what would have been certain death in the first few hours of the beach assaults, Archie heard and felt a loud bang and the whole ship shook. The ship had hit a mine in the water and was sinking. Below decks in his bunk, Archie later confided to his brother that he kept his rifle ready and was prepared to take his own life rather than let the water close in on him in the pitch dark and drown him. Fortunately, an English ship arrived in time and Archie and his surviving shipmates were evacuated, transferred to a British destroyer and then put on to landing barges.

Their destination ... Utah Beach where the bloody battles of the Normandy invasion were waged just days before. *(Memories are based on the notes he wrote for the Eisenhower Center for the University of New Orleans and interviews and notes with/from his brother Gerald.)*

The landing barge set them off in neck deep water and they had to swim and wade ashore without guns or a helmet — since they lost most of them when the ship sank. Fortunately, by the time they landed, para-

troopers ahead of them had established a good beach-head, facing only sniper fire and three Germans planes.

It was near Utah Beach that Archie saw his first dead German soldier, a very large man whose size concerned the young Wisconsinite. "I hope they aren't all that big!" he thought.

His first night in France was spent "cold, wet and hungry," a trio of misery he numbed to as the war dragged on. They hid in trenches that night as German planes bombed the area and lit up the sky with the deadly fireworks. The next day, Archie finally got a helmet and gun to fight with, reissued into service off of dead soldiers.

The unit pushed its way into Cherbourg, where he saw many German prisoners of war taken.

"There were hundreds marching in step guarded by MPs. At last, we had a seaport that could bring supplies to build our forces for the big push to drive Germans out of France."

That big push came in what was called the St. Lo Breakout.

"The last week of July six of us were assigned to outpost duty near St. Lo. The Germans had built up their defense forces there. I was on guard duty early one morning when the Germans launched a bombardment of huge mortar shells on us.

"A mortar shell differs from an artillery shell in that a mortar is dropped into a barrel after a fuse is pulled and then sets itself off and propels itself into the air and explodes when it lands. Its range is rather short and is used mostly by infantry. A mortar doesn't give much sound warning like you get from artillery. It's sort of a 'swish-bang.'

"That's the way it was that morning and I threw myself to the ground so fast my rifle barrel hit a man in the head who had been sleeping near where I was standing. He woke up at the same time the mortar exploded and thought he'd been hit. We all ran for cover and crouched along a building. Another shell exploded and

a man hollered that he'd been hit and clutched his seat. I had to laugh because I saw it was from a flying stone and all it did was sting him."

The big breakthrough at St. Lo was set for July 25 and was preceded by saturation bombing of German front lines. Archie's unit pulled back almost a mile to create a greater bomb safety zone as the area to be bombed was five miles wide and two miles deep, just south of St. Lo-Periers highway.

"It was a scene I could never forget. First came the roar of the close formation of bombers flying low overhead. At the same time, aluminum confetti was fluttering down, dropped so German radar could not target them. There were Piper Cubs flying higher than bombers trying to spot German artillery.

"From where I was, I had a grandstand seat and saw several bombers get direct hits from German fire. I saw them disintegrate in the sky. I never saw anyone bail out."

Smoke and dust soon engulfed him and the ground trembled underfoot from explosions up to a mile away.

"When our infantry advanced, the dug-in Germans were waiting with machine guns. When our trucks moved through the bombed area, I noticed a dead American infantry officer lying on his back with his boots missing. This was not so unusual. Officers, as well as paratroopers, were issued high top leather boots. They were the envy of all regular soldiers. So, when someone with these boots was killed, somebody would always steal them off their feet."

During a break in the action one day, the unit stopped for a quick C Ration lunch near where a German truck had been hit. Some men began going through pockets of dead Germans near there.

"That was one thing I could not bring myself to do, although later on I did take a combination fork and spoon from a dead German's mess kit, lying next to him. I carried it in my sidepocket and used it when I ate my C Rations."

It was a scene Archie wanted to get away from. He spotted a huge boulder in a field of tall grass and headed for it as a good spot to each lunch.

"For some reason I felt uneasy and turned around. In the tall grass I saw a dead German soldier sprawled on his back with his open eyes staring at me. His helmet was off and he had red hair, unusual for a German. I could only think he must have run for cover under fire to the boulder and was killed there. I don't remember if I finished my lunch."

By Sept. 1, 1944, the 294th had reached the city of Melun, France, with Gen. Collins' 7th Core of Gen. Hodges 1st Army, where they were ordered to build a Bailey Bridge across the Seine River. "We named it the Dinah Shore Bridge because Dinah put on a performance for us."

From there, it was on to a small Belgian city where Archie got a little time off. "Some of us bought an ice cream cone from a street vendor. It was quite a treat. Then, we went to a movie and I was surprised they sold beer in the lobby. That was the first good beer I had since leaving the states. While we strolled around, we came across a shoemaker shop and I asked him if he would sew some leather tops on my shoes. His price was cheap and he did a good job. After that, we came across a photography shop and I had my portrait taken."

By Sept. 16, the 294th was near the mighty German Siegfried line. "It was a long line of huge concrete tank obstacles sticking out of the ground. It looked like little shark's teeth."

They were ready to cross and keep the push into Germany going but ran short of supplies and had to wait in the heavily forested area called the Hurtgen Forest.

"Our outfit was called on there to serve as infantry and my platoon was sent out to man an outpost in this densely wooded area. My squad was sent up a hill where we dug in and two other squads took up different loca-

tions.

"In late afternoon, a patrol of Germans came over a hill and opened up on our men down the hill with rifle fire and a machine gun. I was kneeling in my slit trench waiting for an attack on our side. Less than 100 yards away, I saw three figures moving towards us through the brush. I sighted my rifle on the man in the lead and waited. Suddenly I saw he was one of ours. I found out later that our lieutenant had sent these men out to man a roadblock and had neglected to tell us. When these men heard the shooting, they got scared and were running back. I am sure glad my grandpa taught me never to shoot unless you're absolutely sure what you're shooting at!

"Our radioman had contact with an artillery outfit back of our lines and gave them the Germans' location. They fired one shot, which was close but off target. They corrected their fire and zipped in just fine. The Germans took off but one left his overcoat behind."

The next day, the German artillery, now aware of their enemy's position, returned the favor.

"We reorganized and I was given a position behind a machine gun. It was a 30-caliber, water-cooled gun and I was dug in on a hillside where there were a lot of trees and brush. My friend Cutico and another man and I took turns sleeping. It was so dark you couldn't see your hand in front of your face. We never had any more action. After about a week, someone else took our position and we moved back to our base."

FOREST WOUNDS

Archie found what he thought was a good spot to pitch a tent and went to work on small fire to heat up his C-Rations.

"Apparently some Germans had dropped some bullets that got covered with leaves and I built my fire right over it. All of a sudden, 'BANG-BANG-BANG!' The bullets exploded and their brass casings became small shrapnel and cut three knuckles on my right hand."

A week later, about Oct. 20, 1944, the platoon was sent to patrol between posts.

"I could have gotten out of it because of my fingers but I never liked to chicken out. Our truck driver took us as close to the front as he dared go and Lt. Jackson led our platoon through the woods. He was relying on his compass to lead us to the next outpost but somehow took a wrong turn and led us straight to the German lines. Up popped two German soldiers who were on lookout, about 60 yards away. We were too surprised to shoot at them and they disappeared into the brush.

"A few seconds later, they gave a warning whistle to alert their men. It sounded like a referee whistle, only this time the opposing team was shooting at us. We hit the ground and crawled until we were out of their sight, which wasn't hard in the brush. We made it back and gave the artillery their position and they fired some shells into the German line."

Soon the platoon realized it was missing three men. The sergeant asked for volunteers to look for them. Only three volunteered — Archie, Cutico and a corporal. The truck carried them back to their original position with the driver warning that as soon as he heard shooting he was out of there.

"We started walking through the brush with our rifles ready to fire and, as we got in a ways, 'BANG!' There was a big explosion and I could hear shrapnel zinging through the brush. At the same time, I felt pain in my right knee, like someone driving a hot nail into it. I fell and discovered the corporal had set off a trip wire. He was hit in the hip with a small piece of shrapnel, as was Cutico. I was wounded the worst and couldn't walk so the corporal walked back to the outpost and brought two medics and a stretcher."

The medic cut open Archie's pants leg, gave him morphine and bandaged the knee. They carried him to their Jeep and he was taken to an aid station where he had to wait until an ambulance was available to take him to a field hospital.

The Hero Next Door

"As I lay there, a Catholic priest came up and asked me what religion I was. I said Protestant and he asked if I minded if he said a prayer for me. I said 'not at all.' He did and I thanked him.

"I was loaded on an ambulance where another man, who was badly burned, screamed and groaned all the bumpy way. At the field hospital a medical officer and his aid looked at my knee, which was very swollen. As he touched it, blood came squirting out and he quickly told his aid to bandage it and give me another shot of morphine. As I lay on the stretcher, a medic came and said they were going to take my clothes before my operation and I asked if he could save my shoes because of those leather tops."

Archie was soon transported to a hospital for an operation. Fighting continued around him and lots of wounded were brought in, American and German, soldiers and civilians.

"We all had to wait our turn with no preference. So it was around midnight before I got into the operating table. I asked for a drink of water and the doctors were surprised when I sat up and drank it. They opened my wound and took out the shrapnel and gave it to me before cleaning it and sewing it up.

"I was taken to a huge medical tent and my cot was placed between two wounded German soldiers who moaned and groaned the rest of the night. They couldn't have been hurt that badly because in the morning they were chattering away with one another.

"Later that day, I was loaded on an ambulance and asked the driver if they still had my wallet and watch that was taken from me before my operation. He went back and checked and came back without them, saying this happens all the time. A year after I was discharged, I received my money in the mail but never did get my watch."

A few hours later, Archie was in a giant warehouse building, filled with several hundred soldiers on cots. While there, an entertainment group put on a show.

"I remember there was a black man who was moved to the front so he could see better. He looked like a mummy because he was bandaged from head to toe, just two holes for eyes. He had been a truck driver hauling cans of gasoline and had a wreck where the truck caught on fire."

The next day, Archie went to a Paris hospital where he stayed one week before being loaded onto a C47 cargo plane with other wounded men heading for England and the 107 General Hospital.

"I finally got a clean bed. The room was very long and filled with about 10 beds on each side, all occupied with wounded. At night, you could hear some of them moan and cry. After a week or two, my cast was removed and my knee operated on again, this time more for cosmetic reasons. In a month, I was walking around with a cane."

One thing Archie remembered most was all the stories he heard from other wounded.

"One man told me how he pretended to be dead while a German soldier stole his wrist watch. Another told me he took cover behind a wall but his rearend protruded just beyond it and a German machine gunner raked it with fire and cut his butt to pieces. Another infantryman told how three captured Germans were brought into his camp during the Hurtgen forest fighting. The infantryman asked his captain what he wanted to do with them and the captain replied, 'I don't care, take them out and shoot them.' So the man did. About a week later this man and the captain were both killed.

"And, a French man told us how he watched from his basement as Germans ambushed an American patrol. He said an American lieutenant had been shot in the leg and was lying on the ground. He watched as a German walked up and shot him dead."

While in the hospital for two months, Archie was awarded the Purple Heart, before he transferred to a rehabilitation barracks for a month of physical exercise to get back in fighting shape.

"About mid January, 1945, all of us had to be checked

by a doctor to see if we were fit for active duty. We were all lined up and there were men with tears in their eyes who complained about their wounds so they wouldn't have to go back.

"I was very happy where I was, sleeping between clean sheets and the food was great. It felt so nice and secure.

"My knee was still a little stiff and I was going to complain about it when my turn came, but I thought it wouldn't do any good. When the doctor said 'what's the matter with you?' I said, I had a cold, which I did. I am sure the doctors had their orders because they wanted to get men back to the front for the big spring offensive. A day later, they had a big parade of men who were wounded and were now going back. There must have been over 1,000 of us who passed in review, marching to band music."

From there, Archie went to the 10th Replacement Center.

"It was a very cruel place. They had a stockade for men who were being disciplined, mostly for going AWOL (absent without leave). It was a very cold winter and there was snow. These men had their winter underwear taken from them. All they had on were cotton fatigues and they couldn't wear coats or mittens. They were also forced to run everywhere. We heard stories of men being beaten by guards. I guess the Army wanted to make an example out of them."

BACK TO COMBAT

Still, combat wasn't a much better option, though that's where Archie was headed, aboard an English troop ship.

"It was an English crew and the food was lousy. The night we left port I was assigned firewatch in the lower hold. Before we went on duty we were served cocoa. As I stood watch, the combination of the ship movement and the smell of the hold made me sick and I ran for the head (toilet) but I didn't make it and sprayed

the whole wall with chocolate."

Archie finally made his way back to his unit, now in Germany.

"Everyone was surprised and glad to see me, especially Cutico who had been wounded with me. I learned the three missing men had made it back themselves. And, I learned we were getting ready for the big push."

Archie's platoon was to construct a floating bridge for a late February, 1945, assault across the Roer River. Since the Germans were heavily dug in on the far side of the Roer, Archie's platoon and about 1,000 more men fell back some 20 miles to another river to practice the bridge construction.

"We had to wait until dark before we could begin our practice session. I remember I said to a friend, 'Just think, in a few days a lot of these men will be dead.' And he said, 'Yes and one of them might be you.' 'Or you,' I added."

The bridge was made out of two assault boats interlocked back to back with a sort of large door hinge. Treadways (to form "roads") were laid on top of the boats.

"When it got dark we started construction. It was a mess because it was almost impossible to interlock these boats in the dark and we were not permitted to use a flashlight. I don't remember if we ever completed the bridge and we went back to base cold and tired."

The night before the actual attack, Archie's platoon moved down to the river and slept restlessly in sleeping bags.

RIVER ROER

"I tried to sleep but couldn't. I had a feeling this was going to be our worst battle of the war. Just before 3:30 a.m., I crawled out of my sack to relieve myself. The date was Feb. 23, 1945, just three days after my 22nd birthday.

"There was a loud roar when scores of artillery pieces opened fire and the heavens above just screamed when

hundreds of shells flew overhead and landed on the far side. This lasted about 30 minutes. When it stopped, our platoon sergeant hollered 'Come on men, let's move out!

"We grabbed our rifles and moved down to the river. Smoke from the burst shells burned our nostrils. The current of the river was 10 miles an hour because the Germans had released water from a dam upstream. The infantry was attempting to cross the river in boats and the Germans were firing with machine guns and mortars. It was still very dark and we moved further down the river to our bridge site. Our trucks with our boats were parked next to the factory building.

"By that time, it was getting light and, as we were getting ready to unload our boats, a mortar shell came zooming up at us and went through a window behind me and exploded inside. The explosion blew my helmet off and some shrapnel wounded the man next to me in the rearend. Tiny bits of glass struck my legs and back but did not penetrate because I had on a heavy wool coat and two pairs of pants. Our lieutenant came running out of the building with blood running down his face and he hollered that he was going to the medics and we were to work without him.

"There were more mortar shells coming in. Cutico, another man and myself dove behind one of our boats as the shell exploded. This young man started screaming 'I'm Hit! I'm hit!' and his face turned white; he passed out. I looked and saw he had a hole in his shoulder and I hollered 'Medic! Medic!' We started to carry him out but he was quite heavy. Cutico had caught a small piece of shrapnel in his cheek from that same shell. He was a large, strong man and said 'Here let me take him.' He picked him up like he was as light as a child and carried him away to the medics. Cutico got his face treated and returned to the bridge site.

"In the meantime, a dense smoke screen was laid on our side of the river so the Germans couldn't see us and there were some of our infantry on top of a build-

ing firing a 50-caliber machine gun at the Germans across the river.

"The bridge site was where I saw the first German jets flying overhead and our ack-ack was firing on them but the planes were going so fast the shells were exploding far behind them. They released their bombs, which came screaming down. Cutico and I took cover inside some huge steel pipe lying around. The bombs were off target so we were all right.

"Since our platoon no longer had a lieutenant and was under-strength from other casualties, we joined the rest of our company trying to build a floating steel treadway bridge further upstream. Another engineering outfit came and took over our job. We later learned they had casualties too, one sergeant was killed. They managed to get the bridge up but then shrapnel cut the steel cable that kept the boats in line and the whole bridge went floating downstream.

"We joined the rest of our company at their bridge site alongside a bridge the Germans had destroyed. The Germans were firing artillery shells and our men dug their slit trenches to protect themselves. I didn't have my trench shovel so I used my steel helmet to scoop out a hole to lay in between bursts.

"Towards evening, about six or seven of us were asked to go upstream and join some infantry and cross the river in a boat to clear out German snipers.

"As the small group moved along the river, a German plane dropped a bomb and one man was wounded and sent back. The rest proceeded on to the boat site. Just then, several German planes came overhead.

"We all dispersed and hit the ground. The plane dropped a lighted flare which drifts down on a small parachute and lights up the area bright as day. If you don't move, the enemy isn't supposed to be able to see you. So, I lay very still on the ground. Suddenly I heard a hissing noise overhead and I was afraid the flare would land on me. I couldn't let it burn me so I peered over my shoulder to keep track of it and it landed about three

91

feet in front of me. I waited until the flare burned out then got up and ran away. I didn't get far before the plane released its bomb. As it came screaming down, a bomb crater loomed up in front of me and I quickly dove in, followed by another man. As the bomb exploded, the ground shook and dirt came down on top of us.

A few seconds later, another bomb hurtled in Archie's direction.

"The scream of a bomb is far greater than the scream of an artillery shell. You feel like your eardrums are about to break before it explodes.

"As the dirt was still falling, a plane flying over was strafing us and a falling rock hit my wrist numbing it. I thought for a second I was shot. I have to admit that I prayed silently to God to let me live so I could start a family some day."

The planes finally let up and the group continued inland.

"We came to a house, could hear men in the basement and went downstairs. It was pitch dark and a medic called out ' Do you guys have any matches?' I did and he said to come over and light them so he could patch up a guy. I lit the matches while he worked on this wounded man stretched out on a table. In the gloom from lighted matches I could see other men had taken refuge in the basement and some had their rosary beads out and were praying."

After the aerial bombing and strafing was over, Archie returned to the company.

"When I got back everyone thought I'd been killed or wounded and I learned that Cutico was missing.

"At daybreak, everyone got orders to go back to the bridge site but I stayed behind to look for Cutico. I found the bomb crater I'd taken shelter in and was surprised to see five dead men about 20 feet from my hole. Shrapnel from the bombs had gone through their steel helmets and they had looks of horror frozen on their faces like they saw the devil himself before they died."

Archie didn't find Cutico but learned he had been

wounded. He never saw him again.

"We finally got our bridge built and then were sent back to our base to rest. I had gone three days on very little sleep and food. When I got to the house, I looked in a mirror and hardly recognized myself. After going through the chow line, I found I couldn't eat very much and, when I tried to sleep, I would wake up every little while.

"This was the worst of the war for us. I was fortunate not to be wounded or killed. My platoon had the most casualties in our company, 30 percent (all wounded, nobody killed)."

INTO GERMANY

"The next day we crossed the Roer River and could see a lot of dead soldiers snagged in the brush along the riverbanks. When we got to the German trenches there were a lot of dead bodies scattered around. We went into the city of Duren and it was in complete rubble. The only thing standing was an iron statue of Bismark.

"We moved on to the Rhine River where we helped build a heavy pontoon bridge. We then stayed in houses on the far side where I found a German book and found a good supply of wine, which we enjoyed.

Once across the Rhine, the 1ˢᵗ Army made steady progress across Germany.

"A friend and I came upon an abandoned farmhouse with a couple beehives. He wanted to get some honey. I was pretty skeptical, but we made a smudge fire that created a lot of smoke, which made the bees sleepy. We were able to steal about a pound of honey from them and neither of us got stung."

The Army raced through Germany so fast its supplies couldn't keep up so the company was given permission to get food from the Germans.

"One day we came upon a farm village with a lot of chickens. We climbed down from our trucks and started to chase these chickens all over. We were laughing be-

cause it was funny to see these men running after squawking chickens. It didn't take us long to catch quite a few and we climbed in our trucks and left quickly as old German farmers were watching us with pitch forks in hand."

Eventually, the company moved into a town where they were supposed to build another bridge.

"Some got orders to check houses near our bridge site for German soldiers who might be hiding. It was getting dark and, with a man named Joe, I checked a house whose top part was destroyed but we were able to go down into a basement. I came to a door tied shut from the other side. I could see a light through the cracks and I told Joe to cover me as I kicked the door open.

"What I saw at the far end, dimly lit by an old lantern, was a young man and woman sitting on a bare mattress lying on the bare floor. Between them was a newborn baby wrapped in a thin blanket.

"I shined my flashlight at the man's face and asked him for his papers, which he showed me. I saw they were one of thousands of displaced people from other countries moved there to work in Germany. I gave him some cigarettes and her a chocolate bar and told them to stay where they were because they might get shot if they came out in the dark."

Another day, the platoon rounded up some German soldiers and was searching them before loading them into Army trucks.

"One soldier was very young and our sergeant pushed him in front of a tree to search him. At the same time Lester Dorman and I walked across the road to sit on a patch of grass. The soldier must have thought we were going to shoot him because he broke out crying like a baby. I have to admit we laughed as we put him on the truck with the other Germans."

Another day, while traveling the well-kept German Autobahn, the troops happened upon a German ammunition truck bombed by Allied planes.

"There was very little left and the driver's remains were lying on the concrete. It was a shapeless body as if all its bones were crushed to nothing, not a stitch of clothes on it and surprisingly little blood. It amazed me what high explosives can do to a body."

The Army made good progress on fast German roads, with the exception of a few bridges and sections the Germans had destroyed ahead of the Allies. It was Archie's job, at first, to repair those sections and keep the Allies moving.

"At a lot of places, the Germans buried their explosives under the road but for some reason didn't have time to explode it so we were assigned to dig out this dynamite and get rid of it.

"After a while, we figured these explosives might be booby trapped so we went into town and looked up the burgermeister (mayor) and had him round up German men with shovels and had them dig up the dynamite. It saved us a lot of work and we never had any accidents."

For a short time, the company was in Leipzig, a city taken by Americans and later turned over to the Russians.

"Our VII Corps captured the city of Nordhausen and discovered a German concentration camp composed of thousands of slave laborers, both men and women, brought in from Russia, Poland and other conquered areas. They were made to work in a huge bomb factory built on a hillside.

"I think the world should know it wasn't just Jews who died in concentration camps. Thousands of bodies were discovered. Most died from starvation and the living were practically dead. I did not go in this camp myself but one of our truck drivers did and described it.

"Our Army rounded up all male citizens of Nordhausen and made them dig graves in the hillside and carry and bury the bodies in this cemetery."

The 294th came to settle in a small German farm town where Gen. Eisenhower ordered them to stop advanc-

ing.

"I believe we could have reached and taken Berlin before the Russians but I have to give credit to Eisenhower for stopping because he knew we were going to give that territory over to the Russians. Why lose American lives for land we were just going to give away.

"When we took over this village we ordered people out of their homes and took them over as our quarters. Our living quarters were German homes. It sounds nasty now, and I always felt a little guilty when we ordered people out of their homes, but I think they were glad we were Americans rather than Russians.

"The Germans had Polish people as slave laborers who worked in the fields. There was a Polish man who came to our headquarters and told how some SS German soldiers killed a number of Polish men and buried them in a common grave. Our officers had the man show them where it was and then made the German people in town go there, dig up the bodies, wash them and rebury them in a nearby cemetery."

Archie saw hundreds of the German soldiers fleeing the Russian front and deserting.

"They would shed their uniforms and put on civilian clothes. We had orders to round up these men and one day we caught three. While they were being searched, I spotted some Jack rabbits about 400 yards away. They were running fast with huge leaps. There were many of these rabbits around and they made good target practice. When we shot one we gave it to the Germans or some displaced people as they were happy to get meat of any kind. So, I started shooting these rabbits without realizing the noise scared these men so bad they almost jumped out of their skin."

Part of Archie's duties was to inspect farmyards, barns, homes, and outhouses for German soldiers.

"I went up to one farmhouse and rapped on the door. There was no answer so I took the butt of my gun and rapped much louder. This time, someone opened right away. The whole family was lined up facing me. There were two women, an older man and a younger man, who I turned to and asked to see his papers. He could have been a former soldier but I didn't want to take him from his family because as far as I was concerned the war was over.

"I gave him back his papers and told the man who was with me to stay there while I checked upstairs. I went up and opened a bedroom door. There in the room was a man in bed, in broad daylight. The covers were pulled up to his chin. I told him to get out of bed and show me his papers. When he pulled back his covers and got out of bed I could hardly believe my eyes. The man was huge over six and half feet tall and dressed in long white underwear. He went to a chest of drawers and opened it. I was wary with my rifle but then he handed me his papers with his huge hands. I saw he had been a Russian soldier and was probably placed on the farm to work. I never could figure out why he was in bed except he impressed me as sort of retarded and when I rapped on the door maybe the family told him to go hide upstairs.

"All the time I was in the Army I never got any real eggs, only powdered. So, when I went to a German farmhouse, I'd ask 'habenseire' and they usually gave me two eggs which I fried myself. It was a real treat. One time we were combing the countryside and I was almost run over by two deer. I shot one of them and the cook prepared it for a meal. It didn't go too far in a company of men."

A FINISH WITHOUT END

The war in Europe ended May 9, 1945. The war in the Pacific still raged and, at first, Archie got orders to go there and prepare for an invasion of Japan.

"It didn't seem fair to us to survive our war and then get killed fighting in Japan. But, in the Army you do what you're told."

The orders were to move to southern Germany first,

as an advance party to take over German homes to house the rest of the company, set to follow.

"There again we gave German families short notice to move out. One woman wasn't going to leave anything to the Americans and she went outside and picked all the gooseberries off her bushes even though they weren't ripe. But then, a few days later, we got a change of order to return because the 294th Combat Engineers was going to be among the first American troops to enter Berlin. I wondered how that woman felt about us after picking all the berries but at least she got her house back."

When Archie returned to the farm village, he learned the rest of the outfit had left for Berlin and noticed the town was preparing as best it could to welcome the Russians soon arriving there.

"They were supposed to be taken over by the Russians in the Yalta agreement. The town's people were scared out of their wits. They had big signs out that said, 'welcome to the victorious Russian army.' They also had red flags hanging out their windows. The funny part of that was that you could see where the German swastika had been removed because the red background had faded.

"We continued on our way to Berlin and crossed the Elbe River. We met hordes of the Russian Army. They were a rough looking bunch and even had women with them. They were traveling in horse drawn wagons and even driving livestock with them. They were friendly and we waved to each other as we passed. I couldn't help feeling sorry for the Germans where this Army was going to settle."

OCCUPYING TIME IN A DIVIDED CITY

"It was hard to believe such a big, beautiful city could be destroyed like it was, but everywhere I looked, there was rubble. Berlin was divided into zones and the Russians had the zone on the other side of the Brandenburg Gate. The Russians had big, red posters and banners

98

everywhere displaying their propaganda. On the op-
posite side was the British zone. The American zone
had the Tempelhoff Air Field.

"We arrived at a residential area where the rest of
our company had taken over all the houses on one
street. The house my platoon had was a nice two story
with a dry basement. We had a grave in the front lawn
as the Russians buried a lot of the dead where they fell.
There was a Russian cemetery down the street and a
lot of their dead were buried there including high officers. They paid a good price to take Berlin.

"The German family took most of their furniture when
they moved out but left a large grandfather clock that
wasn't working. I tinkered with it and got it to work.
Three or four of us shared a room and slept on cots.
Somewhere I picked up bedsheets and it was wonderful to sleep between sheets again. We enjoyed living
there because we no longer had to do KP duty because
German civilians were happy to do the work in return
for leftovers."

In spite of the bombing, Germans kept Berlin's electric trains running and on time, a transportation luxury
Archie took advantage of.

"When I was in their downtown station I saw German
soldiers who had been prisoners in Russia. These men
were young but they looked like old men. They were
ragged, dirty and smelled. A lot of them had their feet
wrapped in rags. I figured they must have walked all
the way back from Russia and they couldn't understand
what German girls were doing going out with American
soldiers.

"There was a lot of other activity, including refugees
from other countries — a lot of miserable people going
some place.

"I rode this train to a resort town outside Berlin, where
they had sailboats that people could take out on a large
lake. Our Army had taken over this spot as a place for
recreation. They had a shooting range, downtown was
a service club for us and there were beer gardens where

the beer was good."

Archie's platoon was among those assigned with converting a huge public building into the "Allied Control Council Building," to be occupied jointly by the Americans, British, French and Russian high command.

"We loaded a lot of stuff on trucks to take to the dump. When we unloaded it, Germans were there to pick it up as fast as we threw it off. In fact, they were even stealing from each other. These were desperate people who would faint from hunger. We had cut down a few trees in front of the building and were going to construct a circle drive. As we cut them into smaller pieces with our chain saws, Germans would dash in and grab the wood before it hit the ground.

"Germans also tried to sell their gold jewelry for food and once a man stopped me and tried to sell me a gold ring. I asked him what he wanted for it and he started off with a long list of groceries and I said, 'what do I look like, a store?'

"When it was chow time, little children would come running with their containers hoping we would share, which most of us did. Once I saw a man, a Jew, tell a little German boy 'get out of here you little shit!' and he dumped his leftovers in a garbage can."

German prisoners helped the Allies with the construction work they did in Berlin. Archie was part of a surveying crew and in charge of watching over some of the prisoners.

"In the morning we had to go the stockade and pick these men up in our trucks. We had orders that every truck with prisoners had to have an armed guard on it. After I loaded all these men, I had to get on with my rifle and we were all packed in like sardines. There was little I could do if one wanted to escape. I was on good terms with these prisoners, I treated them well and let them quit a little early if they did a good day's work. If I was goofing off and they saw an officer approaching, they would warn me.

"Our orders were to check out a clip of ammunition

Archie and Lois Sanderson in the spring of 1995.

in the morning and turn it in at the end of the day but I always guarded with an empty rifle because I felt the war was over and I was not going to shoot anyone wanting to escape.

"One young man came up to me and said his girlfriend was nearby and could he leave for 10 minutes to talk to her. The rest of the Germans looked to me to see what I would do. I pondered the question because if he turned up missing I could get in trouble. But then I figured what could they do to me, I was only a private. All I could get was company punishment. I told him he could go. Ten minutes later, he reported back."

As the Americans got to know the German prisoners better they found they shared some common ground in the hell of combat they both had crossed through.

"We learned they were just as scared as we were and

we felt we had a lot in common. That's when I felt how stupid war is. If the political leaders had to lay their lives on the line, there would be no war."

Though the war was over, the death and destruction were daily reminders. "There was destruction as far as you could see.

"And, one day, I was eating lunch in front of the Allied building when I saw a man fall from the top of this three-story building. He never screamed nor hollered. He hit a pile of lumber and bounced about six feet and landed on concrete. I was one of the first to reach him and could see the back of his head was bashed in and blood was pouring out his nose like water out of a faucet. He was loaded in our Army ambulance and taken to a hospital where the doctor pronounced him dead. We figured he'd committed suicide."

On Sundays, Archie was free, except for occasional guard duty, to roam Berlin. He and a friend would occasionally take a train downtown.

"There we came in contact with Russian soldiers in front of the Brandenburg Gate. Russian officers were not friendly but the regular soldiers were. I was surprised to see so many Oriental soldiers.

"There was one public building that had been burned out and had a very high dome. Inside Russian soldiers had scrawled their names in every square inch of space. We heard a lot of stories about how the Russians had plundered and raped the city. They had gone into office buildings that had leather covered furniture and cut off the leather to send home.

"Near the Brandenburg Gate was a huge wooden park, called the Tiergarden, where all the black market operation took place. American cigarettes would sell for $10 a pack in American money. Regular German money did not have much value. We were paid in German occupation money, printed in America, and they must have printed the same for the Russians, as the only difference was theirs had a dash after the serial number. Most Russian soldiers had not been paid for years.

When the war ended, they were paid all at once. The biggest craving for a Russian was to own a wristwatch so any American with one could sell it to a Russian for $500 occupation money. They would even buy a Mickey Mouse watch.

Compared to combat, post war Berlin was safe duty, though it had its hazards, as Archie nearly discovered when he decided to travel downtown alone in the Russian Zone.

"I passed through the Brandenburg Gate and walked Unter Der Linten Strasse which went into the Russian zone. I must have walked several miles looking at the ruins when I decided it was getting late and I better start getting back. Shortly after turning back, two Russians in a beat up truck came along and asked if I wanted a ride. I pointed and said Brandenburg Gate? They nodded so I climbed in the back.

"After driving a short way, they made a left turn and started down a deserted street. I shouted for them to stop but they kept going. I was glad I had my loaded rifle with me and took the butt of my gun and banged it on top of the cab. This time they got the message and came to a halt. I jumped off and made my way back. It was very dark by the time I got close to the Brandenburg Gate. Even in the dark you noticed all the displaced refugees roaming around the ruins. It looked rather ghostly.

"There were several American soldiers about 100 feet in front of me and they must have been mean. A refugee must have bumped into them because I heard them curse and then 'Whack-Smack!' and a man's scream. There were running footsteps towards me and the man almost ran into me as he passed."

Still, there were some things Archie was rather fond of in Berlin.

"Though we could get in trouble for it, Adam and I dated German sisters. We had several dates and always went to the Berlin Zoo, which didn't suffer too much damage. I was surprised it still had animals and wondered how they fed them. I remember a man and woman who had a small baby with them were looking at the lion. The lion saw the baby and paced back and forth and roared. He was hungry and wanted to eat the baby; it gave me the creeps.

The sisters lived deep in the Russian zone and did not want the men to walk them home. Instead they met and said goodbye on Sundays at the Brandenburg Gate.

After a few dates, the men received their orders home.

"Before we left Berlin a huge supply of whiskey came in and every man got a bottle for his ration, most foolish men had to drink it all at once, which was a bad idea because of all the fights it caused."

As exciting as it was to be going home, Archie remembered the train rides through Germany with no great fondness.

"It was long and bumpy and I said 'I thought the train was going to jump the tracks last night' to which someone responded, 'what made you think we were on the tracks!?'"

Once they arrived in France, the meanness of a few American troops returned.

"A French trainman hollered at some men to move back from the cars and one man got mad and hit him on the head with the butt of his gun making it bleed. We had some mean men."

The boat ride home from LaHavre, France, was just as bumpy, though this time Archie knew better how to handle the high seas.

"Our ship moved out of the harbor and we were on our way to the states. We soon ran into rough weather and I got seasick again but wouldn't let it get the best of me. If I got sick, I would throw up and go back and finish my meal. After the second day, I was OK. It was a good thing because we ran into a winter storm where the waves were washing over the top of the carrier and water was coming down the elevator shaft used to bring planes up to the top.

"I got stuck on KP duty and another man and myself

had to dump the garbage over the side. We lugged the heavy garbage cans to the outside door and opened it and were greeted by a strong wind. It was starting to get dark but we could still see and it was a scary sight to look out at this huge wall of water surrounding us. We dumped it quickly and went inside; it was no time to get washed overboard!

"A few days before we reached New York, we had some snow and some men made a snowman on the flight deck. Then, when we got near port, a welcome ship loaded with women, came out to greet us. They were coaxing us men to jump overboard and swim to their ship. I was surprised someone wasn't dumb enough to do it."

Instead, they boarded a ferry boat that took the war-weary troops past the Statue of Liberty. "It was getting dark by then and it was a great sight to see."

Everyone went their separate ways from Camp Kilmer, N.J.

"I finally boarded a train to take me back to Ft. Sheridan, Ill., where we started out. There was a lot of paperwork and a counselor briefed me because I was wounded. He said I should apply for disability pension. I was reluctant but have to be grateful this man convinced me I should as I was declared 10 percent disabled."

From Ft. Sheridan, Archie took a train to Milwaukee and then caught the North Western to Elroy as his brother Gerald had done just six months before.

"I can't remember my thoughts on the train but it was December and very cold with a lot of snow on the ground. The train pulled into Elroy and I got off with my big duffel bag on my shoulder and started walking home. It was very late, after midnight, and I knew every one was sleeping. The door was even locked but I remembered I could unlock it by twisting the doorknob.

"I walked in and went into my bedroom where my brother was sleeping. He woke up and we hugged. I crawled into my side of the bed and we talked awhile.

"The next morning, my mother came in followed by my father. They were quite surprised. We were greeted with a hug and kiss and I said I was looking forward to some good home cooking.

"My long hard journey took me three years to complete. I wouldn't want to go through it again but I saw and learned a lot and was grateful to come back healthy and alive."

HOME TO THE MOON

In all, Archie had fought his way over the thousands of miles from Elroy to Berlin and back again. Little did he know when he returned how far his dedication to a new American goal would carry some of his countrymen — all the way to the moon.

He soon found work at Allis Chalmers in Milwaukee, where he met and married his wife Lois in 1953. Then, Archie took a job with General Motors in Milwaukee where he was a designer and drafter in engineering on the company's contract with NASA for the Apollo space program. He was part of a team that designed the guidance system for the first spacecrafts, including Apollo.

In 1973, Archie was transferred by General Motors to Indianapolis, where he worked on jet engine designs for the military in the Allison Gas Turbine Division, until he retired to Florida in 1986.

He was also an architect of his own homes, working with his wife Lois on the designs for them and their three daughters, and settling for a long time in Greendale.

Archie was long active in his churches, serving as youth group sponsor, junior high teacher and usher for the United Church of Christ in Greendale. He also joined the Mount Auburn United Methodist Church in Greenwood, Ind. before he retired and moved to Sun City Center, Fla., where he joined St. Andrew Presbyterian Church.

Archie lost his final battle, one against cancer March 13, 1997, living 52 years longer than he thought he ever

would while slugging it out in the European trenches of World War II.

BOMBER BUGLER

Equally grateful to survive the war and get a second chance at life was Archie's older brother. While Archie was dodging bullets in battlefields,Gerald Sanderson was dodging flak in the European sky as a toggelier and gunner on a B-17 bomber out of Italy.

Before he was a toggelier, Sanderson was a bugler.

At his high school graduation in May, 1940, Sanderson played a cornet version of "The World is Waiting for a Sunrise," an appropriate tune he surmised as Elroy was just coming out of The Depression. "If only my classmates, my brother and I had known the hell we'd have to go through in the next few years."

That hell was far from his imagination as Sanderson went to work for the Hercules Powder Co. in the spring of 1941. After the Japanese bombed Pearl Harbor, Sanderson knew he'd be signing up for the draft. Rather than be drafted into the Army he and three co-workers enlisted in the Army Air Force. He was assigned to the 95th Infantry Division for basic training with his friends Warren Winn and Don Ormson.

Instead of making war, however, Sanderson soon discovered the Army wanted the high school cornet player to make music for the military. "I told them I hadn't played a cornet in almost a year. When I played for the band leader I didn't play very well but they asked me to join the band anyway. After a month of practicing, the leader told me I was the most improved player."

The Hero Next Door

Life as an Army musician was good, as the military musicians practiced band music in the morning, dance band in the afternoon. Sanderson continued to play after the 95th was transferred to Fort Sam Houston, San Antonio. The tempo of band life was good but Sanderson still wanted to serve in the Army Air Force. "So I asked my captain if I could go and take the Army Air Force test. He said I could if I passed a written test but I failed one of the eye tests so I did not get transferred."

Instead, Sanderson, and the rest of the band, stood guard as the 95th went to Louisiana for maneuvers.

"Then, one day, my first sergeant came to me and told me to pack my bags. I was going to the Army Air Corps and I was very happy because I just didn't think doing guard duty was my way of fighting the war."

The switch meant Sanderson got to do basic training all over again, this time at Sheppard Field, Texas, before he went to the University of Nebraska for classes and some Piper Cub pilot training at the Lincoln Air School.

After a few months at the university, Sanderson learned he had been eliminated from the cadet program. The air corps asked him to pick which school he wanted to go to, engineering, radio or armament school.

"I asked which one was shortest. They said 'armament school in Denver, Colo.' So I went there and learned about bomb racks on B-17s and all about explosives and 50 and 30 caliber machine guns. While at Lowry Field, I even joined the boxing team, which kept me out of KP duty."

In short order he was off to Laredo Gunnery School where he learned about B-17 and B-24 bomber gun turrets and more about 50 caliber machine guns. "I learned how to take them apart and put them back together with gloves on and also blind folded, which you might have to do in combat in very cold weather."

After training, Sanderson went to Lincoln, Neb., where he became the waist gunner for a B-17 bomber crew of:

tailgunner Hank Vaslovik, waist gunner Dick Brehm, engineer Milo Kelsey, radio man Bill McCarl, co-pilot Donald McCormich, navigator Bob Louden and pilot Bruce Waltz. The crew was sent to Pyote, Texas, to train and practice bombing runs and air-to-ground gunnery.

"One day, the co-pilot wanted to shoot at targets with the 50-caliber so I sat up in the co-pilot's seat. Pilot Waltz let me fly the B-17 over the gunnery range and it seemed more like driving a big truck than flying an airplane.

Sanderson soon learned he and his crew were Africa bound. It was September, 1944.

"I remember we flew over Chicago on our way and I though that this was as close as I was going to get to Elroy, Wis., in a long time, maybe never."

With a stop at Gander Bay, Newfoundland, and the Azore Islands to gas up, the crew arrived in Marrakesh, Morocco. "Everything was very dirty so a few of us slept in the plane."

Things weren't much better at a stop in Tunis, Tunisia, which was covered with shot-up planes.

"Finally we arrived at our airfield in Italy, 30 miles north of Foggia. As we flew over, the landing field looked more like a mud field. This would be our home for the rest of the war.

"Home was a tent that housed six: our pilot, co-pilot and navigator had tents in a different area of the 815 Bomb Squad. Our tents were heated with 100-octane airplane gas. The runway was made of metal matting and the airstrip wasn't very level. If a plane did not lift off the ground soon enough, it would go into the valley and crash. One time a plane did not get off in time. It crashed and burned. All 10 men inside it died."

A PAPER DOLL

Sanderson's first mission out of that homebase was to Innsbruck, Austria.

"There was a railroad marshaling yard we were to bomb. The plane we had was named Paper Doll. It was one of the older ones as new crews got older planes so

those who'd flown a lot of missions could have newer ones."

Most of Sanderson's missions were to oil refineries, marshaling yards, ordinance depots, railroad bridges and troop concentrations.

"On days we'd fly, we'd have a wake-up call at 4 a.m. As we flew, we'd see other planes blown up or shot down by anti-aircraft fire and all or some of the crews killed or parachuting into enemy land. All this made for hard sleeping the night before we'd fly. I would often wake up and find our waist gunner Brehm smoking a cigarette and sweating out the mission already.

"After waking up and rubbing what little sleep we got out of our eyes, we'd dress and head for the Mess Hall where breakfast would be dehydrated eggs, coffee or milk out of dried skim powder, which I hated! To this day I can't stand skim milk.

"We would always dress in winter underwear and our winter shirt and pants. Then a truck would take us to the flight line where our plane was parked. We would get a flight bag which contained a heated flying suit, heated gloves and boots, a parachute and an oxygen mask. I had a sheepskin jacket with a high collar to wear over my suit. We needed all these warm clothes because it would be 20- to 40-degrees below zero at 30,000 feet.

"Once in the plane we'd make sure we had flak suits to wear when we were over the target. The thought was that, when parts of German anti-aircraft exploded around us and flew into the plane, it would bounce off our flak jackets.

"After we were in the air and had assumed formation we'd fire our 50-caliber machine guns to make sure they were working properly as we headed to our target for the day. On the way we were on constant look out for German fighters such as the FW-190s and the MC109s; those planes were good and their pilots had lots of experience. After that, we flew through flak from between 200 and 400 anti-aircraft guns and the fighters would return to go after the planes damaged in the flak bar-

rage; they were easy pickins.' On the way back we saw many airmen bailout into enemy land and many planes get shot down."

Once the planes were out of enemy territory, crews could tune into big band music over their earphones. "I will always remember the Christmas of 1944 because we were coming back from Brux, Germany. We'd been hit by a lot of flak and had many holes in our plane. Then, we heard Bing Crosby singing 'I'm Dreaming of a White Christmas.' That was the only time I can say I was homesick and shed a few tears."

After the first few missions, Sanderson was checked out on dropping bombs as a backup for the bombardier, a role he filled on a Jan. 21, 1945, mission to Vienna, Austria.

"That day, I was flying up in the nose of the plane as top gunner in place of a bombardier so we were short a waist gunner. It rained the day before and all the planes were saturated.

"We had been kidding our ground engineer, Don Speigle, daring him to go along on a mission to see how it was to get shot at because he kept telling us we had it easy. So that day, he went and got a flight bag and, as we were taxiing off the runway, he jumped in!"

It was probably a ride he regretted since the Paper Doll came close to crashing from engine trouble on the return ride.

"As we neared Trieste, Italy our No. 2 inboard engine began to pump oil out the breather all over the wing. When I saw it and told the pilot, he feathered the engine. We soon began gaining altitude and caught up with the rest of the formation. As we were nearing Graz, the No. 3 engine also began losing oil and eventually froze up with the propeller blades flat against the wind. Now, we could not keep up with formation so we left the group without breaking radio silence.

"We had to look for German fighter planes as we continued but, fortunately, we did not encounter any. As we neared the city of Wiener Neustadt near the Hun-

garian/Austrian border we did see some gunfire directed at us but weren't damaged. We dropped our 10,500-pound bombs on this city. It wasn't a military target but it was our target; that has bothered me all these years about civilians getting killed.

"Our pilot asked the navigator to give us a heading to the nearest Allied (landing strip) since we were steadily losing altitude. As we approached the Adriatic coast we broke out of the clouds at 6,000 feet with the two remaining engines smoking badly. We didn't know if we would have to ditch in the Adriatic Sea or if we'd make Italy.

"When we sighted the Italian coast we were at 3,000 feet. We saw the Falconara landing strip ahead and made a straight in approach to land just as a B-24 was taking off! Since I was sitting in the nose, I had a pretty good view and we didn't miss him by much!

"Bruce Waltz made a perfect landing with no flaps on a short fighter strip. After parking the Paper Doll, we looked around. It seemed that we were in an aircraft graveyard, surrounded by a lot of damaged planes that made it back by sheer luck, just as we had."

They were safe on the ground, but the ground did not provide the warmest reception.

"The weather was very bad, snow piled high, and it was cold. We weren't too far from the front lines and our lines of communication were out from the cold so we couldn't tell our airfield where we were. Our tailgunner found some gasoline to try to make a fire but burned up the tent in the process.

"Other crews on our mission reported they saw us leave formation with two engines out. As a result, Lt. Waltz' crew on #043 were listed missing in action. The crew chief that had flown with us was listed as AWOL. He was demoted when we returned but he stayed in the service and eventually became a top sergeant."

Three days later, the crew finally got a call through to the airfield. In the meantime, it snowed another 10 inches and they struggled to keep warm with little heat

Gerald Sanderson played in the Army band before exhcanging his trumpet for a bomber gun sight in the Army air force.

in their tents and only one thin blanket each.

"We slept in our jackets and winter clothes and were still cold. It was another seven days before the plane could come to pick us up; so for 10 days we froze our butts off!"

When they finally did get back, the crew chief was demoted to private for hopping aboard without permission. He didn't get his sergeant's stripes back again until September.

"Two days later, we had a new plane and were headed toward Regensburg to bomb an oil refinery. This was a rough trip since they had more than 200 anti-aircraft guns shooting at us."

On another trip, Sanderson found himself hanging out the open bomb bay doors with his crew's life in his hands. "One time, we had to turn back from the mission because of a problem with the plane, I think. Anyway we had to turn back right after I had gotten ready to release the bombs. So, I had to get in the bomb bay, with the bomb bay doors open and put the pins back in all the bombs. Believe it or not, I was more concerned about having enough oxygen than falling out."

Those missions were tough but not as rough as a lone wolf — extra-hazardous mission — the crew flew in February 1945.

The Hero Next Door

"The weather was so bad they couldn't get a group of planes in the air because they would run into each other. They said these missions were flown by volunteer crews but don't believe it. Our target was the city of Bleckhammer (sic) near the border of Poland, which had an oil refinery. We hid in the clouds all the way to the target and didn't encounter any German fighter planes; I guess the weather was too bad for them too.

"Being a lone plane, with no others for fighter protection, it was the most scary mission I was on. When we got to target, we ran out of clouds. They told us at the airfield that if the sky cleared, we should abort the mission and return to base. Our pilot asked us all what we should do and we all agreed that, since we had come this far, we wanted to do it. 'Let's go get them!' we told him.

"We got as much altitude as we could and started the bomb run. The German gunners opened up as we dropped our bombs and peeled off to the right trying to get back into the clouds. Those German gunners were really accurate as they followed us into the clouds. I can remember our tailgunner Hank Vailavick telling years later that he saw two bursts of flak behind us and figured the next burst would get us but it missed. Koehn the ball turret gunner had some flak rattling around inside the turret but none of it hit him; he kept a few chunks as a souvenir.

"We stayed in the clouds all the way home and no fighters attacked. When we landed we found that the main spar (main support) of our right wing had a good chunk missing. In the right waist, there was a big hole near my head; it's a good thing I'm short. I can remember that while we were trying to get back to the clouds after the bomb run, I was shaking so badly I couldn't control myself. I don't know how we stayed in the air, but we were soooo happy when this mission was over. We must have had some help from above that day!

"We all prayed, I'll tell you that. You've got to talk to somebody and God was a good one, maybe the only

one then, to talk to. Us guys never talked between us when we were flying, though some crews did. And, when we got back, we never talked about the mission. We'd take a couple jolts of whiskey, talk about anything else and go to sleep."

By this time, the crew was closing in on 35 missions, the magic, "get-to-go-home" number.

"Our last mission was to bomb German troops dug in trenches in northern Italy. We carried 20-pound fragmentation bombs that would explode 20-feet above the troops and blow down in the trenches filled with infantry. I heard later that we killed some British troops; they were supposed to have some flags around on the ground to mark their area. I don't know what happened but no one saw the flags or someone in the group ahead maybe released a little early; it is one of those sad things of war.

"Since this was our last, on return, we left formation and headed for base. When we came to our airfield we were at treetop level and buzzed the control tower. We were one happy crew to have completed our missions alive."

To celebrate the end of their missions, Sanderson and Milo Kelsey got passes to go to Rome. On the way through the mountains around Naples, Sanderson ran into an old high school classmate Paul Rusten, who was in charge of an Army photo lab and who showed the two fliers the first jet plane to arrive in Italy.

Though the Rome furlough was good times, the deadly seriousness of war was not forgotten then, or now.

"Some friends never made it back from Germany; you tried not to make too many friends because it hurt when you lost them. We did not lose any of our crew, though Kelsey earned a Purple Heart when flak hit him in the head. The pilot and I had to drag him out through the bomb bay doors and along the narrow walkway into the radio room; I'm still not sure how we did it but then I took over the top turret for him.

"We also went through three B-17s, so we were very lucky. We all got the Air Medal with three oak-leaf clusters, the European African Middle Eastern Campaign medal with six battle stars, the Good Conduct medal, the Victory medal and the Presidential Unit Citation. The Greek government awarded everyone in the 483rd Bomber Group the Greek commemorative medal, the highest medal they can give to those other than their own soldiers."

Shortly after returning from furlough, the war in Europe was over and Sanderson was going home. He was eventually transported to Camp Kilmer, N.J, from where he caught a train to Chicago. In Chicago he hopped a Chicago Northwestern train headed for Elroy, which happened to be conducted by family friend Harley Kopenhefer. "He said, 'you're sitting with me' so I did and we visited all the way back to Elroy."

Sanderson was home on a 30-day furlough but was still in the service, so near the end of his "party time" at home, he and a friend drove to New Mexico where he caught a train to Los Angeles and the Santa Ana rest camp, contemplating but doubting he would be sent to the Pacific since it appeared that war too would soon be over and he knew he had enough points to get out.

"There was quite a bit of partying there too. I visited Hollywood and the StageDoor Canteen where Phil Harris put on a show for us soldiers and I saw some movie stars.

"That's when, one night while we were coming back to camp, my pilot Bruce Walz said to me 'it's like we just woke up from a nightmare.' I surely agreed with him."

By July, 1945, Sanderson had enough points to be discharged and was eagerly welcomed home for good by his parents, though they still waited for word of when his brother Archie would return from Europe — that reunion would wait six months.

"Both us boys came back home alive from the war after three years. My parents were very thankful be-

The crew of Gerald Sanderson's Paper Doll, pictured in Italy, included Gerald (left), pilot Bruce Waltz, Bob Louden, Bill McCarl, Milo Kelsey, Dick Brehm, Emil Noehm and Hank Vaclavick.

cause ma and dad had been through a war and bad times themselves."

Sanderson spent his first six months home "running around a lot and drinking some" in between his full-time job at the Hercules Powder plant in Elroy. Then, one night at a bowling alley, he met Rosalie Ennis, a girl he'd met two years before on a ride from Dreamland to Wonewoc. "I had thought about her even when I was overseas in Italy so I asked her for a date."

But, because so much had changed since he went to war — including where Rosalie lived — their first date was "a fizzle."

"When I arrived at the house where we'd let her off two years before, nobody was home. I didn't know her parents had moved, so I went home."

The Hero Next Door

The next week Sanderson was able to explain himself, so well that by Christmas, 1946, the two were engaged. They were married June 21, 1947, in Wonewoc. On July 10, 1948, they had their first son, named Bruce after Sanderson's bomber crew pilot. Eventually, the Sandersons had four children, which they raised in the early years on a mink farm they operated while Sanderson worked various other jobs, including Ray-O-Vac. When he was laid off there in 1955, Sanderson started with Wisconsin Dairies Cooperative in Union Center, where he stayed for 30 years, 10 as plant manager.

Through the years, Sanderson served his family and his community well. A life member of the American Legion and VFW, he also was on the foundation board of St. Joseph's Hospital, the Elroy museum board, the library fund-raising committee and in the Lions Club. Sanderson is also an avid golfer and his team won the local championship three times.

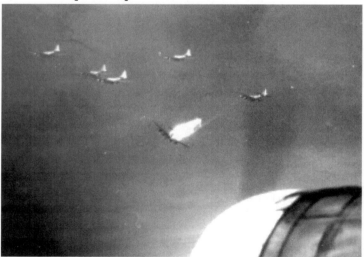

A few seconds after this photo was taken by Horace Small, the bomber with Gerald Sanderson's good friend Michael Hornack rolled over, engulfed in flames, and went down. There were no survivors.

And, he still likes to blow that horn now and then. He plays at Devil's Lake Lodge with the Hal Edwards Band in the summer and plays in the Elroy community band, the Town Tones.

He retired in 1983 and soon found himself following another soldier's footsteps overseas — those of his father. He has twice gone to Russia to retrace the steps of his parents' courtship and flight to freedom.

RELIVING RUSSIAN MEMORIES

Sanderson's father Carl was born in New Lisbon, Wis., in 1894, and went into the Army, serving along the Mexican border before heading for the fighting in France in W.W. I. He fought in the second battle of the Marne and the drive on the Scissions front. He fought often hand-to-hand in No Man's Land, killing a German solider with his bayonette. He was gassed with mustard gas and, near the end of the war, was captured and held prisoner of war — where he was nearly starved and "walked to death."

After returning from the First World War, Carl Sanderson volunteered to go to Siberia, Russia, to guard food supplies along the Trans-Siberian Railroad. He was eventually sent to Posolskaya station, 60 miles south of Ulan Ude, in Irlinka. It's there he met Sanderson's mother Ekaterina Romanov Mikhailova, one of 11 children born in the village of Naryn, 30 miles north of the Mongolian border. She was working for a Jewish family near the station and tipped off Sanderson as to who had opened fire on the box cars one evening. The two fell in love and married in Russia, knowing that Ekaterina would have to leave the country or be killed for helping Americans. They eventually returned to the U.S. and settled in Elroy.

Carl Sanderson committed suicide in 1947, haunted by his own war memories.

"My father never told of his experiences. I think that was probably from getting gas that the Germans sprayed on our soldiers and all the effects the war had

Gerald Sanderson and his wife, Rosalie.

on him in his short life. I know from my experiences in World War II that those experiences never leave you."

All the more reason Sanderson appreciates everything his parents, his friends and he sacrificed.

"Life seems to go in a circle. My parents fled Irlinka for a safer, freer world in America. As their children, me and my generation, survived the hard times of the 'Great Depression.' Those tough times made us able to survive the hell we went through during World War II. It gave us the stamina to fight the war that freed the world's people from the atrocities of Nazi Germany and Imperial Japan. After retirement, I was free to return to Irlinka to meet my relatives and gain an appreciation first hand for what it is to live with a lack of freedom and opportunity."

It is that freedom and opportunity that Sanderson is proud to have fought to secure, and prouder still of those who sacrificed even more than he for freedom.

"I had hardships, but I have to consider myself luckier than them. As Ernie Pyle said, 'there are no atheists in foxholes.' So I'm sure the men on the ground prayed as much as we did over the skies of Germany.

The War in Europe

"I still think of my friends, of Mike Hornak who went down in flames, 75 miles south of Berlin; about Roy Milner who bailed out over Austria and walked back to Yugoslavia; about my Chinese friend Herbert Ginoz (sic) who went to the UW before the war, was shot down over Vienna and held prisoner of war until it ended; and about my brother who was wounded twice and suffered the cold and mud with nothing but the hard ground to sleep on.

"The challenge is for this generation to guard those freedoms, my friends suffered and died for."

BATTERED JUMPER
Joe D. Reilly
Janesville, Wis.

Private Joe Reilly, a Janesville, Wis., native, didn't walk, nor run, nor ride into W.W. II history. He jumped into the European Theater's biggest battles, as a paratrooper with the 101st Airborne.

Born May 7, 1921, the oldest of two, Reilly graduated from Janesville High School in 1939 and went to work in a defense factory in Delavan. His work there was important enough to the war effort that he got a deferment from the draft, automatically renewable every six months. But in March of 1943, Reilly's patriotism drove him to give up that promised safety, enlist in the Army and parachute into the greatest battles of the 20th Century.

Near the end of his basic training at Camp Robinson in Little Rock, Ark., two paratrooper lieutenants came to recruit men for airborne. Reilly leapt at the Army's offer to jump into battle, often behind enemy lines with little but his rifle, a parachute and a prayer to keep him from harm's way.

The War in Europe

"They told us training would be tough. *(In fact, like many veterans, the first time Reilly rode in an airplane was the first time he jumped out of one.)* "We'd have to go through jump school to get our wings. But, you got an extra $50 a month for jump pay which seemed like a fair exchange."

Training was tough. It had to be to prepare Reilly for the rigors of his first day — his longest day— in battle, the D-Day Invasion of Normandy, France on June 6, 1944.

Having earned his paratrooper wings and the right to blouse his trousers to show his jump boots — "very important to a new paratrooper," Reilly joined the 541st parachute regiment for advanced training and maneuvers, as a private first class 81-mm mortar gunner at Camp McCall, N.C.

In February 1944, he boarded a troop ship bound for Europe as a replacement for an airborne unit, wondering which division he would land in, the 82nd or the 101st.

Reilly continued training during a three-week stop in Belfast, Northern Ireland, before shipping out and eventually took a troop train to Southern England. Once there, Reilly's question was answered when he first saw the sign of his new unit — a Screamin' Eagle patch. He was now with the 101st Airborne Division, assigned to headquarters company, 3rd battalion, 501 Parachute Infantry.

From March until the last days of May, the new replacement trooper had practice parachute drops and more training which included a lot of dry run field exercises. In early June, the troopers were trucked to an airbase with restricted barbed wire enclosures.

"There, we were issued weapons, ammo and K-rations and were housed in an airport hanger, which was better than the tent we lived in the last three months. We enjoyed the public address system that played good old big band records like McNamara's band and Paper Doll." The best part of his stay was the Air Corps chow. "The food was so good it made us feel resentful for what we'd been eating. There was no comparison. I'd always felt the Army paid us extra for jump pay but they shorted us on a lot of other things."

But there was little time for the finer things anyway. "We were kept busy learning the terrain we might land on." They were drilled to memorize the rivers, locks, roads, rail lines and villages they would encounter since they were not permitted to draw nor carry maps.

And, there were other challenges. "We were issued a complete new jump outfit that was impregnated with a peculiar odor which was supposed to keep us dry and insect proof. It failed on both counts."

LEAPING INTO D-DAY

The day the paratroopers had been preparing eagerly and apprehensively for was soon at hand. They would be among the first Allied troops in battle, parachuting into Nazi occupied France along the coast near Normandy. Their objective was to help knock out Nazi defenses and clear an easier path for thousands land-ing on the beaches. *(D-Day memories are based on Reilly's transcripts for the Eisenhower Center for the Uni-versity of New Orleans and interviews with this author.)* About 6 p.m. on June 5, 1944, Reilly and the rest of the Screamin' Eagles replaced their treasured uniform patches with an even more treasured symbol, the American flag.

"Then, we had showers. Church services were close by and well attended as every one was becoming aware of their mortality. I am Catholic and church was no stranger to me. My company was very conscious of what we would be called on to do."

Reilly and company watched three white stripes be-ing painted around the tails of the planes. That after-noon, all the divisions' helmets had been painted. "We used a well-known mark on all the helmets — the 501 was a diamond, the 502 a heart, 506 a spade and 327th, a glider infantry, was a club."

Then, the troopers tried to catch some sleep.

"It was impossible. Some of us pretended but we were

kidding ourselves. It was obvious we were going into combat and, for the most part, we were in good spirits. It's an old adage that young men make the best soldiers because they believe they are not going to get killed."

Shortly after 10 p.m. the company filed out to the runway.

"We put on our chutes and checked our equipment bundles assigned to each plane. We carried about 150 pounds and, as a member of the 81-mm mortar platoon, I jumped with guns and ammo as well as K-rations.

"My best buddy Tom Chapman, from Kentucky, and I talked briefly about our pilot who said he too was from Kentucky. This made Tom feel good. He said, 'Joe, we have a good one here; he'll take us right to the drop zone.' That was important because if we'd missed the drop zone we'd have been separated or killed by falling in the ocean."

All his equipment, especially a folding shovel for digging foxholes made climbing the narrow ladders of the aircraft extra challenging. The design of the C-47 aircraft determined how the troopers were carried and released to their drop zones.

"There are two sticks in each aircraft of 12-18 men each. The No. 2 man in the door (the second one out) carries the heaviest equipment. That is the best position from which to leave the plane."

Reilly's plane was in the third wave to take off in a tight formation that night.

"Unfortunately, tight formation means we cannot ride out the numerous coastline air pockets. This caused the plane to roll and pitch. It made some men nauseous and the floor very slippery.

"As we climbed in total black out, sparks from some engines bothered us because the gas tanks are so close to the engines. We knew the C-47s as firetraps. As we started over the French Coast, some anti-aircraft fire was coming up. Not much at first but it only takes one to bring a plane down. Some planes ahead on the right

and left got hit and the blaze that erupted only confirmed our firetrap fears .

"It was dark and seemed windy, probably due to the prop blast of so many planes. There was little conversation as each man had his own thoughts of anxiety and fear. My thoughts were dominated by hoping the pilot would bring our plane into the drop zone."

The troopers were waiting in quiet trepidation for the stand up and hook up signal. "Just above the door on the right hand side are two lights, one red, one green. When the red light comes on, troopers know they have five to 10 minutes to get ready. So you stand and hook your static line and check the parachute pack on the man directly ahead of you. You slap his back to let him know you see that his static line is hooked.

"The No. 1 man stood in the door with hands outside the door edge over the taped hinges. The No. 2 man is very close behind him as are we all close behind each other. When the red light goes out and the green light goes on, it's time to leave the plane in a hurry."

Watching for the lights, Reilly first heard the motors throttle back and he knew he was about make his 12th jump ever, the most important jump of his life.

"The flak increased as we drew close to the Normandy coast and we were ready to get out because we believe in the law of averages where flak is concerned.

"The planes all dropped as low as possible. With all my equipment, I knew it wouldn't take long to reach the ground. As the wind fills the chute, you feel the familiar snap on your harness and I quickly said a prayer hoping I didn't have too many blown panels because at 800 or 900 feet, if your main chute has any problems, forget the reserve; you're too close to activate it.

"As soon as you leave a plane, I am always surprised by the sudden change in noise level. It gets quiet for a few seconds, peaceful."

R-4775 ARMY EXCHANGE RATION CARD - ETO

No. _____ Date issued _____

Name _____ ASN _____

Signature *Joe D. Reilly*

Organization _____ APO _____

Signature Unit C.O. *John A. Ford*

A 6

Joe Reilly's airborne ration card from Oct. 22, 1945, which kept track of how much he was issued in tobacco, matches, toothpaste and other goods.

THE LONGEST DAY

The peaceful quiet didn't last long, for in the distance Reilly could hear sporadic gun and small arms fire.

"It was a dark night and the ground came up to meet me just as my eyes saw some trees outlined in the dimness. As quick as I hit the ground, I got a knife and cut a couple of panels from the chute. They were nylon and almost airtight so they made great blankets and were easy to carry."

It was 1:40 a.m. when Reilly hit that ground, located behind the Normandy beaches.

"We were all supplied with a little toy called a cricket that makes a click sound when one presses it. I heard a noise nearby and gave two clicks; two clicks answered me so I took the safety off my M-1 rifle. The regimental commander of the 502nd landed close to me. I never met an officer that wasn't friendly in a tight spot.

"I was soon joined by eight or 10 troopers. I was happy as they were that we were in one piece on the ground.

The Hero Next Door

My drop was on target, four or five miles inland from Utah Beach for the 3rd Battalion of the 501st regiment. It was then I remembered Tom was right; that pilot brought us right in our drop zone. Some pilots got so frightened when flack got heavy that they pushed the green light and dumped all the troopers in the water!"

Reilly and the rest of the troopers from his group hunkered down in the pasture they landed in until the dark got a bit lighter, around 3:20 a.m.

Then, Reilly's long day really began; it didn't end until midnight. In a way, it never really ended.

"We could hear some more small arms fire and then some heavy artillery in the distance. We came through a hedgerow and walked up a hill. When we got to the top, we kept a low profile and what we saw was awe-inspiring.

"About a mile away, we could see a coastal gun emplacement. A few radiomen from the Navy, who jumped with us, were just beginning to give us a show I'll never forget. On their radios, they contacted some battlewagons offshore. Their firepower was very impressive. When I saw the projectiles come and land near the heavy concrete Nazi pillboxes, first I saw the blue ball of fire and then heard the explosion. They fired for about an hour and I just thanked God they were on our side.

"I didn't know if they'd penetrated until later that day when we got up there and saw there were six or eight Krauts inside with just a little blood from their noses and ears. The concussion from the 16-inch shells had got them."

Reilly and a group of 30 started down a road toward the coast, hearing some small arms fire to the right and left.

"It was about 6 a.m. but it seemed it should be at least noon. We knew soon that we'd face the Krauts and, as we came around the bend, I saw the first dead man in a ditch. He was a German with the side of his head blown away and his brains hanging out over the side of his face. It's common knowledge you always remember the first dead man you see but not many more very vividly, unless it is your own troopers."

By then the group was nearing a causeway behind Utah Beach. "As we drew closer to a crossroads, we were joined by quite a few officers and troopers, about 50. The officers decided we would circle in two groups and advance to take a little village nearby, Pouppeville.

"After a cautious approach, we went building by building clearing out snipers. We had some wounded troopers but I was beginning to get the feeling this was too easy.

"But combat experience makes boys old very quickly and I was about to get another lesson. I prided myself on learning in a hurry and this was to be a very valuable asset all through combat.

"A wounded trooper lay in an apple orchard at the edge of the village. He was hit bad enough where he couldn't get on his feet. A medic with his Red Cross band and first aid kit bent over him.

"Up a tree, not far away, was a German sniper. He started firing on the medic in the open field. He fired four or five times and forced the medic to retreat.

"I watched the medic run back and start to work on the soldier again. The sniper started to fire again and this time he drew fire from about 10 of us — a barrage of probably 60 rounds. I remember being criticized for spending too many rounds on the sniper, but that just made me more trigger-happy.

"When it was over, the medic was dead beside the wounded man. The sniper was riddled before he hit the ground. Lesson taught: The Geneva Convention was an empty fraud. The enemy would kill an unarmed medic as fast as they could.

"I now knew we could not expect any mercy. After all, we were really spies. We were behind enemy lines, which afforded us the opportunity to see all their defenses, movements, supplies and numbers."

Reilly knew that kind of position was especially dangerous, even deadly. But it was not the fear of death that scared him most. A devout Catholic, Reilly explains "nobody likes to die, but if you have a strong faith you think even death will work out; God will take care of you. I felt sorry for people that didn't have a strong religious background. We all had the same apprehensions but I had that extra faith to help carry me beyond them."

Two things scared Reilly more than death that long day and every battle-weary day after — the pain of being wounded and the agony of being taken prisoner.

Thankfully the rapid-fire life of a combat soldier leaves little time to ponder much more than the next minute. There were towns to fight for, like Pouppeville.

"Pouppeville was a pushover in every way except the physical and mental strain that accompanied every advance.

"Think about carrying 30 or 40 pounds of equipment, getting up and running about 20 yards, keeping a low profile, dropping down, getting up, crossing a road, and crawling along a ditch for another 50 yards on your elbows and knees, peeking up over the ditch to see if any Krauts are nearby. Then, if they outnumber you, quietly digging in and hoping no one has seen or heard you until more support comes up. Then, if support doesn't come, going back and getting help without being detected — all the while wondering if a German bullet has your name on it or if some of your own shells might land close enough to get you.

"I and the rest of the troopers moved five or six miles, dug in several times, lost some good men, watched some wounded men suffer the loss of limbs and blood."

Those images are still vivid as are many of the often-repeated phrases from that day.

"They still tie knots in my stomach: 'Get that sniper!' 'Move out,' 'Oh, God not him!' 'Medic!' and 'We're going to lay down a field of fire right now!'"

"People often ask me how I can remember what happened to me over 50 years ago and I answer that 'if you

ask people where they were when (President John F.) Kennedy was shot, they know exactly.' Well, combat is very stressful. If someone was trying to take your life every day, you'd remember some details."

And Reilly vividly remembers the tiring battle over his own exhaustion. " I was constantly hot, angry, hungry and tired.

"It is difficult to put into words what it means to go into combat, to lay your life on the line every day. The only comfort is knowing other paratroopers will back you to the last man. I want to explain that we had only small arms fire, 30-caliber and mortars to face artillery and tanks and German fighter planes. I would be derelict if I didn't give the highest praise I can bestow on the American soldier, especially the paratrooper. He has the guts and isn't afraid to give the most he's got, sometimes his life. I know our behavior was not the best in garrison but on the battlefield, we proved we could stand against anything the Krauts had."

"My opinions were never asked on the battlefield. I was told what to do and was expected to carry out orders no questions asked. It is the private who puts his life on the battleline every minute and gets no credit. I hope people can understand how important the guts of the American foot soldier are in battle."

Those guts were courage wrapped in instinct, a combination Reilly quickly sharpened.

"I was very anxious to stay alert, observe everything. Of all the senses, hearing becomes the most important. Your ears start to tell your mind a lot. I know one can tell, for example, when you hear the muzzle charge first and then the louder explosion a few seconds later that you are near the gun. How close? The sound can register that too, depending on the size of the projectile. I soon became aware of the distinct differences in some weapons' sounds. The Germans had a famous gun called the 88 with a shell about 3-inches in diameter and about 20-inches long. Its sound was a unique high pitched noise."

A bombed-out church in Holland, where Joe Reilly fought during the fall of 1944.

It's sounds of a different kind — the sounds of dying men gasping for life — which haunt Reilly's memories still.

"We were dazed-alert and the shadows were getting long as we went over a hedgerow. We dug in and posted guard. I got picked for an early morning shift. Nearby was a makeshift medic headquarters in a little shed with some badly wounded men.

Without sleep for nearly 36 hours, Reilly pulled his parachute panel over himself in his foxhole and lay there trying to sleep. He still remembers the sounds of death coming from the shed.

"Do you know what soldiers cry out when they are dying? Some say it softly, some loudly, they say: 'Mama, mama.'

"From the medic's shed I heard that call again and again; I didn't sleep long."

And, by the way, Reilly adds, Germans he heard dying cried the same.

"It was indeed the longest day, my first day in the killing fields."

NAZIS IN RETREAT

There were many more days in the killing fields for Reilly, more than a year's worth.

After the initial Normandy assault on D-Day, it took the Allies more than a month of hard fighting to penetrate the hedgerows and drive the Germans to retreat.

One of the hardest fought battles for the 101st was capturing the large city of Carentan, France. "Our battalion had the dubious honor to try and take and hold it. Our first attempt was met with very heavy resistance ... and we were beaten back. The only other way in was through heavy swamps, which the Germans didn't think we'd do. That's exactly what we did. We lost quite a few men to get there but we captured it."

For their bravery some Army brass wanted to reward some in the 101st with medals and lined the men up in parade fashion a few days later, learning the hard way

that the enemy had an ever-watchful eye even after battle. "As the presentation was about to start, Kraut artillery opened fire and we dispersed in quick order; some French officers were wounded."

After six weeks in Normandy, and a furlough to England, Reilly parachuted into Holland, and back into combat, Sept. 17, 1944, in a daytime jump operation named Market Garden.

The Market Garden mission in Holland was for two American airborne divisions, including Reilly's, and a British airborne division to secure bridges across canals and rivers, like the Rhine, before the Germans had the chance to destroy them and delay the Allied advance. With Dutch intelligence and some tough fighting, Reilly's division held the bridge near Eindhoven. The British weren't so lucky, losing more than two-thirds of its 9,000 men in the battle for a bridge near Arnhem on the Lower Rhine. (*World War II,* p. 520.)

Reilly's duties had changed since he last saw combat and he was now a 300 radioman for the entire 81 mortar platoon, advancing ahead to observation points with sergeants to spot targets for mortars and help out rifle platoons and other units.

Finding observation points to spot from was difficult and dangerous in the flat Holland terrain. "We found out we made a big mistake using windmills as observation posts because the Germans had every windmill zeroed in and we lost some good men."

And observation posts, once found, were best approached under cover of darkness. Approach by daylight was often painful as one of America's top officers quickly discovered, Reilly recalls.

"One afternoon I was very surprised to see some men coming toward the observation point and sure enough the Germans opened up a barrage. The men coming turned out to be General Taylor and his entourage. As they ran back, the general caught some shrapnel in his rear end. Medics attending him told us where he got hit and we liked having this particular first hand knowledge and we were all grinning when we got together for them to give him his Purple Heart."

There were other, "lighter" moments too.

"We were at rest in a Dutchman's house, writing letters, playing cards and sampling the 'local supply.' Suddenly the door flew open ... and there was General Taylor. Of course we flew to our feet with pots and canteens flying all over the kitchen. He looked around and said 'at ease men ... is there anything you men need?'

"Well our sergeant Al Charpentier had been in the Army longer than most and was quick on his feet. He said 'Yes Sir. We need razor blades!' Well, we all had plenty of razor blades but we hadn't taken time out to shave and looked kind of scruffy. General Taylor turned to one of his men and said to see to it that 'these men get razor blades.' We had more damn razor blades than you can ever imagine after that!"

Another time, shortly after the troops received orders that they no longer needed to forage for food (sometimes killing Dutch livestock), a colonel approached a canal near Reilly and saw two men on the other side with a newly slaughtered cow. He said, 'haven't you men heard the order?' One man said 'yes,' but the other knew they were in deep trouble and said, 'Colonel the cow stuck her head up over the dike and she had a German helmet stuck to her head and before we knew what happened, we shot it.' The Colonel just said 'that's the best damn story I heard all day but don't let me catch you again.'"

Away from the water, the 101st liberated many Dutch villages, like Eerde. But, it wasn't always easy. "We had several of what we called 'rat races,' where we'd capture the town and the Krauts would circle around as we were leaving and retake it and then we'd circle around. It was both humorous and tragic. "Still, people were so happy to see us they had national flags out and a little parade."

But not all was festive. "I remember in the town square a bunch of men had gathered some girls and shaved

their heads. They were Nazi sympathizers and the Dutch had a strong opposition to anyone who collaborated with the Nazis."

And like every combat solider, Reilly had his share of close calls. Perhaps the closest happened when Reilly was literally saved by the luck of a draw.

"We were in a static area one night and drew cards to see who would go on guard duty. I got lucky and drew a higher card than Ed Dixon from Burmingham, Ala. He went out and 30 minutes later, an artillery barage hit and tore the inside muscles of his leg away. I never saw him again after that, but imagine my joy when two years ago I saw his name in a newsletter and knew he had survived!"

BATTERING BASTOGNE

After Holland, on Dec. 1, 1944, Reilly and company were stationed back in France at a camp called Mourmelon LaPeite, not far from Rheims. "With my new job, I was assigned a Thompson sub-machine gun as my personal weapon which I carried through the end of my days in combat.

"Most our weapons had been sent back to ordinance for repairs and most of our equipment was being checked out at quartermaster. In addition, many of the men were on furlough in France."

While the Allies had dwindled numbers and supplies they had too much of just one thing the last month in 1944: confidence. The Allies had the Germans on the run and little anticipated the Germans still had the strength or desire to counterattack. But on Dec. 16 the Nazis did just that, and with a vengeance in what became one of the most massive, hardest fought battle of the European war — The Battle of the Bulge. Between Dec. 16, 1944, and January 16, 1945, the Americans lost 76,890 killed or wounded, the Germans 81,834 (*World War II*, p. 324).

Reilly was right in the heat of that battle, fighting

nearly to death in the infamous, besieged town of Bastogne.

SIEGE IN THE BATTLE OF THE BULGE

Reilly's entrance into The Battle of the Bulge, like most Allied soldiers, was awkward.

"We were awakened very early [that day] and I remember some troopers complaining very bitterly since they had hangovers. There was a good deal of profanity in the air when we were told we had to go up to the front as we knew what that meant."

The troopers knew they were going somewhere up to Belgium. And, they also knew they were going into battle woefully ill-supplied.

"We knew we didn't have much equipment going with us. A lot of us had no helmets, very little ammo. A lot of our weapons were back in ordinance and it was cold, dark, dreary and foggy as the trucks rolled out for miles. We also had just a few K-rations with us because we had to pack in one heck of a hurry.

"Some guys did have Christmas packages from home and did it ever seem good to share a cookie with somebody because we knew we weren't going to get very much for quite a while.

"We knew we were going back into battle, and that leaves a pit in your stomach, especially when you're a veteran as I was, going into my third campaign."

As they neared the front after 13 hours on the trucks again, Reilly could hear artillery in the distance. "That sound makes you feel low."

They soon felt lower as they saw a stream of people rushing down the road, away from where the soldiers were heading. "We said, 'My gosh, what's happening?' Here's all these troops coming down the road toward us. They were a ragtag looking bunch, rear echelon people, people from quartermaster, nurses and small groups of armor. There were even tank destroyers and a mobile artillery. They were all coming right at us and

they were in one hell of a hurry!

"We shook our heads and kept going toward the hill. When we got closer, we saw the town sign 'Bastogne' though we didn't know what the heck Bastogne was or even how to pronounce it; we had about 15 different pronunciations. We just thought: 'All these people are all coming out and we're going down. What's happening now?'"

So many were leaving that the narrow roads were getting clogged. "We started thinking, 'Well, we must be going down there to clear something up.' And we sure as hell were!"

His division arrived in Bastogne Dec. 19 just before the town was completely cut off from other American forces. The 501st was given an area around Mont, and soon found itself in the "thick of things."

"We started to lay out our lines. Things were rather quiet for maybe the first half day. Then, the weather started getting even colder and foggy. I guess the fog helped us on several occasions because it was harder for the enemy to see our movements. Of course, we couldn't see theirs either. Maybe it was a wash.

"And the Krauts were a bit surprised too because they didn't realize who their formidable opponents were going to be. They'd been pushing units all over the place until they hit the 101st. The Germans believed they could just keep right on coming and they had a pretty good record of doing just that for a while. They'd already gone through three divisions.

"But we were seasoned troops and when they came at us, it started to snow and was getting even colder. Our troops were hungry and tired and add to that we were angry is a mild way of putting it. We were not in a very good mood. We knew we had to dig in and hunker down.

"We were told to hold this little area between Mont and Neffe and knew very soon that we were outnumbered. There's been many guesses about by how much but I would say four to one would be a fairly honest

assumption."

Reilly and the 501st was in the northeast section of the city where the regiment faced off against two or more German divisions at any one time. On Dec. 20 Bastogne was totally cut off and became located behind enemy lines. The Germans bombed the besieged city every night while artillery kept up the carnage by day.

The 101st soon realized they were not facing a defeated Germany army, they were up against some of the toughest soldiers in the Nazi ranks.

"We were facing the Panzer Grenadiers, so it was going to be a long, hard fight. We knew we'd have a tough time keeping it going against the Krauts. They had tanks and we didn't. We had mortars and 30-caliber fire power but that's not too much against a tank."

Though many had left the battered city, the Catholic nuns in the town were bold enough to stay. "The nuns had an aid station and sort of a hospital area in that particular part of Bastogne. We'd always admired their courage and compassion, especially for our wounded."

In fact, Reilly's personal hero, the division's chaplain Father Francis Sampson, featured in the book *Paratrooper Padre* (1948) and *Look Out Below* (1958), was taken prisoner by the Germans as he tried to help the wounded in Bastogne. He spent the remainder of the war as a prisoner of war. "I admired him because he always stayed with the enlisted men and stayed behind to pray with the wounded, pray over the dead and help the medics. He had a different code of ethics; he had a lot of courage and didn't give in to his captors." The chaplain later became Major General Sampson, the Army's chief of chaplains.

Reilly and fellow troopers held up for a time in a small shed near the Catholic aid station. "It was getting even colder and there was a woodpile in the shed. One time I was so exhausted that I went to sleep right on that woodpile. When I got up the next morning, I thought, 'My gosh how could I have ever slept there?' But I did.

The Hero Next Door

When you get that tired you can crawl in where the elements can't get you quite as much and sleep. It was better than trying to dig your way into the frozen ground outside."

Every Allied who could hold a weapon used one to fight for Bastogne, seasoned troops or not. The ranks included the 501st barber, Mike Herta from Pocatella, Idaho, who provided one of the only comic moments during the siege.

"We had a little slit trench which is where you relieve yourself. Well, Mike was out near this slit trench and the shelling got very, very heavy. When a shell came in and landed close by he was completely covered by dirt. He called out and we thought we heard a noise but it wasn't very loud. So we started to look around and my gosh, if he wasn't buried, completely covered up. He said, 'Help! Get me out! I'm your company barber!' By gosh, we did dig him out. It was a little relief for the seriousness that we had faced."

Comic relief didn't last long. The fighting continued to intensify as the Nazis tightened the noose around the hold-out city.

"They had us surrounded. We could tell because your ears remember what the 88 sounds like, the smaltzers, the machine guns and incoming shells from German tanks. No matter which way we fired, they fired back.

"It got so intense, at night especially, when they made an attack that we got the hand grenades out and had some friendly fires — a nicer way of saying some of our own people were wounded by our grenades."

The situation was desperate, especially given the low supplies. "We knew the Krauts were advancing and that they were going to try and take the whole ball of wax. Our ammunition was getting very low."

About this time, General Tony McAuliffe was given the opportunity to surrender Bastogne to the Germans and made a name for himself with his famous reply: "Nuts!"

"The Germans didn't understand exactly what that

meant so Col. Joseph Harper with the 327th Glider Infantry told them through an interpreter that it means 'Go to hell!'"

Christmas Eve was soon upon them and the troops were hoping for a holiday reprieve. The Germans made it quite obvious that would not come.

"I was observing that night when we heard some bombs go off. We knew it was close by and it was. The Germans were bombing Bastogne and — intentional or not — some bombs hit the first aid stations and hospital.

"I was in a hole with Jesse Matlock from Spokane, Wash., who we called 'chief' because he was supposedly part Indian. Jess and I came out of the hole. I said, 'You know — and I think I used quite a bit of profanity — those SOBs will never win this war! Look at what they just done!' And, Jess agreed with me. It was one of those emotional things you see and just get the feeling there's no way in the world someone who could do that could possibly win."

Then, on Dec. 26, Reilly heard tanks that didn't sound German. To his great relief, they were Gen. George Patton's tanks.

"Were we happy to see our own tanks, especially his tanks! History records Gen. Patton had a lot of respect for the airborne troops, especially at Bastogne. Retreat and capture were his greatest dislikes and we had done neither against great odds and still saved the town."

Reilly and his group rode on the outside of the tanks for a few days. "The only problem is when you're riding on the outside of a tank and it hits a personnel mine, fragments spray around the tank quite a bit. So this is definitely a disadvantage."

But there are advantages for cold, tired troops. "The engines are warm and that's better than leaning up against a frozen tree. And, you didn't have to walk through the deep snow."

On Dec. 27, the sun broke the fog and the troopers finally got some air support, firepower and supplies.

And, word came down that the troops could forage. "That meant we could get a hold of any food we could use. This was part of what you might say was the panic button because they knew our supplies were running out as fast as the ammo. So, we corralled what we could no matter if it was moving or flour or what it was. We were, by this time, experts at making up food out of nothing. Our previous combat missions had fortified us in being able to quickly turn supplies into something to eat because it's cold and food becomes quite important when you're in traumatic situations.

"About this time, the cooks decided they were going to give us a treat. And, the cooks hadn't had it easy as a lot of them were forced into front line duty too. They got a hold of some flour and made a lot of pancakes. As I said, their intentions were good but by the time the pancakes got to us on the line, they were frozen solid. Some time if you want a reality check, make some pancakes. Let them freeze outside for about eight hours and then try to eat them. It's the same as eating cardboard."

Shortly after, the planes came in. Because it had snowed a lot the bombers couldn't see the orange panels the troopers set out to denote their front lines. "I was sitting with my little radio in a very well-bunkered hole with Jess. They came over and dropped a 500 pounder not very far from our hole. We were lying in the hole face down but when that thing went off, our rear ends hit the top of the bunker and I said, "Oh my God, that was a close one!

"We crawled out of the hole and quickly got the snow off that orange panel so the bombers could see where our front line was."

For their determined fight to save Bastogne, the 501st Parachute Infantry and 101st Airborne Division were presented a special unit citation by General Dwight D. Eisenhower.

In the unit citation, Lt. General George C. Patton wrote the following about the fighters his tanks rushed to re-

lieve:

"The enemy attempted to seize Bastogne (Belgium) by attacking constantly and savagely with the best of his armour and infantry. Without the benefit of prepared defenses, facing almost overwhelming odds and with very limited and fast-dwindling supplies, these units maintained a high combat morale and an impenetrable defense, despite extremely heavy bombing, intense artillery fire and constant attacks from infantry and armour on all sides of their completely cut off and encircled position. This masterful and grimly determined defense denied the enemy even momentary success in an operation for which he paid dearly in men, material and eventually morale. The outstanding courage and resourcefulness and undaunted determination of this gallant force is in keeping with the highest traditions of the service."

In the same citation, Gen. Eisenhower added, that the position Reilly and the rest of the 501st held was of "the utmost importance to the Allied forces."

"You in reserve were hurried forward and told to hold that position. All the elements of drama — battle drama — were there. You were cut off, surrounded. Only valor, complete self-confidence ... knowledge that you were well trained and only the determination to win could sustain soldiers under those conditions. You were given a marvelous opportunity and you met every test. You have become a fitting symbol ... . As it is my great privilege to say to you here today, to the 101st Division and all its attached units, 'I'm awfully proud of you.'"

News about the heroics in Bastogne by Reilly's division spread fast. "The press now called us rather famous paratroopers: We were known as the Battered Bastards of Bastogne."

And, the name rang true. Reilly earned a Bronze Star for his heroic, stubborn fighting during the siege. Between Dec. 19, 1944 and Jan. 17, 1945, the 101st saw 982 killed in action. *(U.S. War Department, W.W. II).*

BASTOGNE PART 2: THE FOREST

Reilly remembers the Battle of the Bulge in two parts. First was the savage defense of the city Bastogne itself, for which his division was so highly praised. Then, came the battle of the snow-covered Hurtgen Forest area around it, where German troops fought dressed in white to help camouflage their positions.

"There's a lot of forest surrounding Bastogne. And you know when you get in the woods — if you've ever been in the woods in wintertime, and being from Wisconsin I'd been there — it's a lot warmer in the woods than in an open field. The snow was almost up to our waists.

"So when you advanced during the day, you were always checking the forest for a good bunker so if you return to that area as it gets dark, you know where to stay for the night. I remembered passing this area and thought 'God, there's a good hole.' Sure enough, we were settling in for the night and I found that hole again.

"I always put my Thompson sub-barrel in first and this time it hit a moving body. I didn't know who it was but I suspected it could be a German so I shouted 'Rouse!' He came out and looked like he was very frightened.

"I was tired, and hungry and in no mood to wait to see what was going to happen so I immediately entered the bunker. He walked away into the darkness. Sometimes, you just act on impulse."

Surviving troopers like Reilly were hardened veterans who didn't always have time or energy for the trappings of proper Army protocol.

While preparing food during a down time one day, a command car came along a road nearby and stopped. "Immediately, we could see who was coming. It was General Maxwell Taylor [who had been in Washington, D.C. when his troops were fighting to hold Bastogne]. He had his entourage with him, a couple of captains and lieutenants. He rubbed his hands together and said,

The War in Europe

"I want to compliment you men for a great performance."

He was ready to get into some more eloquent statements. But we had a cook from upstate New York named Emerson who was not very shy. He was dirty, as I'm sure we all were, gaunt with a beard and anxiety in his eyes. You could tell by looking at a man in that condition that prudence would probably be best.

"He said, 'General,' and got everyone's attention. His next words were devastating. He said, 'How was the States?'

"Well, that shook him. He turned and walked quickly away. The officers with him glared at Emerson. When they got in their vehicles, we all shook Emerson's hand. He said what we all thought. We knew that any time a general is away from his troops that are engaged in a major combat it is, shall we say, an embarrassing moment for him.

"We also had a saying, 'a 25-cent speech to a nickel bunch of soldiers.' Many times we received this from the brass. This time, it was a 'nickel speech to a 25-cent group of troopers!'"

The Battle of the Bulge remained a hard fought struggle but now, with the armor support, the Allies made progress and were soon chasing the Germans through Germany.

It was during the chase, on Jan. 17, that Reilly happened upon a hero of another sorts. "We walked down a road to get aboard some more trucks. As we walked, I was chewing tobacco, more convenient than smoking in combat but it's a nasty habit.

"Some war correspondents were standing along the road and one of the men became rather famous. He was Walter Cronkite."

After fighting in Alsace-Lorraine elsewhere in Belgium, France and Germany, Reilly was on his way back to England for furlough from March 23-April 5, 1945. He took advantage of the respite to marry the English girl he loved on March 31.

The Hero Next Door

The honeymoon was short, however, as Riley was called back into action after April 5.

Soon after he returned, Reilly caught yellow jaundice and spent four weeks in the 110th general hospital in Bar-le-Duc, France. He caught up with his unit in Lintz, Austria about May 5. They made their way down Hitler's famous autobahn — amazed at the many planes and vehicle parked along the road simply because they ran out of fuel. The 501st ended up in the Berchtesgaden, the host town of Hitler's infamous SS Guard and his summer home, The Eagle's Nest.

"I remember riding a military truck through Munich, the birthplace of Nazism and it was just a pile of bricks.

"We bivouacked in a modern hospital for the times in Berchtesgaden. It was built there so young, blonde German girls could come and get pregnant by the superior SS Guard in order to build the Arian race.

"Many Germans by this point in the war had turned against the Nazis, but not in this region. They were true to the Nazi movement right to the end; they hated our guts."

Being in the land of some of Hitler's elite guard, Reilly's division was able to capture some high ranking Nazis such as General Kesselring and Berger and Nazi "big wigs" Ley, Streicher and Schwarz. "We got Robert Ley, Hitler's labor minister. He was a short, little, fat man and we watched him 24 hours a day; he didn't blink without one of us there to see it. We wanted him to live and not kill himself before being tried.

"So, we were very disappointed when we learned that, after we had turned him over to Nuremberg, he hung himself with his belt."

The war ended on Reilly's birthday May 7, 1945, though Reilly's service was far from over. He had spent two months in Berchtesgaden, arriving back in France just before the end of the war in the Pacific, in August, 1945.

"General Maxwell Taylor got our division together and said 'men I have great news for you ...' we were to go to

The War in Europe

Japan and help end the war there. Needless to say, he didn't get any applause at all. We were so sick and tired of fighting and getting wounded and getting killed ... we didn't want to do it all over again."

The war ended before Reilly had to face the reality of those thoughts. In all, the 101st had 1,731 killed in action, 5,584 wounded and 273 mission from its battles in Europe, Reilly recalls.

The regiment was disbanded in September 1945 in France. Though he had spent all his combat in the headquarters company, 3rd Battallion of the 501st parachute regiment, Reilly was transferred to the 327th glider regiment for the remaining months of his service.

Reilly's part in that fight officially ended when he was discharged Dec.31, 1945, and returned home to Janesville, with a war bride from England and new baby daughter following him home in 1946.

Reilly worked at Parker Pen as a journeyman toolmaker and retired in 1985.

A lifetime member of the VFW, he's served on the firing squad the past three years and enjoys time with his three daughters, four grandsons, two granddaughters, one great grandson and one great granddaughter.

LOVE IN WAR

Reilly was one of hundreds of Americans who brought more than memories home from World War II. He returned with a "war bride" to start a new life in America with.

Reilly found the love of his life in England while on a seven-day furlough following his D-Day battles. Eileen Campbell and Reilly met at an amusement park in Manchester where she reluctantly agreed to go with some friends. "I told them, I'll go but I'm not talking to any Americans. They're too wild!"

But Reilly was quiet, a real gentleman. "Americans sort of had a reputation of being aggressive but Joe never tried to kiss me until I wanted him to."

He won her heart and she his.

After courting throughout the war, the two were engaged when Eileen came down to Newberry in early September 1944. "We got engaged over a little bridge along the Thames River."

Their happiness was short lived as Reilly returned to fighting soon after, in Holland and the Battle of the Bulge, and she returned home to wait and worry constantly for his safe return.

In March 1945, Reilly did return again on furlough and they worked to finish the extensive paperwork needed

to get married. "Her priest and her father were suspicious. They didn't know me. So, I wrote our pastor in Janesville and he wrote that I was a good boy."

That letter helped and the paperwork was finally arranged and they were married March 31, 1945. Following a four-day honeymoon at the Blackpool Resort in England, Reilly left

Joe and Eileen Reilly were married at Darwen Lancashire, England on March 31, 1945. his new wife for his old job — fighting the Nazis, this time in Germany.

Though the war ended on his birthday, May 7, 1945, Reilly would not see his bride again until October, after serving in post-war France before he was officially discharged Dec. 31, 1945.

By then, Eileen was six months pregnant and the sepa-

Joe and Eileen Reilly.

ration was very difficult for both. He returned to her again for a seven-day furlough in November before shipping home.

His daughter was born in England on Jan. 4, 1946. He did not see either of them until Eileen was able to get passage to America, arriving on Mother's Day, 1946, aboard the final voyage of the Queen Mary.

"It was horribly sad for me to leave. My dad went with me to London and they put us on a train to Tisdbury, which is a dirty place. I stayed one week with all the brides and babies until we boarded the Queen Mary in South Hampton. It was the most heartbreaking thing you can imagine with the Royal Guard and the band."

When she arrived to her new life in America, Eileen eventually took a job at St. Mary's school where their three daughters attended high school.

The Reilly's had found love in the ruin and horrors they each faced in World War II; it's a love that's lasted 55 years of the future both thought so uncertain so long ago.

PRESIDENTIAL PILOT
Ernie Tresch
Oregon, Wis.

When Ohio farm boy Ernest Tresch, now of Oregon, Wis., enlisted in the Army Air Corps Nov. 7, 1941, he just wanted to find a job that would let him do what he loved — fly. Little did he know the flying job he enlisted for would take him soaring with the highest ranking military official of World War II, and the future president of the United States, Dwight D. Eisenhower.

After flying 40 combat missions over Africa, Sicily, Sardinia and Italy, as pilot of a Martin B-26, Tresch was flying shuttle runs of supplies to Paris and wounded soldiers back to the U.S. as part of the Air Force's Crescent Airlines, based at New Castle Army Air Base in Willmington, Del., and flying supply planes out of LaGuardia Airport in New York. It was during a down day after one of those runs, in November, 1945, that Tresch got a call from Gen. Eisenhower's staff. They needed a pilot for their crew and wanted him to interview for the job.

"I was at home when I got a call from the colonel at the base who said Gen. Eisenhower's pilot was getting out of the service and he wanted me to come in for an interview. But, after the interview, I came back through operations and told the operations officer that I didn't expect to hear anything more. I never expected they'd pick me."

Then, about 7 a.m., the next morning, Tresch got a wake up call from General George. "He asked if I had any relatives in Germany. I said 'no;' he said 'thanks' and slammed down the phone."

That afternoon, the farm boy received orders to join General Eisenhower's crew in Frankfurt, Germany.

"How I wound up on that crew I could never tell you because I had absolutely no political or military pull."

Tresch started flying with Gen. Eisenhower during the six weeks before the general returned stateside after the war and when he was serving as Army Chief of Staff. Tresch was co-pilot and pilot on Eisenhower's C-54 aircraft (similar to a commercial DC-4) for a year until the fall of 1946.

From day one, Tresch was impressed with the general not only for his military achievements in World War II but for his personal character.

"The first time I saw him was when I reported to his headquarters in Frankfurt. It was rather a good feeling. My first introduction to him was just a very formal one in the office with the general's aide and me as the new crew member."

Shortly after that, Eisenhower was needed in Berlin and Tresch's career, flying the top brass of World War II around the world, took off.

Tresch says the general was a great boss and a great man. "He was really a wonderful fellow to work for. The reason I say this is that all the time I was on his crew he was continually doing something for somebody else instead of tooting his own horn. I've made the comment many times. General Ike was the most man in one indi-

vidual that I ever had the privilege of meeting."

Tresch recalls the general was serious most of the time, yet sensitive. "He had great character and little ego. Look at General Douglas MacArthur who was a hell of a showman; General Ike was just the reverse. He was always concerned about the other guy. I admired that."

As an example, Tresch recalls one very personal thing the general did for him.

"About six weeks after I joined the crew, my father was taken with a heart attack. We'd brought Gen. Eisenhower back to the states before that and were returning to pick up more of the supplies from his headquarters in Frankfurt, Germany, when my family called his office trying to get a hold of me to tell me my father had died.

"Word caught up with me on a shuttle flight down in Bermuda. He had the base commander come to meet the airplane and tell me. We refueled and went right to Washington.

"When I got there, Colonel Jim Stack, the general's aide, was there to meet the plane with a personal letter of sympathy from Gen. Eisenhower and his personal offer to have his staff take care of travel arrangements and, if necessary, Gen. Eisenhower wrote: 'use my plane to your better advantage.' A five-star general just doesn't have to do that for a first lieutenant!"

But that's how Gen. Eisenhower was all the way through, he adds.

"The general had a sense of humor too but he was always so doggon busy that most things were business. He'd sit in his plush quarters poring over important documents or spend time reading a Western.

"When he was on board, he'd come up to the cockpit and pat the breeze with us though. He was a regular kind of guy. Sometimes Gen. Eisenhower would even take the controls himself on long flights as he had a commercial pilot's license."

Tresch recalls another telling incident when Gen. Eisenhower made the line of command very clear to

his crew.

"One time when we first brought him back to the states, we were supposed to land at Logan Airport in Boston. But, coming from the Azores we were getting bad weather reports. So, I went back to tell the general we couldn't land at Logan and to ask if he had an alternative.

"Then General Ike said something impressive. He said, 'When we are on board this airplane you don't ask me any questions. When we're on the ground, it might be a different story.'

"He was saying 'while we're in the air, you're in charge.' Again, a five-star general doesn't usually let others be in charge let alone admit it in front of everyone!"

The general wasn't back in the states too long before Tresch was flying him on a tour inspection in the Pacific. "We took him on that run through the islands, to Japan, to Korea to Shanghai, China, all in just three weeks!"

"After the Pacific, he made a good will tour to Rio de Janeiro with other generals for a week and came back through Mexico City for another week. To my knowledge there hadn't been that much rank on one aircraft before or since. At the time it created a big stink. As I recall there was Five-star Gen. Eisenhower, Three-star General Hoyt Vandenberg from the Air Force, and three Two-star generals.

"People worried that if we'd gone down we'd have lost all that military intelligence and experience. That's why they don't fly them like that anymore."

Keeping all that heavy brass safely in the air did weigh some on the young lieutenant's shoulders. However, Tresch is quick to note that he was equally motivated to keep the plane safely in the air for personal reasons. "I was in that same damn airplane!"

There were fun, relaxing times on the general's crew, though they were few and the general rarely participated.

"When we were in Rio de Janeiro, we went to the beach a lot but Gen. Ike stayed back in the room to work. He also insisted that his crew be invited to the lavish parties thrown for him in Rio. I remember that at those parties more than a few gorgeous women tried desperately to win the attention of Gen. Vandenberg, who was tall, well-built and extremely handsome. That rarely happened with Ike though."

As to the rumor that Gen. Eisenhower had some fun of his own with his personal secretary Kay Summersby, Tresch says the details now appear pretty clear but, as close as he was to the general then, he still can't believe he had an affair with "dear little Kay."

"All the time I was with him I didn't see anything out of line whatsoever. If there was, it was very discreet. General Ike was working 15-18 hours a day; I don't know how he found the time, or the energy."

After their year together, Gen. Eisenhower accepted a job as president of Cornell University in Ithaca, N.Y. Tresch was assigned to the special air mission squadron out of Bolling Field in Washington, D.C., where he continued to fly top brass and politicians — including congressmen, Army brass, and Secretary of War Patterson — on domestic trips for another year and a half. He had, by this time, achieved a green instrument reading, the highest instrument reading available in the service.

Then, in 1948, Tresch heard his old boss was running for the biggest job in the country, president of the United States.

"I was very glad to hear he was running. I was out of the service and flying a corporate plane out of Marietta, Ohio."

Knowing the general as well as he did he was sure he'd make a great president. "He was always thinking of the other guy and what he could do to make it better for the other guy, whether that was an individual or the whole army. He was truly selfless."

OUT OF AFRICA

Long before he was entrusted with the lives of the military's top brass, and a future president, Tresch was entrusted with the lives of some other American heroes, the crew of a Martin B-26 bomber flying missions against the Axis powers in Africa.

It was a love of flying — born watching barn stormers as a child and fostered at Ohio State University where he earned his commercial pilot's license — that drove Tresch to the Army Air Corps on Nov. 7, 1941, just one month before the Japanese bombed Pearl Harbor and America went to war. It was a love of country that drove him to risk his life flying 40 bombing missions over war-torn Africa and Europe.

"I just wanted to fly, period, and figured my best chance was in the military so I applied for the aviation cadets and was accepted." Tresch did most of his training in Texas.

Tresch was commissioned July 3, 1942, and was first assigned on active duty at MacDill Field in Tampa, Fla. Originally, he was scheduled to go into Europe with a new group of B-26s but orders were changed to Africa with the 320th Bomb Group, 443rd Squadron.

In December, 1942, Tresch started flying sub patrol in the Mediterranean Sea out of Oran. "You'd fly out 1,000 feet off the water over a prescribed pattern looking for subs," he remembers of the job he did for three months. "We never did see any."

On April 1, 1943, Tresch and his crew started regular combat missions chasing the German's Gen. Rommel north out of Africa, bombing Rommel's supply routes and ammunition dumps as the German general was nearing Cairo, Egypt. Then, Tresch's group moved further up the coast and started combat missions to Sicily, Sardinia and Italy first out of a desert base and then further north still from an airstrip 20 miles outside of Tunis.

"Our average missions were daylight runs and would

last about four hours. We bombed ordinance supply and heavy artillery, supply depots, etc. We hit a few airports in Africa but it was predominately troops and supplies.

"In other words, we were always trying to hit a moving target."

Tresch's plane flew on the bombing of Rome's airport and railroad depot in the summer of 1943, hitting the airport just outside the city. "We were on the mission the first time Rome was bombed; it was a coordinated mission. We were to wipe out the airport and another railyard but none of us used the town itself as a target until the middle of summer," he remembers, adding his crew also helped clear the troublesome gun batteries from the hills around Anzio during the Allied invasion.

89 HOLES A DAY

Anti-aircraft fire was always heavy and Tresch's plane "got shot up every mission."

They took the worst of it on May 9, 1943, when they bombed Palermo, Sicily. "I remember the date well because it happened to be Mother's Day. I was flying the wing on the lead plane in our group of 36 planes. We were one of two B-26 groups bombing that day, with us were three groups of B-24s, three groups of B-17s and two groups of B-25s.

"When we went across the target, the anti-aircraft smoke was so thick that we couldn't see one-third of the planes in the group ahead of us. When I saw that we couldn't see the planes, I just reached over and hit my co-pilot Pete Graves on the arm and said, 'Buddy, here we go.'

"I didn't take any evasive action while on the bomb run. You had to stay on target.

Fortunately, Tresch and crew returned safely to base, though not safe by much.

"When we came off that target and returned home

Ernie Tresch poses at the controls of General Dwight D. Eisenhower's plane at the end of the war.

and went to fill out the reports, somehow no one was injured in our crew but we counted 89 holes in the airplane!"

A LOT OF LUCK AND SOMETHING MORE

Tresch says luck — and the help of a higher power — had as much, if not more, to do with his crew returning safely from every mission than his skill as a pilot did. "When I left the outfit Nov. 30, 1943, we had a 126 percent replacement of aircraft rate. We'd patch them up and away we'd go again.

"I was very, very, very fortunate that I never had a man on my plane wounded and that we always made it back. You had a feeling there was a higher power riding with you sometimes; that's the only way I can say it.

"For example, one day my bombardier was down in the nose of the plane and a chunk of flak came up through the plane and took the bill right off his hat. Another time, my waist gunner had a hunk of flak come through and hit the buckle of his parachute. And, later

The Hero Next Door

Anne and Ernie Tresch

the tail gunner had a close call too. One came up through the floor and went through the seat and into the parachute he was sitting on, but not into him."

Tresch reports his aircraft "ran into a lot of enemy fighters and had a lot of flak from 88-mm anti-aircraft guns.

"Both were hard to fly through. Flak you can see where it was after the shell exploded and could see they were throwing a pattern at you. If you got a direct hit you could feel the flak but normally the sound of the plane and your own heart beating drowned out the flak noise. But you could sure see it everywhere.

"On the other hand, there isn't anything uglier than a German 109 flying at the same altitude but out of range of your 50-mm gun. And then, you see his leading edge of his wing light up and watch the tracers coming your way and there's nothing you can do about it."

Though each mission was different, the Martin B-26 was generally loaded with part 500-pound demolition bombs and part anti-personnel bombs. And, formations were flown extra tight, adding to the danger. "We never took our eyes off the planes in front. We never crashed

into each other and went down unless one plane took a direct hit and pulled into the one next to him."

It was high pressure flying all the time. And, that kind of pressure took it's toll.

"We were flying tight, concentrating on what we were doing all the time. It was very stressful; we were under tremendous pressure. I wouldn't say I was afraid but if a crewmember ever said they were never scared they're a damn liar. And, I was always in complete control in the air. I was doing my job."

However, the stress eventually caught up to Tresch on the last few of those 40 missions. "We'd get back in the parking area and I'd park the plane fine but then I always had to get someone else to write the mission report (after the last few runs) because I'd be shaking too badly to write it." So shaky in fact that, when he first rotated home to the states after his last mission in November, 1943, "I had to use both hands to pick up a glass of water."

But, after a short stint training South African and French pilots in Constantine, Algeria on B-26s and a 30-day leave, Tresch regained control on the ground as well as in the air. He was soon assigned to the New Castle Army Airbase, where he flew for the air transport command outfit, ferrying planes from one field to another, before receiving General Eisenhower's call to duty.

HOME AGAIN

Five years after he started flying combat missions in Africa, on April 1, 1948, Tresch left the service to fly a commercial twin engine Beech for a concrete company in Marietta, Ohio. The next year he married Lydia Given, an Army Nurse Corps captain who also left the service in 1948. They had two daughters.

Tresch flew for 10 more years until the company sold the plane and Tresch went to work as an assistant manager with the farm silo division, moving in 1963 to Bal-

timore as a plant manager. He came to Madison, Wis., in 1970 after several company mergers. He was then in charge of concrete production at all eight of Martin-Marietta's plants. He lost his wife Lydia to cancer in 1977 and retired in 1981 as production manager for Madison Silos Co.

Tresch continues the tradition of service he began with his military flying career in 1941. However, that service now is civilian. He's very active in the Madison Lapidary and Mineral Club and pursues that as a hobby. He served in the American Legion for 25 years and belongs to and is active in the People's United Methodist Church in Oregon, Wis.

Though he no longer flies, his love of aircraft remains strong. However, no love is greater than the love he has for his country and his family. Tresch remarried in 1988 to Anne Fluckiger adding four stepchildren and, today, eight great-grandchildren to his family.

The emotions he feels for the men he served with, and the future president he served, nearly 55 years ago, remain strong too. It was a privilege to serve his country as he did. "I wouldn't do it again for a million dollars though, and yet, I wouldn't take a million dollars for it either."

THE WAR
IN THE PACIFIC

THE WAR IN THE PACIFIC

In this section, you'll come to know a small sampling of the Wisconsinites who fought with hundreds of thousands of Allied units to free the Pacific Islands and much of Asia from the stronghold of Imperial Japan. These Heroes Next Door include:

• **George Kinsler,** a PBY flying boat gunner who helped rescue downed pilots and wounded soldiers before returning stateside as a aircraft engineer and trainer.

• **Clyde Stephenson,** a Marine on the U.S.S. California battleship, who had a unique vantage point of the Japanese attack on Pearl Harbor from the Fleet Machine Gun School at the harbor entrance;

• **John Topolski,** a radar operator with the 20th Army Air Force out of India during the China-Burma-India campaign who survived 29 hours alone in the Indian Ocean after the B-24 he was riding in was shot down;

• **Glen Hanusa,** a Navy intelligence petty officer who met President Franklin D. Roosevelt while serving in Adak, Alaska;

• **Russ Kohloff,** a 5th Division Marine who fought in the jungle islands of the Pacific and withstood the bloody sands of Iwo Jima;

• **Garvin Kowalke,** a B-29 bomber pilot who flew testing missions for the atomic bombing of Hiroshima in a plane he named for his hometown, "The City of Baraboo."

• **Eugene Skaar,** a utility maintenance man for the 382nd Army Battalion who was stationed in New Guinea and who fought the Japanese in the Philippines.

FLYING BOATER
George R. Kinsler
Tomahawk, Wis.

Navy seaman George Kinsler of Tomahawk, Wis., fought his World War II battles in the Pacific, not to invade an island or capture an airstrip, but to save the lives of the men who waged those battles.

Kinsler was an aviation machinist mate first class on a PBY air-sea rescue aircraft, skimming the wild waves of the Pacific to pluck downed airmen from the sea and pick up stranded soldiers from island beaches.

In all, his squadron rescued 460 injured Marines and Army servicemen in the six months the squadron served in combat.

Kinsler's service to his country began months before the U.S. entered W. W. II, and lasted until well after the last shots were fired. He served from June 16, 1941, until June 18 of 1947.

Born in Redgranite, Wis., on May 27, 1924, as the second youngest of eight, Kinsler entered the Navy soon after his Oshkosh High School graduation in 1941. He was just 17 years old when he enlisted on June 16, 1941, in anticipation of serving his country in a war he says he knew was coming soon. His first stop was boot camp at Great Lakes Naval Training Center in Great Lakes, Ill. until Aug., 25, 1941. Enlisted to be in Naval aviation, he was then sent to an aircraft mechanics school at the Naval Reserve Armory in Chicago.

Kinsler was home on a weekend pass from the armory when the war he knew was coming finally hit home, Dec. 7, 1941. The Japanese attacked Pearl Harbor; America, and Kinsler, were at war.

Upon completion of mechanic training, Jan. 23, 1942, Kinsler was shipped to Goat Island in San Francisco then on to Pearl Harbor, Hawaii, arriving here Feb. 17, 1942.

"I was stationed on Pearl Harbor's Ford Island at Oahu and joined the VP24, a PBY Catalina Squadron. The PBY is a flying boat that weighs 20 tons, has a 110-foot wingspan and holds an 8 to 10 man crew. Our role was to fly patrol and search missions."

VP24 was assigned PBY 5As and moved to Kaneokae Bay on Oahu Sept. 5, 1942, where they flew training and sub search missions.

He recalls his first training flight well since it was the first time Kinsler was ever in a plane. "I made the first flight of my life in a PBY5A. We took off at 0610 Oct. 16, 1942, and flew 12 hours, returning at 1830. It was extremely long for a first flight."

After gunnery school in February and March of 1943, Kinsler was sent to the South Pacific for combat duty on May 1, 1943. There the VP24 squadron was one of many PBYs the GIs nicknamed the "Dumbo Squadron" because of the elephant-like appearance of the flying boats.

"Essentially we'd do rescue missions in the open sea and pick up wounded off islands where fighting was in progress."

Kinsler almost didn't get the chance to rescue others in the South Pacific. The plane crew he was assigned to nearly became casualties themselves on the trip from Hawaii.

The Hero Next Door

"We were flying with squadron VP44 and our crew was split up in several planes because we were to receive our PBYs when we got there. After 10 hours of flying we were supposed to see a small sand island built with a dredge and used as a refueling spot.

"When we didn't see it we knew something was wrong. Our navigator checked and rechecked the heading, which he was sure was right. So, we figured something must be wrong with the plane navigation system itself.

"After some searching, we figured it out. We had a package of knives sitting too close to the master compass. Incidentally, we were carrying knives in the first place because, when war broke out, the military didn't have enough knives to go around so sailors were asked to write home and have their parents send them a knife, which mine did and I still have the knife. And I was also sent to the South Pacific, like a lot of guys, wearing dress Oxfords because there weren't enough combat boots to go around. I'm glad I didn't have to fight in the jungle in those!

"Anyway, we pulled the knives away from the compass and watched how much the compass would swing. By doing this we were able to recalculate how far off course we were. We eventually found the island and when we landed we just had a half hour of fuel left. We were 30 minutes shy of dropping into the ocean!"

But, Kinsler had little time to relax after the near miss. The next morning's take off from that tiny island bay had its own problems.

"When you go to start the engines on a PBY you always have a guy — me — standing by with a fire extinguisher, in case the carburetor floods and starts a fire. So I was out on the wing with the fire extinguisher when the engines were started the next morning. There was a strong wind blowing the plane toward the beach when it released from the buoy.

"The pilot hit the engines and put the plane on the step (meaning moving to about 40 miles an hour) and started across the bay with me still out on the wing! I

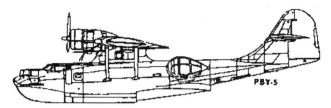

Here is a sketch of a PBY-5 search and rescue "flying boat."

dropped to the hull and put a foot on each blister and my head under the wing and held on while we crossed the half-mile bay. Then someone mentioned to the pilot I was out there and I was able to come back in before take off."

The perils of Kinsler's missions began from the aircraft tender U.S.S. Wright, anchored in the New Hibrides Islands. It had cranes that could pick up the 20-ton flying boats and put them in place for repairs.

The squadron was soon moved to Florida Island, across from the Guadalcanal airstrip in July, 1943. They lived in tents set up on the beach and flew air-sea rescue and sub and enemy aircraft search missions around Guadalcanal and the other islands north.

"On several occasions we could see the Japs bomb the airstrip and the ships unloading supplies on Guadalcanal. One time they hit an ammunition ship; it was like one big Fourth of July extravaganza."

At this early stage of the war, Kinsler recalls watching in frustration as American planes tried to fly as high as the Japanese. "Our anti-aircraft guns and fighter planes could not shoot or fly as high as the Jap bombers at that time. All the good stuff was going to Europe first."

The enemy wasn't the only danger Americans faced on the Pacific islands. Many fell ill to malaria and other strange diseases. Kinsler joined those ranks too.

"Malaria was ever present and we took Atabrine to suppress it. Still, some men had attacks and lost blood and needed transfusions. Our radioman Andy Ander-

son was one of those. So, I went to give blood for him only to find out I had malaria too. I was grounded for the last weeks of August, 1943. They put me on Quinine for the malaria. Then, I got a really bad case of shingles, from which I still have scars. So, they put me on Phenabarbathal for that. The blisters from the shingles were so large on my side that the Navy took pictures of them because they were such a 'good example.'"

Before and after his bouts with malaria and shingles, Kinsler flew approximately 1,400 hours in the PBY 5.

Though they flew as rescuers, PBYs didn't go into the precarious situations unarmed. "We had depth charges we could drop and carried 500-pound bombs and we were designed to carry a one-ton torpedo though we didn't. We also had two, 50-caliber and two, 30-caliber free machine guns."

The Dumbos needed the armament, as they were often attacked by Japanese fighters when they tried to pick up wounded airmen and soldiers from combat.

"There were several times while the planes were on the water that the Japs strafed them. Several PBYs were lost trying to save others. Fortunately, our aircraft was always able to keep flying."

LIFE FLIGHTS

"Our PBY picked up wounded Marines from island beaches, landing on the water, paddling into shore on a raft and back out again — sometimes under enemy fire — and transporting the wounded to evacuation hospitals."

He vividly remembers the job they had of cleaning the aircraft after those trips.

"We noted maggots in the bilge (bottom of the plane). That's because the medics didn't always have antiseptics so they would put maggots in the wounds until the wounded could get back and be properly cleaned and treated. The bilge of the PBY would have blood and maggots that had to be cleaned out."

One mission especially sticks out in Kinsler's memory

because of its unusual cargo, a Japanese POW.

"On one Dumbo mission we picked up 20 wounded Marines from an island north of Guadalcanal that had been strafed by a Japanese fighter and their landing craft had been bombed and mortared. They also brought out to our plane a Japanese fighter pilot that had been shot down. After we had the Marines forward in the plane, my plane captain cocked his 32-caliber automatic pistol and handed it to me because the Marines for obvious reasons might have liked to kill that Jap pilot if they could have.

"We put the Jap behind me in the tail section and the plane captain [head of the enlisted men on the plane, not the pilot] said 'shoot anyone who tries to attack the Jap,' because he is a prisoner of war.

"It was good that he survived because we heard later that the Jap did help with finding out where the Jap fighter airstrip was, which we were then able to bomb."

The Japanese weren't the only danger. Landing an aircraft on the large swells of the Pacific Ocean presented peril enough.

"If you had good water, like in harbors, you could do a hot land which was like using the water as a runway, but most of the time in rescue work you were trying to land on the swell of a wave; if you missed, you could be in trouble."

Rough waters made tough rescues even more dangerous. Kinsler recalls one Dumbo mission that especially looked bad when his PBY arrived at the scene.

"We were sent out to rescue a fighter pilot who was in the water off a small island south of Guadalcanal in August, 1943. The fighter pilot later told us that he was checking out a new P-39 and fell out of the plane when he rolled it over because he had forgotten to close the hatch and fasten his seatbelt! He was lucky to have landed close to an island. We arrived to see that he had made it to the beach. We also found that the wind speed was rising and there were five to eight-foot swells.

"Our pilot, Lt. Norris, figured we could land but would

find it very difficult to get back off the water. About then he noticed a small lagoon about two miles down the island from where the pilot was and decided to try to land and use the lagoon for a take off. Then, two of us — this time, me and another mechanic Taylor — would take our five-man raft and get to the pilot.

"We had noted that the pilot on the beach was trying to launch his own small seat raft to come to us but he couldn't beat the winds and swells, so bringing our bigger raft to him was looking more and more dangerous. But it was the only way to get him to the plane, so that

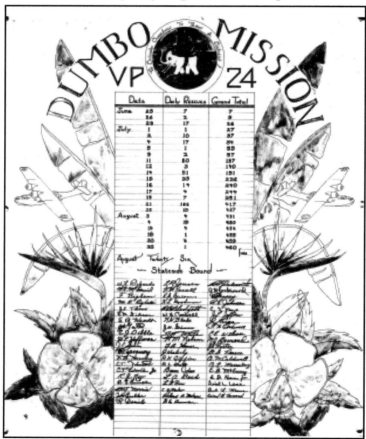

A VP24 mission log, partly from during the time that George Kinsler was ill with malaria.

was the basic plan.

"The pilot decided to stall the PBY about ½-mile out in the ocean. He did a great job and we dropped on a large swell. We only popped a few rivets but we plugged them with golf tees (which we carried for this purpose). The props on the engine were biting into the water as we bobbed up and down in the wind and swells, which caused the plane to take water over the front turret.

"We made it as close to the beach as was safe. When we were just about to inflate the raft for what would surely be a dangerous attempt for Taylor and I to get the pilot, we noted a large, native canoe coming with about 14 men paddling it. We had not seen it from the air. It had extremely high ends on it and could handle the swells and wind a lot better than a raft.

"These natives went in and picked up the pilot and brought him out to us. Thank God, as I doubt that we could have fought our way back to the plane against the swells and wind. Fortunately, the natives on this island were friendly to us. Most natives were friendly but they weren't friendly on every island.

"In fact, we generally carried large cans of Spam and gallons of fruit cocktail that we would drop to the natives whenever we would see them while on patrol as a way to thank them for their support of us and encourage their friendliness.

"We had about eight gallons of fruit cocktail in the plane this trip and we gave it all to this one group of natives, along with other odds and ends, for helping us out of this dangerous situation."

The danger was far from over. The PBY still had to fly out of that small lagoon.

"The plan was that as soon as we entered the lagoon we would drop two sea anchors over one side and ole' George — me — would get out on the wing on that same side and put the float in the water. Then, pilot Norris would gun the other engine. As the plane came around (in a half circle) I would run down the wing and get in the plane so Norris could hit the engine wide open, find

a swell, and we'd be in the air.

"The plan was good, but when we got to the opening of the lagoon, it was smaller than our wing span! As we went through the opening, our pontoons were dragging in the mud. But a big swell lifted us over and into the lagoon. We carried out the plan as the plane came around. They dumped the sea anchors and I ran down the wing and got in the blister. Norris hit the throttle and we were in the air on the first swell thanks to the skill of our pilot and a crew that worked together as a team. It was quite an effort and shows how important everyone was to the success and safety of a mission."

During such dangerous times, Kinsler trusted the teamwork of the crew, the skill of their pilot and his faith to help pull him through. "I carried a small Bible with me and attended Navy church services when I could; ... faith was and is important to me."

In addition to the Dumbo missions, Kinsler and crew flew regular 12-hour search patrols, covering about 1,200 miles each, scanning for Japanese submarines and Imperial Navy ships.

"We generally flew at about 110-knots-per-hour. On convoy patrols we'd idle back to about 90 knots and stay out for 20 hours, floating above the convoys looking for subs, before having to return for fuel. We never did spot any subs but we sure searched a lot for them.

"A typical day on patrol, like to Vanikoro Island, we would fly a triangle 800 miles east out and 400 miles north to Vanikoro for about a 12-hour flight. In the bay there, a ship called the Mackinac — named for the Michigan tourist island — was docked. We'd stay one day and do a similar track the third day.

"We enjoyed those trips because there were friendly natives there and families that we became friends with after several visits. We took an Army photographer on one trip and he took a lot of good pictures of us and the natives. Several PBYs would be there at a time. The Mackinac had been there over a year and served us a fresh fruit pie for our flight back and we always had fresh eggs and bacon for breakfast. How they did it we never could figure out."

SAN DIEGO TRAINER

In October 1943, after six months flying in the South Pacific, Kinsler's squadron was rotated back to the states. He was assigned to the Naval Air Station, San Diego. In a maintenance unit for 2Y2 Corando, a very large flying boat that could carry up to 70 men and was used in the battle on Midway, among other aircraft.

By coincidence, it was Kinsler's privilege to service the plane of one of the most famous men in world aviation history, the first man to fly across the Atlantic, Charles Lindberg.

During World War II, Lindberg flew to the South Pacific to train fighter pilots in P-38s. Lindberg flew there from San Diego and Kinsler got his plane ready for the journey.

"I had the pleasure of servicing that plane and watching him go aboard. I remember thinking that he always looked like a large man in his picture and he *was* a big man in size and legend."

It was during his time in San Diego that Kinsler was able to return to the Midwest for hydraulics training in Chicago. He married his high school sweetheart who'd been waiting and praying for him for three years, Patricia Ann Wood.

From Chicago, he was assigned to a maintenance unit at Camp Kearney, Calif., near San Diego, working on B-24s and 4Y2s, the Privateer, the Navy version of the B-24.

Kinsler was assigned to a PATSO Unit, a large aircraft training services unit, as a hydraulic specialist with a rating of Aviation Machinist Mate Hydraulic Specialist First Class Combat Air Crewman. His combat air crew designation gave him flight pay which was 40 percent more pay for hazardous duty. The role of his unit was to take a squadron of 15 4Y2 bombers or patrol planes and maintain them and train the crews to service and

fly them.

"It was expected we would have a squadron ready for going to the South Pacific every three to four months. The crews flew day and night as they were trained in all types of weather as well as day and night flying. We worked long hours and had small base crews that did the training."

In the spring of 1945, Kinsler learned he would have to rotate back into combat, a fate he did not relish but a reality he knew may come.

"They were going to recycle me back to the South Pacific. So, they sent me to Oklahoma for PBY gunner school and then in April, 1945, on to the Naval Air Station in Jacksonville, Fla., where they were assembling new PBYs."

As the summer of 1945 approached, Kinsler faced a difficult decision. He had served his four years in the regular Navy and was asked to reenlist. Though victory in Europe was all but sealed, victory in the Pacific was still in doubt. Should he get out now or re-up for an uncertain future?

"If I stayed, I got a $600 bonus and Pat and I were enjoying our stay in the Navy. Just before the war in Europe ended, I signed up for two more years. I'm glad I did because, after the war, so many guys were coming out at once and there was a lot of confusion. By the time I got out in 1947, they had the GI Bill system all set up and everything was ready for me."

SEARCHING THE BERMUDA TRIANGLE

The war in the Pacific ended in August, 1945, before Kinsler's training was over. Though he never returned to combat, Kinsler did risk his life one more time trying to rescue airmen lost at sea.

This time it was not the South Pacific waves he was scanning but the mysterious waters of the infamous Bermuda Triangle, just south of the Florida Keys.

"We had a big storm in the Bermuda triangle and they lost five carrier planes; they just disappeared without

174

The crew of George Kinsler's VP24. Kinsler is at left, back row. The crew included: J. Foster, J. Button, H. Norris, L. Mackell, D. Voss, R. Stone, K. Anderson and M. Peck.

a trace or explanation."

In his book, *Unexplained Mysteries of World War II* (1997, John Wiley & Sons Inc.) William B. Breuer writes, on p. 174, about the mysterious disappearance as follows:

"On the afternoon of Dec. 5, 1945, five Avenger torpedo bombers lifted off from Fort Lauderdale, Fla., on a 320-mile navigation training mission. They were scheduled to fly east, then north, over Grand Bahama Island, then southwest back to their base. Leading Flight 19 was U.S. Navy Lt. Charles C. Taylor, one of two experienced airmen aboard the planes. The other 12 — pilots, radio engineers and gunners — were all still in training.

"Less than two hours after the 2:10 p.m. takeoff, radio messages were received back at the Fort Lauder-

dale base indicating that Lt. Taylor, a veteran of count-less flights, had become disorientated.

"'Both my compasses are out,' he said. 'I'm over land, but I'm sure I'm in the Keys [on the southern tip of Florida], but I don't know how far down and I don't know how to get [back] to Fort Lauderdale.'"

Actually, the flight plan should have had Taylor's group ... 200 miles northeast of the Florida Keys.

"For the next two hours, bits and pieces of radio messages reached Flight 19's base. Then the home base heard Charles Taylor's final orders radioed to his five craft. 'All planes close up tight. We will have to ditch unless landfall. When the first man gets down to 10 gallons we will all land in the water together.'

"Then there was silence. An exhaustive search by air and sea over 250,000 square miles of ocean failed to find any trace of Flight 19, yet another tragic and mysterious victim of the ill-famed Bermuda Triangle."

Kinsler was aboard one of the PBYs sent to look for the missing airmen and planes.

"We were sent out in this storm to look for them. I was the plane captain of the crew for the flight and it was the worst storm I ever flew through. We flew through some terrible weather in the Pacific but it was nothing like this. The pilot and I were the only ones on the PBY who didn't get airsick.

"It was just horrible flying. We were going up and down like an elevator, up 500 feet, down 500 feet, over and over. And, once in a while, you could see the water but it was so rough that if there was anything in it, you'd never see it.

"We never saw a thing and they never found even a scrap from any of those planes."

After surviving the jolts of the storm, Kinsler left the seas behind and went to Hutchinson, Kansas, a major 4Y2 four-engine bomber training base for the Navy. Though the war was over, the Navy decided to train as many four-engine bomber pilots as it could before they shut the base down.

"So, with my experience in 4Y2s from Camp Kearney, they sent me to work on this mission. I just flew as plane captain. But, they didn't have experienced hydraulic specialists in the maintenance units so they placed me in charge of about 20 men who serviced the hydraulic systems. We maintained a war status because of the small number of mechanics and maintenance personnel available and the number of pilots to be trained. When the base closed in the winter of 1946-47, I was shipped to the Jacksonville Naval Air Station aviation repair unit to do hydraulic work on trainer planes that were being overhauled."

While in Kansas, Kinsler and his wife suffered the loss of their first child, a daughter who lived just four days. It was six years before they had more children, first George in 1953, then John in 1956, Karla in 1957 and David in 1965.

On June 18, 1947, Kinsler's service life ended with his discharge and he was back to civilian life.

DEDICATED VOCATION

Kinsler immediately took full advantage of the GI Bill to attend college, transferring in 1948 after one year at Oshkosh State to Stout State College in Menomonee, Wis.. He graduated magna cum laude in 1951 with a degree in industrial education.

He accepted a position at Lincoln Park, Mich., teaching high school auto mechanics. While he taught, Kinsler matriculated at Wayne State in Detroit and the University of Michigan to complete his masters at Stout in 1953.

In 1954, Kinsler returned to Wisconsin, to LaCrosse, and entered a field of education — which he dedicated himself for the next 30 years — in Wisconsin's post-high-school technical school system. Kinsler began as an auto mechanics instructor at the LaCrosse Vocational School in 1954. In 1960, he went to work as a trade industrial coordinator at Beloit's vocational school.

Moving to Monona, Wis. in 1962, he accepted a job as

177

Patricia and George Kinsler on their 50th wedding anniversary in 1994.

the trade industrial supervisor for the State Board of Vocational & Adult Education and became chief of trade industrial department four years later. It was the beginning of the transformation and elevation of the vocational technical education system in Wisconsin.

Kinsler helped develop state's technical college system as one of the leaders of a process for evaluating associate degree courses to ensure uniform quality statewide. He worked out the politics and logistics of transforming individual city and county vocational schools into a statewide, connected system of districts. He was appointed director of the Bureau of Program

Development for the SBVAE in 1972 and held this position held until he retired to an 80-acre recreational farm near Tomahawk in 1984.

"As bureau director of the state programs, my staff and I were responsible for all the programs, from health to auto mechanics. Our job was to decide whether a school could add a program or not. It was often a heated debate. For each one proposed, the district had to show the means and staff to provide a quality program, the need for that kind of training in the area and prove they would be able to get the graduates hired."

For all he did for the state's vocational education programs, Kinsler had a national impact on the area of education closest to his heart, auto mechanics.

In 1974, as consumer advocates cried for licensing of auto mechanics nationwide, Kinsler was asked to help develop a voluntary auto mechanics certification testing program. Together with 30 selected representatives from vocational education and all levels of the automotive industry, they developed a national certification test and formed the National Institute for Automotive Service Excellence. To this day, the Automotive Service Excellence sign is the mark of a good mechanic.

Soon after, America was looking for national standards for auto mechanic education and Kinsler was again asked to help. He worked as a committee chairman for the American National Standards Institute to develop the D18 standards for training auto, auto body, and truck mechanics. The result was the syllabi for all the components of teaching vehicle mechanics and preparation for Educational Testing Service certification tests.

"Today almost all states use these syllabi in their vocational auto mechanics programs and prepare mechanics to become ASE certified."

By 1976, however, the volunteer work he did for ASE and the ANSI was taking its toll. "It got to the point where I was gone almost one month a year. I still had a staff of 25 working with me in Wisconsin and I said, 'I've got to

179

quit this.'"

Eight years later, Kinsler also retired from his state job, though he hardly stopped working. After moving to Tomahawk, he started a local AARP Chapter and became president of the local Lincoln County Retired Educators group. He remains a life member of the American Legion and VFW and is a member of the Kaneohae Klippers a veterans group for those who served in Kaneohae Bay, Hawaii, during W.W. II. He serves on the Commission on Aging in Tomahawk and was also active with the Methodist Church.

The Kinslers now spend the winter in Winterhaven, Fla. He hunts in Wisconsin every November and, during warmer months, they live in their scenic Tomahawk home. Kinsler golfs four days a week and loves hunting deer and grouse, making firewood, snowmobiling and riding his ATV. And, he enjoys his time with family, especially the Kinslers' nine grandchildren.

PEARL HARBOR SHOOTER

Clyde Stephenson
Appleton, Wis.

The Japanese bombing of Pearl Harbor on Dec. 7, 1941 — the horrific event that dragged the United States full speed into the war already boiling over throughout the world — was deemed the "day that will live in infamy" for every United States citizen.

For one citizen, Clyde Stephenson, of Appleton, Wis. Dec. 7, 1941, is the infamous day that will live forever vividly in his memory.

Born in 1920, in Wauwatosa, Wis., Stephenson moved to Arpin,Wis., when he was six and graduated Oconto High School in 1938. He attended the Oshkosh State Teachers College for one year before joining the U.S. Marine Corps in January 1940.

Following boot camp in San Diego, Calif., Stephenson graduated Sea-School April 1, 1940, and joined the U.S. Pacific fleet in San Pedro, Calif., where he was stationed aboard the U.S.S. California battleship.

The fleet arrived in Pearl Harbor in May 1940.

When Stephenson arrived, Pearl Harbor was still a native Hawaiian paradise, with little hint of the horrendous battle that would be waged there 19 months later.

As a Marine aboard a Navy ship, Stephenson's main duties while in port were to post guard and perform orderly duty for the captain and executive officers. At sea and in battle, he was to help the dozen or so men man one of the five-inch broadside guns on the port side.

The Hero Next Door

The U.S.S. California had been out on a training cruise and had arrived back in Pearl Harbor about one week before that fateful Dec. 7, Sunday morning.

GUN SCHOOL FIGHTS BACK

As luck would have it, Stephenson was among four to five Marines from each of the battleships in port that week sent out to the rifle ranges at the Fleet Machine Gun School at nearby Fort Weaver, located just west of the entrance to Pearl Harbor.

"They would send sailors out there and we would instruct them on machine guns and automatic rifles. We completed that work on Friday, Dec. 5, and got permission to stay out there for the weekend.

"So, we were there, maybe one mile from where our ship was anchored, on Sunday morning when the Japs struck."

Stephenson was already up for breakfast and back in his tent when the first strike hit the harbor at 7:55 a.m.

According to C.L. Sulzberger in his *The American Heritage Picture History of World War II* (1966), the surprise attack began when 353 Japanese bombers, torpedo bombers and fighters swept down on the harbor and caught soldiers and sailors by surprise.

"By 10 o'clock the fleet as a striking force was wrecked," Sulzberger writes. *"Six of eight battleship [including Stephenson's U.S.S. California] were sunk or badly damaged, three destroyers in dry dock were torn by bombs, three cruisers were damaged, four other ships were sunk or damaged. Half the aircraft on the island was wrecked [leaving the Air Corps with just 16 serviceable bombers]. Some 2,400 men had died; almost half were wounded. Japan lost 29 planes and four midget submarines."*

Considering the surprise of the attack, and lack of wartime readiness of the American troops at Pearl Harbor — ammunition boxes were locked, for example — the soldiers and sailors there put up a gallant defense.

Stephenson was among those defenders trying their best to do something to slow or turn back the Japanese.

He had an unusual view of the attack itself, from the machine gun school at the mouth of Pearl Harbor where he could see the first Japanese bombers wing their way toward unsuspecting ships at their docks.

The small contingent at the outpost school both heard and saw Pearl Harbor unfold almost simultaneously, Stephenson recalls.

"We heard an explosion and saw a lot of airplanes. We looked up and there was a squadron of Japanese torpedo bombers 400 to 500 feet overhead. It didn't take long to realize what was happening."

And, it didn't take long for Stephenson and the Marines at Fort Weaver to take action.

"The armory where we kept the guns and ammo was 100 yards away so we ran to it. Of course the guy with the key wasn't around so we tore the door off and got out the automatic rifles and machine guns and just started firing away. Most the guys went down toward the ocean for a better shot at the target."

The first wave of the Japanese attack lasted until about 8:20 a.m. when, Stephenson said, the Marines could see a break in the action. Within an hour they saw the second wave hit.

"It let up a little and then the second wave were the dive bombers (a wave of 54 bombers, 80 divebombers and 36 fighters, according to *World War II* by Ivor Matanle, 1989, Quadrillion Publishing). They flew at a lot higher altitude and we did see a few planes go down."

Because of their location, Stephenson and his fellow Marines could see plenty of the Japanese bombers coming in but little of the damage in the harbor just a mile or so away. "We could see a lot of smoke but that was about it."

They knew, however, the damage would be heavy as they watched the battle rage literally over their heads.

"During the bombing attack some B-17s were coming in on their way to the Philippines and the Japs were firing at them. That was all right over our heads. The

torpedo bombers came right past us. They all had to fly over us to get into and out of the harbor."

Despite the front row seat, no one at the gun school was killed or seriously injured and, as soon as they could, the Marines returned to the harbor.

Stephenson got an up-close look at the damage two days later when he finally made it back to his ship, which was hit by bombs and had listed heavily before sinking (*World War II*, p. 107).

"The California sunk right down in the mud with the top deck out of the water. About 300 men (from the ship) had lost their lives in the attack. The water in the harbor was still covered with oil and things were still pretty disorganized."

Turning away from the destroyed battleship, Stephenson trekked through the carnage in the harbor and checked in at a temporary office on Ford Island. "There, we were given a blanket and slept where we could find a spot on shore until we became members of work parties going over the ships and cleaning them."

In the next few weeks, Stephenson helped remove the five-inch anti-aircraft guns from the U.S.S. California and set them up west of the harbor. Stephenson and the other Marines manned those guns in case the Japanese returned.

After the U.S.S. California was raised, put in dry dock and fixed, Stephenson and its crew sailed the ship to the Bremerton, Wash., Navy Yard for further repairs in October, 1942. Despite the damage, the U.S.S. California was resurrected in time to fight the Japanese in the Battle of Leyte Gulf, Oct. 20, 1944.

In the meantime, Stephenson was on leave home where he married his sweetheart Elayne Storm, who joined him in Seattle and went to work as a "Rosie the Riveter" at Boeing Aircraft there.

Stephenson then traveled through several Marine and Navy schools including the Naval Research Lab in Washington, D.C. where he learned radio and radar.

The Marine did not see combat duty again until January 1945, when he shipped to the Pacific as a replacement for the 45,000 some Marines that had taken Pelelieu in a hard-fought assault in September, 1944. There, Stephenson went to work on electronic equipment on aircraft.

"They really had some bad fighting there, but since I went in as a replacement, I missed most of it. The island had almost all its trees shot off. The only Japs left on the island were up in cover.

"Our main purpose was to bomb other islands in the area that the Japs still occupied and I was mostly repairing radio equipment on the planes that would come in. When the pilot said they were having radio problems, we'd plug in a replacement unit and take the (broken) unit from the plane back to the shop to fix."

The island by that time was "pretty secure," and the greatest challenge Stephenson and other Marines faced was the weather.

"The biggest issue was the heat. We were only seven degrees above the equator and it got to be about 120 degrees during the day. That's something a guy's just not used to."

Stephenson continued his work on Pelelieu through the end of the war and into November, 1945, when he was sent back to the states.

However, he wasn't home as quickly as he expected.

"I got pneumonia on the way back and ended up in the Naval Hospital in San Diego. But back then they were so crowded that they made space everywhere and I was actually housed for two weeks in the monkey cage in Balboa Zoo! It was the nicest duty I had in the Marine Corps!"

He made it home by Christmas, 1945, to enjoy 30 days of leave he had accumulated — and a second son born in September while he was overseas — before he was officially discharged in January, 1945.

After the war, Stephenson founded Town & Country Electric in Appleton and raised four sons and a daughter. In his spare time now he collects and restores old

radios and has about 300 of them dating back to the early 1920s. And, he enjoys his eight grandchildren and two great-grandchildren.

In addition to other community projects, Stephenson has dedicated a great deal of time to the Rawhide Boys Ranch in New London, Wis., since it opened in 1965. Today, the facility serves some 100 troubled boys who are well known for raising money by repairing old cars. "I got involved in it as a community project and I've been involved with them since ... helping out on a lot of volunteer building projects over the years."

A BROTHER'S HONOR

A member of the local VFW, Stephenson aggressively pursues one more act of service in his retirement — the honoring of another World War II hero, his older brother Capt. Glenwood Gordon Stephenson, a 1940 graduate of West Point. The elder Stephenson died in some of the war's earliest combat. The B-25 bomber he was flying — just before the Battle of the Coral Sea in the Pacific in May, 1942 — hit a mountain in Australia during a storm.

Capt. Stephenson and all seven aboard were killed; it was pilot Stephenson's first combat mission. He left behind his wife of a few months, Anne, as a war widow.

"The plane is still up on the mountain and it's never been moved. We were contacted through the Internet that the National (Australian) War Museum in Canberra is planning to remove it and bring it in for display in 2000."

It's a tribute to a fallen hero Stephenson is sure not to miss.

AIRMAN ADRIFT

John Topolski
Milwaukee, Wis.

For 29 hours of eternity Sergeant John Topolski of Milwaukee, Wis., battled waves, loneliness and the terrors of the Indian Ocean he'd been adrift in since his plane was shot down about Feb. 26, 1945.

There was nothing but a Mae West life vest and a prayer to keep the B-29 radar operator afloat as he waited for what became one of the longer air-sea rescues in World War II history.

But before Topolski found himself drifting in dangerous waters he was flying through the battered skies of the China-Burma-India campaign.

Born in 1919 in Chicago, Topolski grew up in Milwaukee with three brothers and two sisters. All four brothers served in World War II, one as a Navy medic who later served as a Marine who helped take Gaudalcanal and a second as a soldier in the Italian campaigns. The youngest brother served in the Army Air Force as a potential B-29 crew member.

Topolski was drafted into the service in 1944 and he was sent to the Steven's Hotel in Chicago for radio mechanics and code training. After gunnery courses in Harlingan, Texas, he was assigned to a B-24 at March

187

The Hero Next Door

Field in Riverside, Calif.

His first assignment was with the 11th Army Air Force which took Topolski into the remote island of Kiska, Alaska, where he did sighting of the island.

After the Aleutian Island missions, Topolski was sent to Pratt, Kansas, for B-29 training and on to Boca Raton, Fla., where he was one of the first to learn about the PP1 Radar Scope, taught by the man who invented it. Topolski was trained to watch for blips on the screen, which brightened when they picked up land. "With the scope you could see an outline. We were taught to pick up the target, outline of the terrain and take pictures of the outline for mapping. Also, we learned to bomb by radar if the target was closed in by weather and we could pick up storm clouds too, which helped pilots bring planes between mountains and storms."

OVER THE HUMP

Following training, Topolski was sent on to India in August, 1944, as a radar operator with the 20th Army Air Force, 58th Wing, 40th Group and 44th Squadron.

Topolski was among the bomber crews flying The Hump — which is what airmen called the daunting Himalayan Mountains — to bomb Japan and supply the Chinese besieged by the Japanese invading their country. Before the Allied Forces captured Pacific island launching spots like Iwo Jima, bombers flew from India and China to bomb Japanese held positions in China and Japan itself, flying 11- to 17-hour bombing missions. Other crews flew supply flights over the hump on six-hour runs to China and flew various reconnaissance flights over other Japanese-occupied areas in the region, such as Singapore. The Allies had an airstrip in Chengtu, China, and had established other strips in the "safe" mountainous areas of China where planes could refuel or land if they had trouble. However, many went down in more highly guarded Japanese areas in the east and their crews were tortured, if they survived. In all, 850 airmen were killed in the Air Transport Command, which included C-47 transports as well as heavy bombers like Topolski's. *(World War II, p. 338)*

Topolski flew 16 such missions, in danger but unscathed, while pioneering in combat the American technology that helped win the war — radar. "It was so new that the first guy that flew with me was a major to monitor the technology."

That new technology proved especially useful in the mountains of China and India. "When we started out with radar, the pilots didn't trust it. I had one officer, Capt. Gray, who was real strict. We were going to Japan and coming into storms and he called to me and asked 'Can you take me around the bad storms?' I did; that was the first time he ever asked. We never bumped a storm and he trusted me from that day on.

"There was another time we were coming back and lost an engine. We had to land behind enemy lines in the mountains (airstrip) in China. The pilot couldn't see well in the fog and told me to look out the windows and you could see mountains on either side. The radar got us through and that's the kind of thing that, afterwards, they started to trust radar on."

Many of those flights took Topolski deeper into China, where he landed to bring gasoline for refueling other bombers for their missions to Japan.

The terrain and location were dangerous and the technology primitive. "But the people were the greatest in the world to us. They built the airstrips by hand and they used to run across our airplanes to get rid of the devil. It was a different, different world."

GOING DOWN

Topolski's 16th run, on Feb. 26, 1945, was supposed to be easy compared to flying Over the Hump. It was just a reconnaissance flight to Singapore to photograph Japanese positions there.

They and another B-29 had made six runs and were heading home when a Japanese fighter came out of the clouds. Try as they might, Topolski's crew couldn't

down it. "There was something wrong with our firing system and our guns couldn't hit him but he hit us again and again and again.

"He hit the nose of the plane and the hydraulic line, underneath where the bombardier Bill Kintis sat, ignited. It burned him from head to toe."

Pilot, Capt. Jim Lyons, burned his hands getting Kintis out of the fire as he and Sergeant Joseph Dimock tried to extinguish the cockpit fire.

"We got orders to jettison everything we could. It was hard to see everything we thought was valuable a moment ago being thrown out to try to save the plane."

To help lighten the load, the crew tried to drop the extra gas tank out the bomb bay doors. Unfortunately, the pilot closed the doors when the tank was only halfway out. After some of the crew gave it a good whack, the tank fell free. However, it hit the doors and they would not close completely. With the bomb bay door partially opened, belly landing in the water was ruled out.

"I was one of those who went back to the bomb bay door to try to kick out the auxiliary tank that was hanging half in and half out. We had no chutes on while we were doing this and I don't know how we had that kind of daring. It's incredible, when you think back, that we were only 19-20 year old kids making judgments like we had to. I know I was in shock afterwards and I know it lasted a very long time."

In a letter to Topolski about the crash, Capt. Lyons wrote, "I was able to maintain a reasonable altitude and speed but the cockpit was an utter shambles. At this time, the other 29 (B-29) caught up and gave us an accurate position and course home. I thought with any luck we would make it home, but two hours later conditions changed radically" with a fire in the wing.

The left gunner, Louis Sandrick kept watch on the left wing waiting for the puffs of smoke to turn to fire. In his recollection to Topolski about that day, Sandrick wrote, "I heard a big explosion and the top half of the wing

All of the Topolski brothers enlisted and served in World War II and all returned home safely. They include John (center) and (clockwise from left) Matthew in the Navy/Marines, Richard in the Army Air Force and Alfred in the Army infantry.

raised up about a foot and settled right back down. That is when I told the pilot we better get out of there and he gave the order to bail out."

Capt. Lyons notes that "Lt. Mills Bale (the co-pilot) had been flying for the last hour because I finally became aware of the conditions of my [burned] hands. When I tried to release the wheel, I left skin behind. We made preparations to bail out, including rigging a line to Bill's (the injured bombardier's) chute. We hoped we could drop him and land close enough to keep him afloat. He was badly burned ... we opened the doors and two of us dropped Bill out and tried to go with him but his chute opened almost immediately and we never saw him again."

Topolski recalls seeing all the crew's chutes open but he did not see all of them again.

"I saw all 11 chutes, plus mine. The instant my chute opened, I saw our plane's left wing blow off and the plane went straight into the ocean. It hit the water before we did. It was about 2 p.m., Feb. 26.

"We were told to bail out in rapid succession so we'd land as close together as possible. Lt. Bales, who stayed behind to make sure we all got out, was the last one out. He landed some distance away.

"Lt. Bales' action was not only heroic but also beneficial to all those who were rescued," Capt. Lyons further wrote. "Unfortunate for him but lucky for us. [Because he bailed out later] he landed several miles north of us. Bale was prematurely bald with a reddish complexion. While he was in the water his head became badly sunburned. The pilot of the rescue plane swore to me that in the early morning they saw a flash off the water and changed course until they could see it was a man with the sun reflecting off his poor head."

Lt. Bales, who had been attacked and nipped by sharks, was the first one rescued by the PBY air-sea rescue floating boat. Others in a nearby raft — Capt. Lyons, flight engineer Lt. Frank Thorpe, Capt. Anthony Peleckis and Sandrick — were found and rescued a short time later. The rescue location tipped off B-29 search planes and a British sub to comb the area for the others.

Though sunburned fate helped rescue others; it

would still be nearly a day before that bit of luck would pay off for Topolski.

ALONE AT SEA

The first problem Topolski had encountered in the sea was his landing. "I didn't release my chute just before you hit the water like we were trained to do. So, when I landed, I looked up from under the water to see this giant chute above me. Somehow, I managed to get free of it. Then, I got rid of my shoes, gun and anything that would weigh me down.

"I was very relieved to see the plane following us had seen us in the water. They dropped all their ditching equipment, including a small dinghy. Dimock and two other crew were able to get in the dinghy. Since we couldn't see each other in the water, it was agreed that we would call out and Dimock would paddle the dinghy to the sound. That's how everyone, but me, got together."

Topolski floated alone in the water for the next 29 hours, though 'float' really isn't the best way to describe it.

"A Mae West doesn't keep you afloat. You have to keep fighting every minute. If they say the water is calm during the day, the swells are horrendous at night. You can feel big swells building an hour before they hit you.

"You can't let your legs drag or dangle because you bob like a cork on a fishing line and go under. If you turned into the waves, they'd swamp you. You also have to keep the back of your head to the waves; if you don't, the waves flip you over. So, you must try to lie in the water with your head to the waves but the waves are never coming from the same direction.

"At the same time you can't swallow salt water because then everything inside you swells up and you're done. It was a constant battle. I kept spitting the water out as I tried to keep my head to the waves and legs up, all while trying not to think about the sharks that bumped me several times, though they never attacked. That's all I did for 29 hours."

That and wave at planes that never saw him; call out to crewmen that never heard him and pray that somehow someone would find him.

"The desperateness of being alone in the water cannot be described. You search in vain for something, anything, to hold on to — a pencil, a twig, something."

All Topolski could grab on to was his faith. In his wallet, he had a small card with a picture of St. Joseph on it, which his niece had given him for good luck when he went to war. "Don't let anybody tell you that we didn't pray; we prayed before every mission and on every mission and I prayed and prayed in the water. I've heard that if you carry St. Joseph with you, you'll never drown. I can't argue with that."

Though Topolski came about as close to drowning as a man can. It was a death he had even eventually reconciled himself to.

He had survived one night in the ocean alone and saw and desperately waved at a PBY search plane and a B-29 as they circled throughout the next day. He kept waving and trying to swim toward search planes as they scanned the waves for him and the crew. He was unaware that five of his crewmen were already rescued and three others were about to be picked up by a British sub as he watched the last rays of winter daylight shine on the last B-29 as it made its final circle (about 5 p.m.).

"That was the worst because I knew they couldn't stay any longer and I knew no one would be looking for me for another night. I said to myself, 'I'll never last another night.' I knew I couldn't give up or I'd be lost, but I was to the point where drowning didn't seem so bad.

"I said out loud to God, 'Lord, I'll never make it another night. I'm ready ...' and then ... a British submarine surfaced right in front of me! I couldn't believe it!

"I was hysterical after being in the water so long and

so happy to have something to hold on to that, when the crew threw me a line, I wouldn't let go of it even as it dragged me toward the stern of the sub and the propellers. One of the crewmen, whom I heard was a champion swimmer, dove in and pulled me away."

The sub, the British Sea Dog, had found Topolski for several intertwined reasons. First, the second B-29 that flew on the Singapore trip had radioed excellent coordinates of the downed aircraft. Secondly, the sub was in the area to shoot up Japanese shipping, not rescue downed crewmen. It had picked up the message about Topolski's plane and decided to search. On top of that, the sub crew did a tremendous navigation job, using the B-29 spotting and figuring in current and drift of the Indian Ocean to determine the spot where Topolski would be. Perhaps more importantly, the same sub had picked up three of the eight, by then already rescued, members of Topolski's crew who insisted the sub keep looking for the others they knew must be out there.

According to a copy of the Sea Dog's log obtained by Topolski, Lt. E.A. Hobson recorded "At 1548 (military time) on 27th February, three American airmen were picked up from a raft, and, as five had already been rescued by a Catalina, this left four still unaccounted for. H.M.S. Seadog commenced an up-wind search, since the four remaining men were known to have only Mae Wests."

In a more detailed accounting in the log, the Sea Dog captain (*there is no name on the copy of the log record Topolski has but it was likely recorded by the captain or other officer*) recorded the following details about Topolski's rescue.

"Sub-lieutenant Fullerton, R.N. made a remarkable sighting of a B-29 at what was later found to be 30 miles away. Altered course towards her orbit and pressed on at full power. For an hour and a half flares and grenades were fired in a vain endeavor to make the B-29 see us. We were receiving her signals to control asking for a relief aircraft or patrol boats to which the reply

was that no aircraft could reach her within seven hours.

"As we were in visual touch, I was loath to break (radio) silence but eventually had to say we were closing her from the south. We were then about 10,000 yards away and still had not been sighted. Finally she closed and obviously regarded us with the deepest suspicion. We were ordered to fire a recognition flare whilst we were being circled in the most furtive manner, and when our last red flare failed to work — all others having been fired on the way in — I was fully expecting that it would be us who needed rescuing. But holding out our largest ensign, and having finally beaten the flare into submission, we were able to close the raft and had the pleasure of welcoming 1st Lieutenant Nathan Teplick, 1st Lieutenant Vernon Lester and Sergeant Joseph Dimock on board in position 13 degrees 10'N, 96 degrees 18'E."

The time of the pick up was about 1600, the captain continues, adding that, in all, eight of the 12 crewmen had been rescued. The sub kept searching for the remaining four, known to be floating only in their life vests.

"It took approximately half an hour to get the (three)

The surviving crew of John Topolski's bomber, shortly after their rescue. Topolski is at the far right.

airmen and their gear aboard. Realising (sic) the raft would be downwind of the men in the Mae Wests, an upwind search was commenced.

At 1825, they "sighted what at first was thought to be a shark's fin on the port bow and wondered if it was after the men in the water. But the shape resolved into a dim, solitary figure of a man feebly waving at us."

At 1850, we "picked up Sergeant Topolski, who had been adrift in his Mae West for 27 hours (actually 29 since the time the plane went down) with the B-29 circling him, but not seeing him, almost the entire day. He was utterly exhausted and clearly would not have lasted another night..."

The log continues... "At 1116, 28th February, a Catalina landed and the airmen were transferred. After the various mediums in which they had travelled (sic), or sojourned in, during the past 48 hours, they readily admitted they did not know whether it was Christmas or Eastor (sic). But after a good night's sleep they had little to show for their experience, except Topolski who was still rather weak."

Up until that point, the sub had continued to search for the remaining airmen — bombardier Kintis; tail gunner Sgt. John Carney and center gunner Pfc. James Moffit. The search was finally abandoned at 18:30 hours on Feb. 28 and Sea Dog resumed patrol off Port Blair. The three airmen were never found.

Grateful doesn't fully describe Topolski's appreciation of all that was done to rescue him and continue looking for the others.

"The danger to the sub from enemy surface ships was great but they stayed and searched for me. I cannot say enough for the British; they treated us like kings."

FIGHTING ON

Topolski and the other survivors were flown to the Army hospital in Calcutta. Though he was too tired and traumatized to remember most of his rescue, Topolski was largely uninjured, save severe physical and psy-

chological exhaustion.

He spent a week at the hospital before a doctor rounded up the surviving crew and took them all back up in the air to determine their combat readiness. He declared all but one ready to return to flying. "There was a war still on, so nobody was going home. Instead, the bomb group was being transferred to Tinian and we were going with them."

"I had vowed to myself that I would never go back on the water but, after we were cleared, we had to take a boat to Tinian — 30 days on the water!"

Topolski, who had never flown before joining the service and had been nervous about flying over water even before the bail out, flew 32 escort missions for P-51s out of Iwo Jima with the 506th Fighter Group. Those missions began June 15 and flew virtually every day until their last mission Aug. 15.

By that time, the danger of flying escort flights had lessened somewhat as Japanese air defenses grew weaker — his B-29 never lost a fighter it was escorting — but they remained an important part of the airwar against Japan.

"We pioneered escorting fighter pilots from Iwo Jima to Japan since they had no navigational equipment in their planes and received a special commendation for it."

That commendation from 40th Bomb Group commander Lt. Col. Harley Brown, read: "During their tour of duty ... Capt. Lyons and his crew worked tirelessly with unbounding enthusiasm in their efforts to raise the efficiency of coordination between the fighters and their escort. It was through their individual efforts that the procedures now used were brought to their present high state of efficiency. I, and all the fighter pilots of this organization, wish to commend these men for their excellent work, their willingness to cooperate and their ability to recognize and solve our problems."

For their ingenuity and determination not to lose a fighter, Topolski and the crew of the B-29 was later

John and Rita Topolski with their six children.

awarded The Distinguished Flying Cross, Aug. 6, 1945, for "extraordinary achievement while participating in aerial flights 15 June, 1945, to 7 August, 1945."

The award cites the following reasons: "During this period, they flew a total of 24 navigational missions, escorting fighters through extreme weather conditions. Good judgment in selecting points to penetrate storm fronts and accurate navigation was essential, due to the low fuel supply of the fighters and their inability to fly (by) instruments for any extended periods.

"This crew developed a new procedure that reduced time in the air and consequently cut down fuel consumption. On one occasion they intercepted radio calls from fighters who had become lost from other B-29 escorts. Although the fighters were never in sight, this crew, by means of directions given by radio, successfully brought all the fighters back to home base.

"On several occasions, they located fighter pilots who had bailed out at sea, and orbited above them until surface craft rescue arrived. Despite adverse conditions encountered in flight, and the great length of these sweeps, no fighter escorted by this crew was ever lost.

"The outstanding record is indicative of the devotion to duty, skill and efficiency of this crew, and also illustrates the extent to which they aided in contributing to the material damage done to the enemy by the fighter planes."

Topolski had a great deal to do with the crew's tremendous record since, as part of his job as radar operator on those escort flights, he had to locate air-sea rescue subs along the route.

But there was more than his training and efficiency involved.

"I located every one of those subs, every trip. I knew better than anyone that they were too important to ever miss."

LIVING A SECOND CHANCE

After the war in the Pacific ended, Topolski went to Hawaii for two weeks to recuperate. His brothers had also survived the war. Topolski was discharged Oct. 12, 1945, but the war was long from over for him.

"I was still lost when I came back. It's very hard to get over, you never really do. Any serviceman that saw action doesn't ever adjust back to what he was before. But after I married my wife Rita Mrotek in 1953, she recuperated me."

With the support of his wife — whom he met dancing at the Eagles Ballroom — their six children and his faith, Topolski put his trauma aside and led a happy life on Milwaukee's south side. He ran an ice cream stand for four years before becoming an equipment operator for the city of Milwaukee, from which he retired in 1981.

After all he did to serve his country well, Topolski continued to serve his Lord, family and community.

The Topolskis were involved in everything their kids did with school and church, including Scouting. They remain active in the Catholic church and with the VFW Post #9469, Cudworth American Legion Post, the Distinguished Flying Cross Society, the China-Burma-India veterans group, Hump Pilots Association, Caterpillar Association for those who had bailed out of planes, the Sea Squaters Club and he and his wife served as editors for the Milwaukee Basha's China-Burma-India newsletter for more than 10 years. He was also a member of the Holy Name Society, serving as treasurer, a Boy Scout helper and advisor.

Still, Topolski reminds himself that the nearly 55 years he's enjoyed are borrowed. They are years of happy memories built on the memory of 29 hours of terror and the knowledge that only faith, luck, and the skill of those who rescued him granted him a second chance in life.

"It's been a good life that I didn't think I'd get the chance to live."

ISOLATED SEAMAN
Glen Hanusa
Reedsburg, Wis.

Standing in the barrenness of Adak, Alaska, on the Aleutian Islands in the summer of 1944, Petty Officer Second Class Glen Hanusa couldn't believe it himself. An 18-year-old Depression-era Wisconsin boy was about to meet the President of the United States, Franklin D. Roosevelt.

He saw the president's car wind its way from the docks to the small row of offices where Hanusa served as a Navy intelligence petty officer for headquarters of the 17th Naval District, Alaska and N. Pacific Ocean.

Only a select few on the admiral's staff and the intelligence personnel knew that the president was even coming, traveling from Washington, D.C., in person to learn what information Hanusa and company had gathered about the outcome of any possible invasion of Japan.

"President Roosevelt's ship, the heavy cruiser Baltimore, had been in Oahu three days before heading north to Adak, which took five days in bad weather. They docked at the Naval Operating Base.

"He rode in a sedan on a dirt road on a ridge from the base to Com17 (as we were known), which was in a separate area, Finger Bay, from the rest of Adak's Naval Operating, Army and Air Corps bases. Our Quonset hut offices were located up 72 wooden steps at the top of a hill."

Because of his security clearance, it was Hanusa and maybe a dozen other intelligence and petty officers that lined up to meet the president's car.

"Our admiral, Rear Admiral Ralph Wood, had his quarters in the level of offices in a three-bedroom bungalow. He had a wooden boardwalk from his living quarters to the office so his sidewalk was on level with the offices.

"President Roosevelt's sedan stopped next to the boardwalk near the Admiral's quarters and secret service officers lifted him out of his car, into his wheelchair and to the boardwalk."

It was not an all together inspiring experience. The president was obviously ill, though still as charismatic as always.

"When I was 20 feet from him my heart just sank because I could already see that he looked so ill. In fact, he died less than a year after (April 12, 1945). But even so, he could project himself despite being so weak."

He was a personable man but had little time to be so. He had come to find out what the intelligence officers had determined about the impact an invasion of Japan would have on the troops and land in their territory.

Hanusa and company had been busy for weeks preparing a detailed and then summarized report for the president on the subject. The report basically concluded that any invasion would result in hundreds of thousands of casualties on both sides, if not more.

"We had two weeks notice he was coming and the admiral directed that a written report be ready for him. So, we worked long hours for two weeks to give him a picture of our part of the world (the northern Pacific) since the job of intelligence is to provide information so the Commander in Chief (then Roosevelt, and after his death, Harry Truman) has as much information as possible to aid in his decision making.

"I read dozens of captured (translated) Japanese diaries. If you consider the mind set of the Japanese during World War II — i.e.: kamikaze pilots who dove their planes onto U.S. ships, and that the Japanese would defend their homeland — it would not be out of line to expect at least a million total casualties (including Japanese). And that may have been conservative.

President Roosevelt died before he could fully react to the report and make the decision about whether to try an invasion or try out a new weapon-the atomic bomb. The decision was made instead by his successor Harry S. Truman. "Our report probably impacted some on that decision but to what degree no one knows."

"From my point of view, President Harry Truman had no real choice except to drop the A-bomb. I always wonder whether he read our report; most likely he did. We did have a summary on top since we knew the president wouldn't have time to read it all."

President Roosevelt left Adak with the report after just a short time. But he apparently left more than his impression on Hanusa behind.

"There's an old story about him leaving his dog Fala on Adak Island and sending a destroyer back to get his dog. And, he got a lot of criticism in the States because of the expense. I find that attitude ridiculous. I admire FDR greatly for what he did during The Great Depression and his conduct of WWII. I think he was the one who invented the G.I. Bill, which was serendipity for me and countless other GIs who were able to get an education, buy a house and start a business.

"Besides, any dog lover will understand why he had to have it picked up. I later heard a most eloquent speech he gave in defense of his dog. I found a copy in James MacGregor Burn's book *Roosevelt: The Soldier of Freedom, 1940-1945.*"

It reads:

"*These Republican leaders have not been content with*

attacks — me, or my wife, or on my sons. No, not content with that, they now include my little dog, Fala. Well, of course, I don't resent attacks, and my family doesn't resent attacks, But (a pause and then quickly) *Fala does resent them.*

"You know, Fala's Scotch, and being a Scottie, as soon as he learned that the Republican fiction writers in Congress had concocted a story that I left him behind on an Aleutian Island and sent a destroyer back to find him — at a cost to taxpayers of $2 or $3 or $8 or $20 million — his Scotch soul was furious. He has not been the same dog since. I am accustomed to hearing malicious falsehoods about myself — such as that old, worm-eaten chestnut — that I have represented myself (he chuckles) *as indispensable. But, I think I have a right to resent, to object to libelous statements about my dog."* (p. 523)

RUGGED INTELLIGENCE

For a poor farm boy to go from scraping money together in after school jobs to compiling reports for the president one year later was an enormous leap.

Hanusa was born a farmer's son near Black River Falls, Wis., Oct. 4, 1926, one of seven children. Hanusa's family lost their farm in 1935 during The Depression and moved to a 7-acre farm in Reedsburg, where Hanusa graduated from high school in 1943 at the age of 16.

"People say everybody was poor but not everyone was *as* poor. We were very poor but we were able to raise our own vegetables and had three cows and some chickens. I got my first paying job when I was 10, working from 4 to 5 p.m. seven days a week for two old ladies who ran a boarding house for railroad men. I was the errand boy, I saved $17 to buy a used bicycle earning 10 cents a day. I bought another for $27 when I was earning $2.50 a week delivering for the *Milwaukee Sentinel.* The owner of the hardware store said 'give me $1 a week.' How much I appreciated that."

Life had been tough and unknowingly hardened Hanusa for the ruggedness, the starkness, of his service in the Aleutian Islands during World War II.

When Hanusa graduated from Reedsburg High School, America was well into the war. It was a foredrawn conclusion that he and many others would soon be in the service, including his best friends: Phil Reinfeldt, who was a military policeman stateside and then fought in the Korean Conflict where he earned the Bronze Star and Purple Heart, before ultimately retiring as a bird colonel in the Army Reserve; and Leland Gander who saw heavy fighting as a telephone man in New Guinea and Biak Island.

"So many were going in the service that the teachers were crying at graduation because three were going the very next day. None of my classmates was killed in the war but there were casualties from Reedsburg.

"Lee once had his canteen shot off his belt. And, another time, he was facing three Japanese soldiers. He aimed his rifle and fired and was rewarded with only a 'click,' since, in the excitement, he forgot to put a shell in the chamber. His nearby buddy opened fire with a machine gun and shot the Japanese, saving his life.

"Lee (who died of cancer at age 42) earned the Combat Infantryman's badge. He was prouder of that than any of his battle stars and decorations. I have great admiration for anybody who earned that decoration. It also is mind boggling when you think of my Air Corps friends who flew bomber missions over Europe time after time, knowing a certain percentage on each mission would not return."

TO A PLACE WITH NO TREES

Hanusa joined his friends in the fight when he joined the Navy Feb. 7, 1944, and did boot camp at Great Lakes Naval Training Center near Chicago.

"They wanted me to be a signal man but I said I wanted to do something that would help when I got out so I went to an eight-week basic engineering school and came out as a fireman first class."

Hanusa went to Schoemacher California Naval Base

and then by train to Bremerton Naval Yard, Bremerton, Wash., where he and 650 sailors boarded the U.S.S. Carl Schurz for an 11-day trip to Adak, Alaska, and an 18-month tour of duty. It was one of the few times in the Navy when he was actually aboard a ship. "My older brother S/Sgt. Roger Hausa served in the China-India-Burma theater in the Army and he had more sea time than I did because I was at the headquarters office of the 17th Naval District, Alaska and N. Pacific Ocean."

The ship stopped in Dutch Harbor on Unalaska Island to pick up soldiers rotating back to the states. "They had been in this godforsaken place for 27 months and when you looked into their eyes, they had what was described as the Aleutian Island stare, caused by isolation and remoteness and monotony."

Of the 650 men Hanusa sailed with, 21 were chosen to interview to serve on the admiral's staff. As part of boot camp, Hanusa took the standard General Classification Test and scored quite high. To be eligible to be an officer, you needed a 58; Hanusa scored a 68 which is probably why, he says, he was originally interviewed for a position on the admiral's staff. That score also put him among seven interviewing for Naval intelligence work.

"They picked me out of those seven. I looked around and said ' Holy Cow! I became a seaman first class, petty officer second class and then acting chief when I was 18 years old. When I first got there I was scrubbing floors and now I was the chief!"

Hanusa was soon stationed at the headquarters office on Adak where they gathered intelligence on Japanese strategies and plans, studying countless, translated, Japanese diaries and communiqués. And, they studied up a lot on one of their own Allies at the time — the Russians.

"We were gathering intelligence on Russians. Yes, we were on the same side then, but we weren't stupid. When a Russian ship came in an intelligence officer went aboard and wrote a secret report. We even had one

officer studying the Russian language."

Hanusa later ran one of the two small offices of intelligence officers, all attached to the Admiral's staff. "We were a very small group; there were four men in my part of the office. All secret papers had to cross my desk both coming and going."

"There were four petty officers in our section: Chief McFarland, who published a weekly newspaper in Jacksonville, Texas, John Healy from someplace East, Frank Royal from Salt Lake City and me. The operational intelligence section was in another room with a large map to keep tabs on all the ships. That's where Commander Freedlander (later Cmdr. Lloyd Kersey), district intelligence officer; Lt. Nathan Fitts, the ADIO; and, as I recall, two lieutenants (junior grades) and three first class petty officers worked. They had to be on duty 24-hours a day."

Chief McFarland tutored young Hanusa and helped prepare him for higher rank.

"He was one of the finest people I ever met. Promotion standards were high on the admiral's staff compared to the rest of the Navy, but I took an exam for third class petty officer and, after another and officer review, I was promoted. I was subsequently promoted the same way to second class petty officer.

"Chief McFarland rotated back to the states a year after I started and I became acting chief. In the Navy, even in wartime, you had to have so many months grade before you could be promoted. So, I had the power and responsibilities of a chief petty officer when I was 18."

Rear Admiral Woods' office was next door, though Hanusa didn't have much personal contact with him. "But I do remember he had a photo of his two lovely daughters on his desk. There were no women on Adak, you know. So, a young sailor would naturally pay attention to such things."

In general, military protocol was a bit lax on the outpost location. "I wore civilian boots from a civilian construction worker, Marine fatigues and a chief petty of-

Three friends on "sunny" Adak Island include (from left) Ray Harris, Frank Royal and Glen Hanusa. The starkness of the landscape caused many to develop the "Aleutian Islands stare."

ficer shirt. We didn't even salute the admiral and, once in a while, we'd get a memo from his aide pointing out this fact. But, since the admiral didn't care, we ignored his memos."

"The admiral was not a stickler for protocol and he had a fine sense of humor. Some guys at Finger Bay, where the admiral's staff was located, had a pet blue fox they kept chained. The staff's mascot was a nondescript dog, named Skeezix. And, we had two sea lions we considered pets. Every evening at precisely 7 p.m., they'd come into Finger Bay for supper. One would chase the fish into the end of the bay and the other would backstop him. Then, they'd reverse positions.

The Hero Next Door

"We also had a pet raven who would come down and land on your outstretched arm, but you had to watch his sharp beak. If you ran, he would fly about three feet above and behind you. When a new recruit came up, a favorite trick was to point at the raven and yell for him to run. When he ran, the raven would fly harmlessly behind him and scare the poor guy.

"The admiral was walking one day to his office and the raven was attracted by the gold braid on his cap. The raven picked the cap off his head and dropped it in one of many mud puddles. As a joke, the admiral called the Marines and had the raven put in the brig for three days. The raven would never land on your arm after that."

RUGGED ISOLATION

Though it was far from combat, the weather and the emptiness of their location were rigid enough.

Adak Island is one of about 150 small islands in a 1,100-mile chain that extends from southwest Alaska toward Russia. Attu Island, the furthermost, was close to both the Russian mainland and Japanese Kuril Islands. Thus, they were strategically important, so much so in fact, that before Hanusa got there, Japanese forces had invaded Attu and Kiska islands June 3-4, 1942. The Americans took back Attu in a bloody battle in late May 1943; they recaptured Kiska with no resistance in August, 1943. (*World War II*, p. 363)

What they won was a bleak, strategic landmass.

"It was very rugged country. It has its own beauty and would be a wonderful place to visit for about two weeks. In the hills you walked on tundra which has a grassy, spongy feeling."

There wasn't much else.

"There was a standard joke that there was a girl behind every tree there, but there were no trees! In fact, in Christmas 1944, someone mailed an artificial tree that unfolded to two feet high. It was our only tree.

"It was complete and utter isolation, the kind that

210

drove men nuts."

And, the weather didn't do much to help the feeling. "Though the weather was not as cold as Wisconsin, it was pretty bleak and miserable. You'd have precipitation at least 20 days a month; when the sun came out we'd take the day off, maybe drive up a dirt road which was usually mud. There was lots of mud because of the precipitation.

"I joined the Navy to see the world and all I saw was Williwaws (snow and rain circles created when the wind blows the snow horizontally as it falls vertically)!"

To add insult to injury, the food wasn't much better, less due to military meals and more due to the cook.

"Our cook was not the best. The powdered eggs, powdered milk and powdered potatoes all tasted so extra bad that I just lived on beans the majority of the time!"

Communication home was difficult, especially for an intelligence officer. "I couldn't write anything about what I was doing or where I was which didn't leave me much to write about."

But Hanusa is quick to add that he didn't have it nearly as rough as any combat soldiers, including those who actually had to fight on the islands he endured living on in what Hanusa terms "a forgotten war."

"People probably don't remember that there was heavy fighting in the cold and mud and isolation before I got there. It was a strategic location for the Japanese." In fact, according to the *VFW, May 1993*, 549 American troops (and 2,400 Japanese) died, 1,148 were wounded and 2,100 suffered hypothermia and frostbite in the battles to regain the Alleutian islands in 1942-43.

RETURN TO CIVILIZATION

Hanusa rotated home for a 30-day furlough Jan. 6, 1946, and coincidentally came home to Reedsburg about the same time as his friends Lee and Phil. "We celebrated for 30 days. After being on an isolated island for so long, I was restless when I got home. I couldn't sit down long enough to read the paper. Our

parents, God bless them, never complained about my coming in at 2 a.m., sleeping until 11:30 a.m. and leaving right after lunch to join my buddies."

On May 20, 1946, Hanusa was discharged and soon settled down and, thanks to the GI Bill, went to the place his classmates never believed he'd go — college. Both he and Reinfeldt attended the University of Wisconsin-Platteville (then State Teachers College in Platteville) where Hanusa had a double major in history and education and a double minor in social sciences and English. They both graduated after just three years in 1950, after each taking a year off to teach. (Hanusa taught at the rural, 38-student Gravel Store School on Hwy. 106 near Edgerton).

"We always went to summer school so it didn't take as long to get degrees and we worked in the summer too. One summer we worked afternoons and evenings at Cuba City Canning Co., another we ran a cement hopper on the highway construction job between Hwy. 12 and Reedsburg."

After they earned their bachelors degree, each became K-8 school principals — Reinfeldt in Milton Junction; Hanusa in Warren, Ill.

They then went on to the University of Wisconsin-Madison. Though Reinfeldt was called to Korea, Hanusa earned a master's degree in elementary education and school administration, which the once-poor farm boy cherishes.

"We worked hard to get that college education. Phil and I got up at 5:30 a.m. and drove to school. He'd pick me up after the last class at 11:45 a.m. and we'd speed to Reedsburg to open the country club bar where we worked at 1 p.m. Since I had my typewriter on the end of the bar to work on studies during slack times, we were known as the intellectual bartenders. We'd tend bar until closing and do it all over again the next day."

It was an accomplishment most former classmates in Reedsburg doubted Hansusa could obtain but a goal Hanusa himself never questioned he would realize.

The War in the Pacific

"There was never any doubt that I would get the education I wanted. In fact, we were so poor, that in school when I got up and said 'I'm going to college,' everybody laughed because they thought it was an impossible dream. But there was no doubt in my mind. I hated hoeing strawberries. I worked every job imaginable and I had the GI Bill. I did it!"

He did it well, graduating with a masters, and honors, in 1951.

He owes more to his college education than just a degree. He had met his wife Ruth "Legs" Sanderson — now a feature story writer — while a student at Platteville.

"I first saw my wife when Phil and I joined the group in English for indoctrination for members of the staff of the *Exponent*, the college newspaper. Ruth was the public relations director for the college and faculty advisor for the school newspaper. I wrote a column called the *Dorms Dallies*.

"Later, the faculty advisor advised me to marry her. Since she was my advisor, I readily complied."

Given that the highest pay for a K-8 principal in 1952 was $3,600 a year, Hanusa opted to change professions and went to work for Travelers Insurance Co. claims department in Milwaukee. Ruth became the public relations director for the University of Wisconsin-Milwaukee.

Hanusa later was transferred to head the Madison claims department. At the time, the company was the largest multiple line insurance company in the U.S. "Which means we handled all lines of insurance from life to fire. This made for a diverse and interesting job. For instance, I was a member of the International Association of Arson Investigations and, since we also insured many national corporations, I handled the claims for Oscar Mayer for three years. I was later called out of retirement in 1992 to work on claims from Hurricane Andrew in South Florida."

Hanusa dedicates himself now to serving his family

well, especially his daughter and two grandsons who he enjoys taking on special trips.

He is dedicated to serving others too.

Hanusa was a Big Brother in the Big Brothers/Big Sisters program in Dane County during the 1970s and eventually served as a board member for 10 years, including as its president, when the Big Brothers and Big Sisters programs were merged and Dane County started the first Big Brothers/Sisters couples program in 1979.

"On July 10, 1974, I became a Big Brother. I felt I could make more of a difference in a one-on-one situation. From the feedback I've received from Mark and his mother I am happy to say it did make a big difference in Mark's life. One person can really have more influence than you realize."

Hanusa was also elected president of the Southern Wisconsin Claims Association, a professional insurance organization. He became a long time member, and president, of the Monona Grove Lions Club and currently belongs to the Monona Grove Businessmen's Association and Eastside Businessmen's Club. He also volunteers teaching ballroom dancing at the Madison Senior Center.

In the early 1960s, Hanusa was one of the early Bethel Series Teachers of Lutheran studies. "This was developed by Rev. Harley Swiggum of Bethel Lutheran Church, a program dedicated to teaching the Bible to adults over a 2-year period with a year on the New Testament and a year on the Old Testament. The program went international under the direction of Pastor Swiggum."

Hanusa says "he was blessed to be a blessing" for all his service to his country and the decades of service to others since. "I was never able to do things for other people without receiving more than I gave in return."

ISLAND FIGHTER
Russ Kohloff
Beloit, Wis.

When Russ Kohloff, born May, 7, 1922, graduated from Wauwatosa High School in 1940 he went to work as a salesman. Little did he know the fate of the world would soon propel him into an organization he would dedicate his life to the United States Marine Corps. Nor could he imagine the horror he would endure for Corps and country in the next four years, as he fought his way through Pacific Ocean islands and into the bloodiest battle in the history of the Marine Corps, the fight for a minuscule, barren island called Iwo Jima.

"When Pearl Harbor broke out (Dec. 7, 1941), some high school friends and I all rushed out to join the Marine Corps. It was Al Jordan, Gordy Krause, Frank Sabatinelli and Whitey Brown. Whitey had high blood pressure so we kept trying to feed him bananas to get it down but it never worked and he ended up joining the Army."

Frank, known as Frankie, was Kohloff's best friend since childhood. "He was only 5-foot, one and a half inches. You had to be 5'2" to join so we tried to stretch him between the bumpers of our cars. Finally, the doctor said 'if you want to get into the Marine Corps that bad ...' and Frankie was in. Frankie died fighting on Guam."

Russ Kohloff (right) and his buddies (from left) nicknamed Bedford, Roachie and Ebby display a captured Japanese flag in Hawaii after fighting on Iwo Jima.

PARATROOPER TURNED JUNGLE FIGHTER

Because of a waiting list of enlistees after Pearl Harbor, the friends didn't get into boot camp in San Diego, until January, where they decided to become tail gunners in the Marine's air corps.

Kohloff nearly didn't pass his physical but the friends, as close as brothers, helped Kohloff out. "I was color blind. As I was completing my physical exam, the doc said he had another exam and we should go out and wait for his return. Gordie, who had taken his eye exam already, suggested that when we went back in he would take my eye exam. He did and it worked."

The friends were now in the Marines and would soon split up for different assignments. Al and Kohloff took to the skies, not in planes but jumping out of them.

"This guy asked if anybody could type and Al and I said 'yeah,' and suddenly we had volunteered to be paratroopers. I'm still not sure what typing has to do with that but that seemed to qualify us."

The War in the Pacific

The private first class soon shipped out to New Zealand over Christmas of 1942 as part of the 2nd Marine Division, 1st Marine parachute regiment.

Kohloff would only jump from a plane as a paratrooper once, in practice, while training in New Zealand and later Caledonia. "New Zealand was one of the nicest places I've ever been and I remember thinking 'if this is war, I can handle this.'"

The Marines finished their training in a not so regular place, Guadalcanal. The fighting there was over when Kohloff and company arrived to stay and train in what was jungle swamp beneath rows of canvas tents.

It was an environment swarming with diseases that Wisconsin boys like Kohloff had never heard of and U.S. medics had little lasting treatments for. "I had jungle rot which is a skin disease that festers underneath and then just eats your skin away in spots."

Malaria and dysentery, also known as cat fever, sickened many. Kohloff had both.

"All they had at that time for malaria was a medicine called Atabrine which made you real yellow. I lost a lot of weight with malaria, it wakes you up at night hot and cold and sweating; it's terrible. And, I remember when I went in I weighed 185 pounds when I came home on leave I was 138. My mother took one look at me and said 'he's not going back, he's not going back!'"

Kohloff was plagued by bouts of malaria fever throughout the war and once in a while for years afterward.

His bout with beriberi — an aggressive form of diarrhea — was, thankfully, more temporary.

"I got that in the middle of monsoon season in the middle of the night. It was raining and we were in our tents. So all night I was getting out of the tent, putting on my boots, sloshing through the swamp, 'digging a hole,' sloshing back through the mud, and over and over."

Between bouts, Kohloff was sent from Guadalcanal into island fighting around the Pacific, working to se-

cure islands along what became known as the Solomon Islands ladder. He fought on jungle islands like Vella Lavella in August, 1943, where Marines withstood strafing by Japanese fighters and inland fighting, and Choiseul Island in November where they faced little strong resistance.

"What I remember from Vella Lavella is actually kind of funny now but it scared me to death then. I was climbing a cliff and all of a sudden I saw two big eyes staring at me from (the rock). It was a big land crab but boy did it scare me!"

Kohloff doesn't have too many other memories of the fighting on the islands he hit before landing at Iwo Jima, not because men didn't die there nor because it wasn't tough going. But, because "once you saw fighting on Iwo Jima every other battle seemed not as bad."

But he does remember Bougainville, the top rung of the Solomon ladder, was tougher than most. "There was little resistance when we landed in Nov. 1, 1943; the resistance came mainly on the island. The jungle was thick and it was scary.

"I remember the first patrol I went on we got lost. It was so hot we were just wearing shorts and a T-shirt. I was the point man. I looked down and saw a huge spider on my leg and froze. My buddy took his shirt and wiped it off but, when we looked up, everybody was gone. There were just three of us; it was very lonely, eerie."

Fortunately, the trio was able to somewhat determine the direction the others had gone since "in jungles you have to cut your way through so you could kind of see a path. Eventually we made it but we got in trouble for getting lost."

They fought hard to secure Bougainville island. "The Japs were the best fighters in the world because they weren't afraid to die but they fought dirty too. They'd capture one of our guys and torture him. He'd be screaming and hollering to us all night to save him. Of course we couldn't do it. That was the hardest part of the fighting, those screams and to hear them when they called for their moms.

"It was all jungle fighting and we were real prepared for it because of all the training on New Caledonia and Guadalcanal. Jungle fighting is so much different than other fighting. It was bad but we didn't realize how good jungle fighting was until we got to Iwo Jima. In jungle fighting you can't always see the enemy but you always have a place to hide; on Iwo there were no hiding places."

It was a stark reality Kohloff would soon come to know.

RETRAINING FOR BATTLE

Shortly after Bougainville the Marine Corps sent the paratroopers back to the states and disbanded them to help form a new 5th Marine Division at Camp Pendleton, Calif.

While Kohloff was re-training, his friend Frankie died on Guam.

It seemed at first that he might have escaped the worst of the war. Kohloff's father Bill, once in the National Guard, even thought his son would miss the rest of the war. "When I was home my dad thought I'd be going back to become a trainer of something with all my combat experience."

Instead Kohloff took all his combat experience right back into the worst combat of the Pacific theater.

In August, 1944, Kohloff shipped to Camp Tarawa near Hilo, Hawaii, for final training as part of the 2nd Marine Battalion, 27th Marines, 5th Division, the Spearhead Division. On Christmas of 1944, Kohloff left the island paradise for the horrors of war, arriving at the battle destination Feb. 19, 1945.

They joined an enormous convoy heading for a mere 7-mile long by 2 ½-mile wide strip of land in the Pacific, Iwo Jima. The small island was less than 800 miles from Japan. So, it would make a much-needed emergency landing strip for bombers and a fighter escort-launch-

ing platform for the U.S. Army Air Force. Before Iwo Jima was secured, many planes crashed in the Pacific and hundreds of crewmen died because there was nowhere but water to land on when they ran into problems.

Kohloff and some 60,000 Marines would give Allied bombers the sanctuary that over 24,761 B-29 crewmen used for emergency landings by the end of the war (*The American Heritage Picture History of World War II*, page 588). It was a small plot of sanctuary bought at an enormous price.

SO MANY HEROES IN SUCH A SMALL SPACE

"We were going into Iwo on the 9th wave, about 10 minutes after the initial landing, and they briefed us on ship about the terrain and where we were going in and what part of the beach was ours. Our destination was to secure the first airstrip on the island in three days and then we would be relined for Okinawa (invasion)."

The plan was to have the 27th Marines cut off Mt. Suribachi from the rest of the island and then pivot north to the airstrip.

Before loading onto the landing craft, each Marine was given two bandoliers, four hand grenades and a gas mask. As a combat veteran Kohloff knew how best to get into the landing craft pulling up along side the ship that d-day morning.

"Marines always want to be the first one in anything, but when you go over the side of the ship and go on these big rope ladders we learned the hard way that you don't want to be the first guy over the net. So we stayed back and picked up some extra bandoliers from a guy handing them out."

The squad got into the landing craft and, as was usual, the boat circled between the big ships for protection until they got the signal it was their time to hit the beachhead.

"You've never heard such racket in all your life; the bombardment of the island was incredible. And over it we heard these Navy guys yelling at us, 'Go get 'em you glory hungry bastards!'

"That charged us up even more. I wouldn't say we were afraid, though we sure had that squeezing feeling you get before combat because you don't know what to expect. We should have been much more afraid."

Though the Allieds had bombed Iwo Jima for months prior, bombing intensified as the invasion prepared. On d-day, at 0640 a massive pre-invasion bombardment began with the Navy pumping tons of explosives onto the island before the air corps bombers took over with bombing runs beginning at 0805. Thirty-five minutes before the set invasion time, the relentless bombardment finally ceased *(The Spearhead: The World War II History of the 5th Marine Division,* p. 43).

For all its furor, the bombing did little to penetrate the deep-dug Japanese fortifications lying underneath the volcanic ash-sand island.

Kohloff almost didn't make it into fight against the 21,000 entrenched Japanese on Iwo. He nearly drowned trying to get there.

"As soon as our landing craft started going fast toward the island, we got hit, not a direct hit but on the side. The force put us on our side and we all went into the water.

"I went under, sinking like a rock with all that ammo and stuff on. I was fighting like crazy to get it off but I made it ashore."

He arrived on the already body-strewn beach battleground, right under Mt. Suribachi with no ammo, no rifle and no helmet. Though the first few waves had gone in with much less resistance than they'd all later endure, Kohloff still had to pick his replacement rifle and ammo from among the "dead guys lying all over the place."

He thought he'd found a helmet too, at first. "I found a guy lying there with his helmet still on so I started taking his helmet off, thinking he was dead. This guy turns around and said 'what the fuck are you doing?!' and I said 'oh, sorry, I thought you were dead.'"

The Hero Next Door

Soaking wet, Kohloff began shaking uncontrollably and soon a medic rushed up to him with a blanket and took him to an aid station. "There was another guy next to me shaking bad too and I remember the medic asking him why he was shaking since he wasn't wet. The man looked up and shouted 'because I'm fucking scared!'"

A corpsman noticed blood on Kohloff's side, a minor injury from either the landing craft or a bullet whizzing by that he hadn't noticed. "Then a colonel came in and said 'anybody that can walk is going back in the fighting.' We could and we did."

Kohloff left the aid station to search out his unit, heading along the beach just east from Mt. Suribachi to where he knew they were supposed to land. He eventually found them dug in as best as they could for cover.

"As soon as you hit the beach you just fell down and crawled around on that soft volcanic ash on your hands and knees. There was nothing to hide behind and you couldn't dig a hole in that soft stuff. There were land mines all over the place just in case the bullets didn't get you. But, the soft ash sand did kind of muffle the mortars when they hit so they didn't throw as much shrapnel as they would have."

Kohloff spent most of that first day and night dodging those mortar shells since "it was strictly artillery against us; there wasn't much to fire at.

"I remember that first night was the worst because they just kept dropping mortars all down the beach. There was a sea wall right in front of us that we were supposed to go over to get toward that first landing strip. We never did get over it that first night at all; it was that bad.

"Boats were trying to come in with more troops and to take wounded out but it was so clogged with sunken boats and bodies that they couldn't get in."

The dead and wounded were piling up fast on the beach, reported *The Spearhead* (p. 53). "Wounded men were arriving on the beach by the dozen where they

222

were not much better off than they had been at the front. There was no cover to protect them and supplies of plasma and dressings ran low. The first two boats bringing in badly needed litters were blown out of the water. Casualties were being hit a second time as they lay helpless under blankets awaiting evacuation."

Then in the night, it got worse for the wounded.

"The tide came in. Since the aid stations had to be set up on the edge of the beach by the water — and there were just so many wounded — the tide washed a lot of them right out to sea."

Casualties that first 24 hours were enormous. "I think everybody got wounded in some way. I got wounded on my arm, hit by shrapnel and went into the aid station. They told us we had to bandage ourselves unless you were real bad, which I wasn't. That's when a guy came in dragging his buddy with him and begging them to help his buddy. And, here was this guy, himself shot in the stomach, and he was more concerned that they treat his buddy. There were so many heroes in such a short space that day."

Who survived and who perished in that short space was as much about luck or fate or the grace of God as it was about heroes.

Kohloff still struggles to explain why he was spared on Iwo Jima when so many died, especially during one mortar shell attack that first night.

He and four Marines from his unit, including his sergeant and good friend Sgt. Darnell Harris— who named his son after Kohloff when the war was over — were dug in as best they could to a shell hole on the beach.

"Sgt. Harris had a nice big hole and it was getting dark and all of sudden this captain came running up to it and said we had to get out, that he needed it to set up a command post in.

"We weren't happy about it but he outranked us so we got out. It wasn't maybe an hour later that they took a direct shell hit in that hole. They were all killed and we were left to ask why we were spared."

The Hero Next Door

Answers like that were hard to find but prayers were plentiful, especially for Kohloff whose childhood was built on a strong faith bolstered by a devout Lutheran father and equally devout Catholic mother.

"I was raised Lutheran but had a lot of Catholic influence. I had a rosary and Catholic prayer book I carried throughout the war. I especially remember this Catholic chaplain that went foxhole to foxhole on Iwo Jima. It didn't matter what your religion was, he was there. He was the greatest guy."

By dawn of the second day the toll of fighting was counted in the bodies covering the beach.

There was little let up as Kohloff and company finally scaled that sea wall and made their way to the first landing strip, arriving as planned on the third day.

"That second day we kept moving up. I remember they were clearing the beach so more boats and tanks could get in. I can still see this guy in a bulldozer surrounded by bulletproof glass, just plowing stuff like there was no war going on. They were incredible.

"The tanks started coming in, which drew more fire. Of course, one place you learned you never wanted to be was near a tank because they drew the most fire.

"After a couple of days we got an interpreter and tried to talk the Japs out of their underground tunnels but they wouldn't give up. Then, these guys with flamethrowers came in to clear the Japs out; it was the only thing that could penetrate the tunnels. Those flamethrowers did a great job."

Though the battle never let up much, by the third day the beach was more secure and Marines like Kohloff were relieved of battle duty for a time, though the task they had was no relief.

"We were helping pick up the wounded and dead. Sometimes that was the worst. We had a burial on the beach and the bodies were stacked like cordwood, 15 to 20 feet high.

"One company had nine people left with all privates first class in command. Some companies were com-

pletely wiped out."

And, they weren't finished fighting yet, not by six miles! The Japanese would not surrender. In all, some 6,821 Marines died taking Iwo Jima *(World War II,* p. 597). Only a small percentage of the Japanese surrendered; the rest fought to their deaths. The 5th Marine Division alone suffered 8,770 casualties between Feb. 19 and March 26, including nearly 2,500 killed in action. Kohloff's division buried 7,710 enemy dead, more than half of all the enemy dead the landing force interred on Iwo Jima; the Japanese reportedly buried 10,000 of their own as well. *(The Spearhead,* p.121)

"I know there are a lot of people that say we should never had dropped the atom bomb, (to end the war with Japan that August) and it killed many Japs. But, it saved over a million American lives. I know this as I've seen how well defended Japan was, on Iwo Jima. That was just seven miles long and we had more than two casualties for every yard of it that we took!

INLAND FIGHTING

"In all it took us 34 days to 'secure' the island. We were fighting all the time. You had a constant buzzing in your ears and the stench from the dead bodies was just terrible. After a while you actually kind of acclimated yourself to death; it was a numb feeling.

"After the third day we reached the airstrip. There were Japs hiding in the bombers and everywhere and we had to get out. Then it was into the island's gorges and hills.

"About the fifth day we were taken off the lines and back to the beach. I can remember the first four or five days on Iwo Jima like it was yesterday. But then as I try to think after that, a lot of the next 30 days or so there seem foggy. I think it's because, by then, we were so tired as we had no sleep for about 100 hours. All the shelling we were under, we were just numb."

A few days rest caught Kohloff and the squad up some on sleep but didn't do much for that numb feeling. They

were soon sent back to the front lines. "That was always tough too as you had to readjust to new surroundings but we had a pretty easy time the next day. We advanced about 500 yards which was very good as our casualties were low compared to other days. But, on our right flank, the 4ᵗʰ Division had over 500 casualties."

It soon got bad for Kohloff's division too.

"When we got to the hill, called 362B, there was a small opening and flat land before the hill. We tried to get through but it was terrible and we were thrown back each time we tried. After trying for a couple of days a message came from the command ship — I'm sure it was from Gen. Holland "Howling Mad" Smith — that told us that if we didn't get through he was going to get a Girl Scout troop to relieve us!

"Of course, that was an insult to us and, lo and behold, the next day we got through because we had help on our left and right flank, and we knew it wasn't the Girl Scouts!

"Once again we had to go and pick up our dead. We came upon a small area surrounded by large rocks, sort of a large horseshoe. As we entered the area, we saw a Marine sitting under a large overhanging rock ledge. It looked like he was reading a letter and his head was bent and it seemed he fell asleep. We went over to him and asked if he knew where there were any more bodies around ... He never answered us; he was dead. We took the letter out of his hands ... it was from his wife and young son. ... That is one scene I'll never forget. It's hard for me to even think about it now."

There are other vivid memories that drift in and out of those foggy days of fighting on Iwo Jima.

"Another vivid memory is when we were attacking caves and pillboxes on hill 362B. Most the time we had to call on flamethrowers to throw fire into them and drive the Japs out. This time a flamethrower was climbing up this cliff to attack. He had some riflemen to cover him from the rear. Just as he pulled the trigger on his weapon a sniper hit him. He fell over backward and

Russ Kohloff and his high school friends rushed to enlist in the service after the Japanese bombed Pearl Harbor. This picture, which first ran in the Milwaukee Sentinel in 1942, captures their enthusiasm to defend their country. They include Al and Bob Jordan, Whitey Brown, Frankie Sabatinelli (center, the only one killed in the war), Frank Riemer, Kohloff and Gordy Krause. *(Photo reprinted with permission of the Milwaukee Journal Sentinel.)*

sprayed the rifleman behind him; he was just a ball of flame. The rifleman came running down the hill screaming his head off. At the time you feel so helpless as there wasn't anything you could do to help him.

"As a life member of the VFW, I have met many men that have been in combat in W.W. II, Korea and Vietnam and a lot of us share the guilty feeling because we were lucky to come back and so many, like that rifleman, were left over there."

Shortly after the rifleman's death, Kohloff remembers they again went back to the command post.

"We were given hot chow and were able to take a shower. It was like heaven! Though there still wasn't a

227

safe place because the Japs still had the island in their sights.

"Every day always was the same after that. Some days you would cover about 100 yards and then the Japs would come out of their holes and you had to turn around and retake the area you just covered.

By this time, the division was getting many replacements. Watching unseasoned troops in battle was "very sad," Kohloff recalls. "Most of them had just completed boot camp and were sent over here without any other training. Their casualties were higher than the seasoned troops."

Finally, after some 34 days, Marines raised the final flag to signal that the island was secure. "But it really wasn't. A day or so later about 500 Japs broke out at night at the second airport and killed many pilots and other Marines while they slept in their tents. Even long after we secured it, those hiding in tunnels underground would sneak up and kill aircrews using the airstrip while they slept. There were many casualties even after the island was secured."

There were few lighter moments in the constant fighting but Kohloff still talks about one thing on Iwo with a smile, an incident involving the chaplain's aid.

"I remembered him from boot camp because he said he was 18 but he seemed a lot younger to me and he had trouble shooting so they made him a driver. While learning how to drive, he put the Jeep in reverse and drove right over the head (outhouse) with five guys in it. No one was hurt but they decided to make him a chaplain's aid instead. He was a loyal Marine and a good guy.

"What I remember the most was the funny way he talked; he ended everything with an 's.' He'd say 'I'm going to write my moms or we're going on furloughs.' On Iwo he came running up to us and said, 'I got the Purple Hearts,' and we thought because of the 's' thing that he got just one. But he really did get two. He got hit in the head bad enough that he went to the aid station. On the way back, a sniper shot him again. So he got two Purple Hearts!"

It was one of the few 'funny' things Kohloff remembers from his 34 days in the hell of Iwo Jima. He left there, bound for rest in Hawaii, as a war-weary Marine longing for home. On March 27, 1945, just 36 days after he came to Iwo Jima, Kohloff said "goodbye to the guys we were leaving behind" as he shipped off the tiny island. Though he had left Iwo Jima, the memories of the massive fight he waged there will never leave Kohloff.

FORCED OCCUPATION

It would be nearly a year before Kohloff would return to civilian life, though he returned to Hawaii for some rest and recuperation from battle.

By the summer of 1945, the war in Europe was over but the war in the Pacific continued. Still, Kohloff had hopes that he would be going home and not back into battle.

"You needed something like 72 points to go home and I had 96," yet he was soon aboard another ship heading to the Pacific from his Hawaii respite.

"That's when we learned that we were headed for Japan. We were going to be the troops for that invasion and, after Iwo Jima, we sure were dreading it."

While he was on ship, Kohloff learned that invasion would thankfully not come. The Japanese had surrendered.

"We were told that when we got to Guam those with 70 points or more like me would be let off and would catch the first ship back to the states." That never happened and Kohloff was still a long way and time from home.

Instead of invading the Japanese islands, Kohloff and company would be among the occupation forces stationed there after the war. He was based out of a former Japanese naval base on Sasebo, on the southern part of the Japanese island of Kyushu.

"We were again told once we got to Japan we would

get the first ship home. But that too never happened and I felt bad. I had served three years overseas and had 96 points to go home. I landed on Japan, like a lot of guys, feeling very bitter.

"We landed on the beach combat loaded like we were going to fight just in case but it was just kids and dogs and the Japanese policemen that met us. It struck me because it was not the welcome we would have received if they hadn't surrendered.

"Sasebo was just flattened; there was nothing left of it and there were very few men on the island. Our main job was to take all their weapons and dispose of their bombs."

There were plenty of arms to dispose of, indications that any land invasion would have been extremely costly for both sides of the fight. According to *The Spearhead: 5th Marine Occupation Edition*, "as they inspected the island they found it heavily fortified with underground tunnels."

It was a defense Kohloff is grateful he didn't have to face. "It would have been just like Iwo, only worse, only bigger."

In his three months there Kohloff adds, "we were treated with a lot of respect but we really wanted out and I finally caught a ship back to the states in late November, 1945."

Kohloff was discharged, in November of 1945, from the Great Lakes Naval Base near Chicago. All of the friends he enlisted with, except Frankie, made it home too. However, lives, jobs and a guilty feeling they all had coming home when their best buddy Frankie didn't, caused them to drift apart in the years to come.

NERVOUS HOMECOMING

As good as home felt, Kohloff had a difficult time leaving his military memories behind and rejoining civilian life. He married his high school sweetheart Jeri Streeter in 1946 and they had a daughter in 1949.

"But I had bad legs and knees and I still had malaria.

Russ Kohloff today with Aaron, his "adopted" grandson.

I had two or three attacks of it after I got out of the service; it was the worst then. Finally I was given Quinine and that seemed to work, though I still, about 15 years ago, had another episode that sure seemed like malaria to me but the doctors weren't convinced.

"I was also nervous. I had the shakes real bad when I got home and it got worse after I was out a few months

231

and had time to think. Jeri taught me to knit to help calm my nerves and get me thinking about something else. I knitted a lot, the nicest pairs of argyle socks you've ever seen."

In the meantime, he eventually took a job selling Kirby vacuum cleaners, a job he developed into a 35-year career. In the early 1970s, he and Jeri got divorced and he married Nan Forbes 25 years ago. His job with Kirby took Kohloff to Beloit, Wis., where he's also sold insurance, for 15 years.

SEMPER FIDELIS

It was in Beloit that Kohloff met a fellow Marine who served in the Pacific in World War II, Jim McKearn. The two started talking. When the conversation drifted to where each was born and Kohloff mentioned Wauwatosa, the two discovered just what a small, sad, world it really is.

"I told him 'you probably never heard of it' but he suddenly looked sad, 'yeah, I've heard of it. I had to go see a family there after I got out. Their son had died in my arms on Guam; it was his last request.' That son was my friend Frankie!"

Even decades later the words choke out as Kohloff struggles to deal with the loss of a good friend and the irony that another good friend had been with him in his horrible final moments.

But born of that emotion, and friendship, was the Marine Corps League in Beloit, which Kohloff and McKearn helped found in 1986 as a tribute to the Marine Corps and fellow Marines they remain so dedicated to.

The chapter began with just 15 former Marines and now is the biggest Marine Corps Chapter in the state of Wisconsin. Kohloff served as its first commandant and has served as chaplain and in other officer positions over the years. He participates in the league's Christmas caroling at nursing homes.

"The Marine Corps League has pretty much been my

life the past 15 years," he says of the place he helped develop so Marines would have a place to go to talk with buddies who'd "been there, done that;" do things to continue to serve their community; and to "just socialize."

The Marine Corps League has helped Kohloff and others remain true to the Marine Corps motto: "Semper Fidelis," ("always faithful").

"I've always been proud to be an American, and especially proud to be a Marine. We're so well trained; it's the greatest thing in the world! They're my best friends!"

HOMETOWN PILOT
Garvin Kowalke
Universal City, Texas/Baraboo, Wis.

Garvin R. Kowalke may well have been born with a sense of duty June 5, 1920, on a farm in North Freedom, near Baraboo, Wis. It was a sense of duty that pulled Kowalke to leave high school his freshman year to help out on the family's farms.

And, it was a sense of duty that bid him to fly for the Army Air Corps, flying support for the smallest and most significant bombing campaign of all of World War II — the atomic bombing of Hiroshima, Aug. 6, 1945.

Garvin and Roberta Kowalke

HIROSHIMA SUPPORT

Kowalke had flown "The City of Baraboo" through many harrowing flights in June and July, 1945 (read on), but none as important as two non-bombing, support flights he piloted in August.

On Aug. 4, 1945, Kowalke piloted The City of Baraboo on a secret weather reconnaissance flight to determine if conditions were right — and to obtain wind direction, velocity and temperature — for an Aug. 6 atomic bombing of Hiroshima.

On Aug. 9, The City of Baraboo flew a secret mission again, this time to conduct radiation level tests over Hiroshima.

"Several of us had received some atomic weapons orientation prior to departing for the Pacific. As a command pilot and copilot I had taken training before I shipped out to Japan in 1945 at Dallas Air Force Base in Nevada when I spent a week there. So this may have been a factor in my crew being selected to fly support missions for the atomic drop.

"Before we were shipped to Guam, we knew something was being developed. Myself and several other pilots had gone through intense orientation about the atomic bomb in a top secret briefing so we were all trained for it, but we had no idea who would fly it or if or when. I suppose I was chosen for the weather flight because I had been briefed and had a better idea than most what to expect."

Two days before the Enola Gay dropped its single bomb on Hiroshima, The City of Baraboo was equipped with special equipment for determining weather information and a meteorologist was also assigned to collect the weather data.

The history changing flight took just under 20 hours, as Kowalke guided the City of Baraboo through a rather uneventful run from the jungle air strip in Guam, across regions of China and Manchuria, over Iwo Jima and to Hiroshima and back. Though Kowalke knew somewhat about why they were testing weather conditions that day, he believes his crew was sure it was just another weather reconnaissance mission. "We did do weather reconnaissance flights before the one for Hiroshima. We crossed Japan up to Manchuria to check wind direction, temperature and speed so the bombardiers would have that information on the bombing runs."

This time such weather information — especially wind speed and direction — would be critical to getting the atomic bomb on target. And, to getting it

dropped before the fast approaching Pacific monsoon season hit. "Our mission came just in time, it turns out, as the weather deteriorated quickly in August and we remained grounded for several days in September."

The real reason for The City of Baraboo's radiation testing mission Aug. 9 proved more difficult to disguise for the crew, who were not privy to the top secret information.

"As aircraft commander, I was the only one aware of what we were doing, but the whole crew was like 'what's going on?' because our plane had all this different equipment besides the regular weather stuff on it. We looked like a flying porcupine."

Different indeed, as the porcupine-like equipment was necessary to measure the radiation levels in the city, assess the damage and determine how safe it was for American troops to enter. A special technician was also assigned to take readings and Kowalke was instructed to fly over Japan at various altitudes to determine safe radiation levels for planning future missions.

How safe the radiation was for The City of Baraboo crew flying in to test it was of seemingly little concern. The crew wore no protective clothing to guard them from possible radiation exposure.

"On that mission, if the level of radio-activity reached a certain point, we were to climb. If it reached yet another point, we were to immediately turn around and go back. The aircraft was completely equipped with radiation instruments and we had all these extra professionals aboard to read it and give me the go ahead to get out of there fast if it was too high. According to them, we were never in danger."

The readings indicated all was safe enough to stay in the area and Kowalke got a bird's eye view of the destruction. "We flew across at 25,000 to 35,000 feet and I saw it out my right wing first. It wasn't much different than a massive fire bomb raid. The city was blackened and looked like it was hit by a massive fire bombing run, but it was gone, completely gone."

From his altitude Kowalke and crew saw "thankfully saw little true detail" of atomic destruction, although they saw enough to know that this one bomb would end the war, he says.

As he looked at the destruction, Kowalke says he was hit with a sobering thought: "What was impressive was that when you'd look at the devastation you knew it would have taken 300 fire bombers one night to do that kind of damage. We thought they can do all that with one aircraft, one mission, one bomb. Then that's the best cotton-pickin' mission they could run. This war is over. The thing was the radiation and what it did to the people and that's hard.

"When that atomic bomb hit, and the one hit Nagasaki later, that gave the Japanese Emperor a way to end the war and save face. That saved thousands of our lives, probably my life."

DUTY CALLS

The idea of one plane with one bomb that could change a war, and a world, was far from the farm boy's mind as he plowed a living for himself and, after June 15, 1940, his wife Roberta (Harpold), back in North Freedom in 1941.

When the Japanese bombed Pearl Harbor Dec. 7, 1941, and America soon found itself fighting a war on two fronts in the Atlantic and the Pacific, Kowalke's older brother Harold returned to the family farm to help. With the farm well in hand, Kowalke and Roberta moved to Baraboo and Kowalke took a job as an electrician at the new Badger Ordinance Ammunitions plant nearby.

But as the war escalated so did that strong sense of duty tug on Kowalke. Duty didn't have to pull very hard for him to feel it. In 1942, he responded to it and went to enlist.

"I really wanted to be in the service, in the air cadets. I loved planes since I could remember, so I went to Madison to take the cadet exams. I did very badly. I mean I think I knew what geometry was but I had never

237

The Hero Next Door

seen it before. I got through the rest of the test with flying colors but the math killed me."

Kowalke would not be deterred.

"I remember the first sergeant just laughed at me for doing so bad. That really ticked me off. So I went next door and enlisted in the Army Air Corps."

He did basic training at Jefferson Barracks in New Orleans. Because his mechanic's aptitude was high, he was assigned to Aircraft Mechanics School for training as a crew chief on P-38 aircraft. His assignment was to be the 330th Sunrise Squadron in Glendale, Calif., scheduled for duty in Africa in 1943.

An accomplished mechanic, Kowalke still longed to be flying the planes instead of fixing them. Air Cadet exams could be re-taken. A friend, Bud Alexander, was a college graduate and also wanted to fly but wasn't doing well at mechanics, so the two decided to help each other get ahead. "I taught him mechanics; he taught me algebra."

Six months later, by the time Kowalke was supposed to go to Africa with the 330th P-38 Sunrise Squadron, he had retaken the cadet exam and scored a 98 percent, which taught him a big lesson about the importance of education in reaching your dreams.

"That's what I try to tell young people. Education should be their first priority. It's your whole life ahead of you. After the war, I was able to obtain a high school GED and two years of college by 1962. It meant a lot of night oil, but I needed all the intelligence I could get to do the job I was assigned and do it right."

Though he knew he was flight school bound, the Baraboo farm boy never imagined how far he would fly nor how big of a plane he'd be flying.

He was re-assigned to the Air Cadet Training near Glendale and Roberta returned to Baraboo for Christmas 1942 until he completed his pilot and advanced training.

By July, 1943, Kowalke was sharp enough to graduate in the upper half of his class and was commissioned

238

2nd Lieutenant, receiving his pilot's wings. Roberta joined him at graduation and for his next four assignments.

Kowalke didn't receive his first choice of assignments to A-20 fighter bombers. His second choice was Training Command, which he got. Kowalke adds it was just one of many times he felt there was something greater guiding him toward his destiny. He later learned that the talents of the 10 top pilots who got that top assignment were not fully utilized as they were soon reassigned to cargo aircraft, C-47s, because there were no A-20s available.

Kowalke was assigned to Randolph Air Force Base in Texas for pilot training, then on to Marfa, Texas, as an instructor pilot at Advanced Flight Training Base. After one year at Marfa, Kowalke was ready for combat and B-29 bombers.

He had put in for a transfer to B-29s feeling more comfortable with some flying experience under his belt.

"I learned how to fly on smaller planes and then they taught me how to fly the B-29 bomber. I guess they say that it's not so much different flying a big plane than a little one, except that's kind of like saying: 'OK you know how to ride a bicycle, now here's a semi truck, drive that instead!'"

A bit apprehensively, Kowalke followed his love of flying and his sense of duty to bomber school in Roswell, N.M. It was June, 1944, when he reported to the 38th Pilot Training Wing and was first introduced to the famous B-17 bomber for his initial checkout in four-engine bombers.

This was also his first introduction to the B-29 and Kowalke was absolutely "flabbergasted about how something so mammoth could fly." He would soon find out how — and how well — as he marveled at the smooth response to the controls and the plane's tremendous power.

"She was as smooth and stable as the dining room table."

The Hero Next Door

Kowalke was accepted and, in October, 1944, was assigned to the 2nd Air Force, XXI Command, 314th Wing, 39th Group, 61st Bomb Squadron at Smokey Hill Army Air Base in Salina, Kansas.

It was here that Kowalke was introduced to pilot Buck Senger and the crew. Senger was Command Pilot of the lead crew and formation. Kowalke was assigned as his first pilot and co-pilot.

Kowalke and crew received their orders March 20, 1945; they were Pacific bound.

All the crews then flew from Salina to Mather Field, Calif. and on to Hickam Air Base in Hawaii, landing in Guam to be assigned to the 20th Air Force, 21st Bomb Command, 314th Bomb Wing, 39th Bomb Group, 61st Bomb Squadron. Kowalke's B-29 had the serial number #773 so Captain Senger named her "Two Passes and Craps."

Though their counterparts in Europe had the Nazis on the final run, the War in the Pacific was reaching its climax in the spring of 1945. Just seven months later that war too would be over and Kowalke would return to Baraboo a hometown hero, with 27 bombing runs to

Bombers fly over Mount Fuji on a bombing run in Japan.

his credit, his pilot's wings, left pocket full of ribbons, and a memory chest full of war scars.

"TWO PASSES AND CRAPS"

As fate would have it, Kowalke flew into a bit of military history on his very first bombing run from Guam, April 12, 1945, as the co-pilot of the lead plane, Two Passes and Craps.

"Our target was a chemical plant in Hokkaido, Japan, the furthermost island to the north. This mission was of special significance because it was over 20 hours long — most runs lasted about 16."

That first run would as one of the longest bombing missions in history. Now that was a lot of coffee!

"We knew it was going to be a long range bombing record and it was our first mission so that was kind of special. Hokkaido was a big manufacturing area. Only a couple of fighters came up after us and there was very little anti-aircraft. I just don't think they expected us to come that far.

"Our waist gunners in formation cut loose and the fighters ducked and ran. It being our first mission and everything, our wingman hung on to his weapon and shot so long he burned it up. And that was a mission where we had everything on — our flak jackets, helmets, everything. We learned better later on about what to wear and when.

Tucked away in the memory of that first run is one of Kowalke's favorite memories from his World War II flying days — the antics of his on-target bombardier George Bucker. "He was responsible for getting the bomb on target and released. George was the best; he hit 70 percent on just that run. But if you look at his picture, you can see his face was round and chubby and he always had a big grin. Well, he could do a great Porky Pig cartoon imitation. In fact, when he triggered the bomb release and bombs away, he would turn to me, grin me his best Porky Pig and shout 'the-the-the-the-that's-all-folks…now, let's get the hell out of here!'

It always brought a grin to my face, still does," Kowalke chuckles.

Even the shorter missions were long enough, Kowalke adds and he and Two Passes and Craps flew both 12-plus hour day bombing and nighttime fire bombing runs over Tokyo and Japanese targets.

"The missions were long and we were tired because we'd get back sometimes from a mission at 6 or 7 p.m., do our debriefing, hit the sack and go up again in a day or two.

"We flew day raids over target for demolition or fire. Day raids were usually high altitude runs at 30,000 to 35,000 feet, 12 to 16 hours total time. It took six hours to get to the target so we had briefings at about 3 a.m. for the pilot, navigator, bombardier, radar and flight engineers (Gunners usually attended their own briefings.). After the briefing, we'd head to the airplane and inspect it thoroughly while the gunners checked their weapons and turrets.

"Balancing bombs and fuel was tricky. The distance you're going to fly determines the number of bombs you can carry. So, on a long mission, you need more fuel and can take less bombs. Sometimes we cut that fuel pretty close but we always made it into the ramp.

"If it was going to be a high altitude formation, then we fly singly to a certain rendezvous point, join in formation and proceed to target. As we got near the target we snuggled in together for better protection against Japanese fighters. It increased our fire power and made it harder for them to get to us, though we were always concerned with Kamakazis. Once in formation, we'd proceed to a spot on the island as our rendezvous point to go directly to the target.

"Our route was to fly from Guam to Iwo Jima and on to target. Quite often, a B-29 would act as navigator to the P-51s on Iwo. They would follow the B-29 to the target and strafe ground and naval targets. Mostly, the only thing we had to fuss about on our flights on the way to Japan was the constant line of thunderstorms between

The War in the Pacific

Bombers fly in formation on the way to Japan.

Iwo and Japan. They were dandies with the tops of the storms over 30,000 feet!

"We had one major incident on our seventh mission, a mid-altitude bombing run on Tokyo. One B-29 stayed at a higher altitude to act as navigator for the P-51s. A Kamakazi spotted him and flew into his #3 engine, causing it to explode. The crew had to bail out. Our wing commander was on that flight. Fortunately, we had a Navy submarine surface just off Tokyo Bay, taking pictures and acting as a rescue vessel. The commander and crew were able to land near the sub, get in their life rafts and paddle in. However, a Japanese Navy Torpedo Aircraft spotted the sub and came out to attack. Simultaneously, our wing leader spotted the fighter and dove down to the surface to take him on. The Japanese fighter lost the battle and the sub was saved from having to crash dive and could proceed with the rescue."

Kowalke flew 10 missions as co-pilot for Two Passes and Craps that spring. Among those missions was a firebombing run Kowalke himself would have a hard time believing the crew or a B-29 bomber would survive.

"It was May 4, 1945, and our target was Tokyo. I was

in the co-pilot's seat and the searchlights were on us and the anti-aircraft was thick. Fighters were coming down at us, following the searchlights. There was smoke everywhere from the bombing and it was thick but we couldn't do anything until the bombs were released.

"We dropped them and decided to turn into the smoke so the fighters couldn't see us and then we got the damnedest ride!

"We hit the smoke and dropped like a ton of bricks. The air speed indicator pegged at the highest rate. I had the control column bent backwards just to keep the nose up!

"Then we got down far enough that the air that fed the fire was going up instead. All the pressure released and — BOOM, up came the nose!

"We actually did a loop and came out over Tokyo Bay at 1,500 feet!!!

"Fortunately, the Japanese were as surprised as we were to come up so low over the bay. It took them awhile to get the guns in position and we were able to climb fast back to bombing run altitude and out of danger."

GOING DOWN

However Kowalke and the crew of Two Passes and Craps did not escape the dangers of war just a 10 days later, on their 10th mission. May 14 — a fateful day for the central fire gunner and their squadron navigator.

Flying back from a bombing run, a spring had broken in the plane's #1 engine, so Two Passes and Craps flew on three engines past Iwo Jima and headed for the last leg home as Capt. Senger had decided not to stop at Iwo Jima to fix the engine.

About 100 miles from the base, the #2 engine coughed and died. The flight engineer feathered the #2 engine to maintain altitude.

"Both Buck and I had all our strength applied to the controls to keep our course home. We notified base of our predicament and put the radar on emergency.

That's what saved us because Guam picked up the radar and plotted our position to keep track of us in case we didn't make it.

"We didn't make it."

To make the ship lighter Capt. Senger had the bombadier open the bomb bay doors and release the bomb bay tank. The crew couldn't get the doors closed again, which dragged on the plane and caused it to lose altitude.

"We were applying just enough power to the left but it took both of us and all our strength to keep on a straight heading," Kowalke continues. "That's when Buck, just ... jammed on full power. The plane started to roll and shudder.

"I grabbed the throttle back, got it under control and realized we couldn't stay airborne and were going to have to ditch. I reduced power for landing in the ocean and hit the ditching alarm so the crew would take their crash positions. It was a little stormy and waves appeared to be at least 10 feet high. I cut the throttle and landed on the crest of a wave. It was about 6 p.m."

A gallon container of coffee, which Kowalke took on flights, was attached to the bulkhead. When they hit the water, it flew forward and hit Kowalke on the left side of his head, dislocating his jaw. (He set it himself as best he could after he found his way out of the cockpit).

As the water rushed in, a wounded Kowalke managed to slip through a cockpit window. The nose of the B-29 was at least 20 feet under water. Kowalke credits making it out alive to another 'interference' from a higher power.

"When I got through the cockpit window, I was under about 10 feet of water. My flight boots kept me from surfacing and I was taking on water. I realized that drowning is an easy, painless way to die.

"Then, I saw Roberta. I could have reached up and touched her.

"I cut my boots off and swam hard to the surface to-

Destroyer Escort U.S.S. Doherty rescues nine of the 11 crew members of Two Passes and Craps. Garvin Kowalke is in the raft at lower left.

ward her, retrieved my life raft, inflated it and climbed in. A moment later I saw Buck. He had no life raft and the heavy seas made it difficult to swim. I paddled over to him and found a life raft among the wreckage, inflated it and he climbed in. Moments later, I heard one of the gunners call out. He too had no life raft, so we paddled to him and pulled him up between us.

"Some time later, I noticed the body of our squadron navigator with no life raft and only one side of his MaeWest inflated. He had drowned. So, I took his dogtags for identification, said a short prayer and deflated his MaeWest. This all seemed so matter-of-fact, a job to do.

"We joined the rest of the crew about 3 a.m. in the 8-man life rafts. One was severely wounded; one missing; our central fire gunner didn't make it."

Kowalke and what remained of the crew floated in the ocean for nearly 24 hours. Though he prefers not to recall it in detail, in a letter to his wife, Kowalke wrote that he spent most of those hours thanking God for their survival and picturing her face and his home against the waves, hoping they would survive and he would hold her again.

"At 6 a.m., we were surprised by two B-29s coming at us at low altitude. They dropped supplies, smoke markers and an additional life raft. Shortly after, a rescue seaplane came to pick us up. The ocean was too rough for a landing, however, so we had to wait for a destroyer escort that arrived about 3 p.m. that afternoon.

"It's arrival was the best sight I have ever seen. They picked us up and we were treated like kings. First we were checked for damage, medically speaking. Then sent to bed and rest. I was awakened by cannon fire outside my window. I looked out and saw old Two Passes and Craps, torn apart with one end still floating in the ocean. The empty fuel tanks kept it afloat. The Navy had to sink it to prevent it from damaging any sea-going vessels. I watched quietly and said 'goodbye.'"

The weary crew returned to Guam the following day. After a debriefing, Capt. Senger was relieved of command. Kowalke and other crew members received the Purple Heart and Kowalke was awarded the Distinguished Flying Cross for his heroic action in the crash.

His jaw healed, Kowalke and the remaining crew were ready to face the war torn skies of Japan again, this time with Kowalke as their command pilot.

The Hero Next Door

He was truly "honored and humbled" because the remaining men had the confidence in Kowalke to want him as their command pilot.

He was assigned a new co-pilot, two new gunners and a brand new B-29, which Kowalke explains "we named The Renegade because our crew was quite a mix of people from all over the U.S."

With thoughts of home — and the heart he left there — fresh in his mind from the crash, Kowalke felt it only appropriate to rename his plane after something he loved. He named it "The City of Baraboo."

"I get asked why did I name it The City of Baraboo when Renegade sounded just fine? I say, 'Well, I wanted to name my plane and I couldn't very well name her Butch.' And, I'm a homebody and that was my home city and I'm proud of it and I wanted everyone to know about my hometown. That's just how I always felt. And, I'm as proud of that plane as I am of the hometown I named her after. She was one great bird!"

The plane's name made Kowalke a celebrity of sorts back home, where the local newspaper, the *Baraboo NewsRepublic* could more easily follow Kowalke's plane — and, therefore, the town's son — through the war.

The City of Baraboo and Kowalke flew the hometown namesake proudly, not only into battle above the skies of Japan but into history as part of the atomic bombing of Hiroshima that helped end the War in the Pacific.

THE CITY OF BARABOO

Kowalke and The City of Baraboo flew more than 15 other missions together as part of World War II history, before they helped make history on the atomic bomb support runs.

In fact, the first mission The City of Baraboo flew was nearly its last.

"My new co-pilot, who we called Plow because he was from a farm in Kansas, was one of two survivors of a tragic plane crash on Guam. They had lost an engine coming in for a landing when a fuel truck drove out on

The War in the Pacific

The City of Baraboo crew including (from left, kneeling) Sgt. Ronald Durbal and Sgt. Clarence Holman; (standing) Sgt. John Tynan, Corporal Eugene Dondero, Sgt. Brooks Harris, Sgt. Marion Conley, First Lt. Edward Bates, First Lt. Ernest Smith Jr., Lt. George Bucher, Lt. David Agner and First Lt. Garvin Kowalke.

the runway without looking, causing the pilot to have to abort his approach. Unfortunately, they erred in procedure by applying full power to the three remaining engines. The two engines on one side overpowered the other engine, causing the aircraft to flip and crash. I was two ships back on the approach and witnessed the accident.

"My purpose in revealing this accident is to note that my new co-pilot was extremely nervous (and also to show that it takes a whole crew working together to fly safely). This was revealed during his first mission since the crash — our first mission together, a weather reconnaissance flight. The aircraft was loaded with fuel. On take off, just as the aircraft came airborne, there was an explosion in the No. 2 engine and the scanner reported that No. 2 was on fire.

"My new co-pilot hit the panic button and every other button and had to be restrained by Ed Bates, my navigator. I couldn't shut down the engine until I had dumped the load of fuel and lightened the aircraft. This I did and then shut it down and brought the aircraft around for an emergency landing. All ended up OK. I didn't feel shaky until I parked the aircraft and disembarked. Then, my co-pilot came over and hugged the hell out of me. His faith restored, he was the best pilot a man could ask for."

After that, The City of Baraboo had many shaky experiences but came through all unscathed, with the steady hand of Kowalke — and, Kowalke is convinced, the overriding strength of another power — at the controls.

"Most missions were firebomb missions where you flew over separately to the initial point (IP) and to the target. We flew those at about 11,000 feet. Altitude was especially important because the Japanese low altitude anti-aircraft fire was accurate only to about 9,000 feet and their high altitude gun was accurate from about 20,000 feet up. As long as we stayed between that, chances were better for avoiding a hit.

"There were about 300 airplanes in night firebomb missions and we kept separated by 500 feet so we wouldn't fly into each other. We had to be extremely careful and each had a specific time to the IP and to the target. Four or five aircraft would be first and they'd hit the target on the far sides, right and left, and we would drop our bombs just short of those fires to completely inundate the target area."

Night firebombing raids proved highly effective, in part, Kowalke says because the Japanese government did little to warn its own people and save them from the devastation. "Our government actually warned them about the firebombs and they did nothing about it. I saw that myself on one of our early firebombing missions to Nagoya near a Japanese Naval Industrial site.

"The distance from the IP to Nagoya was longer than usual so we had ample time to see what was ahead and get lined up. Two things really surprised me: some city lights were still on and the Navy anti-aircraft was so intense it looked like a black field you could walk on. With a solid wall of fire from the guns and marking fire bombs up to 9,000 feet, all I could say was 'Oh My God!' People were out on the streets. This, after President Truman had warned Japan of a strike on that target. Our first pilots going across just shook their head and that was kind of hard to take for us.

"I took another look and directed the crew to put on all protective gear. I told Porky, my bombadier, that I was going to increase speed by about 10 knots. I had distance between me and the aircraft ahead. We were all really charged up. Porky took over the ship and zeroed in on the target, dropped the bombs and then did the best Porky Pig impression I'd ever seen. He turned to me saying, "Th-th-th-that's all folks ... let's get the hell out of here!"

FLYING WITH FAITH

Through all his harrowing missions, Kowalke stresses that he never had time to be scared "But there were a few missions where I was definitely concerned. The thing is you have a job to do — a crew to direct and a plane to fly — you just do the job. There isn't time for fear."

Kowalke feels strongly that during some of those many times of concern during the war "someone else was at the controls with me."

He especially credits a higher power for rousing his suspicions in time to save the crew on one long, night mission.

"We were all pretty tired, so after takeoff and leveling off at cruise altitude, I turned it over to the co-pilot so I could get an hour or two of sleep.

The Hero Next Door

"Then I started having this weird dream, kind of a sinking sensation. I eased my chair back and went to sleep but every once in a while I kept getting a little sinking sensation, not enough to wake me just stir me a little.

"Now I'm quite a Christian and I believe the Lord once in a while will reach down and slap us in the face and say 'Hey! Pay attention!'

"And that's kind of what happened. It was like I heard a small noise and woke up enough to look out the cockpit window and what did I see — water!

"We were only a few hundred feet from the ocean!

"The co-pilot and all the rest of the crew had fallen asleep too. He was holding the controls in his hands; we were just dipping, sinking slowly out the sky. We were still cruising, but the nose had been dipping periodically, taking us lower and lower toward the ocean. I hit the power and took us back up — that sure woke them up!"

"My big worry then was having enough fuel to complete the mission. We did, but the engines sputtered as I parked the aircraft."

On a night mission another such "something" kept Kowalke and crew from flying straight into Mt. Fuji, he recalls.

"We had dropped the bombs and I made my turn. We were supposed to turn away from Mt. Fuji but the navigator gave me the reciprocal of the heading we were supposed to go. So, I was headed right for the mountain. We were at 11,000 feet and the mountain was 13,000 feet high.

"As I looked ahead of us, I saw some pretty strong storms which concerned me enough — though I would have been even more concerned if I'd known that those storms were surrounding the mountain and hiding it from our view.

"Again something tapped me and I just decided to ask about the heading, something I normally didn't do because Ed Bates was a competent navigator. Ed immediately realized his mistake and I started to turn but we were already entering the storm. There was hail and lightning everywhere. It was a night run and you could have read a book inside the cockpit. The static electricity was so great that all the braces in the front were filled with fire. The propellers looked like solid rings of fire.

"We got caught in the storm's updraft. I was really climbing (screaming up the side of the mountain) and it blew us out the anvil of the storm.

"We were shot up the side of the mountain. In about a minute we went from 11,000 to 24,000 feet and then it pooped us out the head of the storm.

"Safe and sound, we changed our heading, checked it twice, and flew home quick. At least with the added altitude we didn't have to worry about fuel this time."

Kowalke adds that many of his and other pilot's harrowing flights may have proven deadly had it not been for one small thing — the tiny island of Iwo Jima.

"On our fifth mission, with me as commander, we had to land at Iwo Jima because we lost an engine due to mechanical problems. Lots of pilots landed there, and if we didn't have that island, the only place between Japan and Guam to land would have been the ocean.

"That Iwo Jima was a real life saver and any pilot or crew member who ever flew missions to Japan is grateful to the Marines and guys who died to get that for us. It brought us closer to Japan and made the difference in the war. It saved a lot of lives, probably mine."

CITY'S LAST FLIGHT
But for all the near misses of combat, The City of Baraboo never came close to death nor destruction. "The City of Baraboo was never seriously damaged; that we saved her from."

In fact the closest The City of Baraboo and Kowalke came to crashing happened not on a combat mission but on a routine test flight after the war.

"About one week after our last mission it began a solid monsoon. When the weather lifted, we went to inspect

the planes and determined they were ready for a test flight.

"When we took a test flight we got seven or eight friends (ground crew usually) to tag along.

"I got her started and everything was good. We taxied out to the runway and I got ready for take off and put her to full power. I kicked off the breaks and the aircraft was very, very light. I rotated the nose up and BANG! the No. 3 engine went off and started on fire. Then BANG! No. 4 was smoking. I was taking off and had just lost two engines!!

"I dropped the throttle back, slammed the nose back down and jammed on the brakes and was praying I could stop before we ran out of runway and had nothing but a cliff and the sea to stop us. We stopped but I took out about 100 feet of coral at the end of the runway (there were only 500 feet of coral to take) to do it. Fire trucks were at the end of the runway and immediately put out the fire."

"We gave those friends a ride they surely weren't expecting!"

After further inspection, Kowalke and mechanics determined the heavy rains had collected in the bottom of the electrical boxes in the superchargers in the wings. "As soon as I rotated, the water shorted out the electrical system causing the surge and the explosion."

The City of Baraboo had been programmed to go on tour as part of the fanfare over Hiroshima and Nagasaki ending the war, but this shut it out completely.

"Though they did get the engines fixed, and I heard they flew her back to California, I never saw her or flew her again. "It was like leaving a very dear friend, not knowing if you'd ever meet again."

THE REAL CITY OF BARABOO

That problem shorted out Kowalke's time with The City of Baraboo, the plane, but certainly not with the town it was named for.

After the war, the squadron was to be assigned to

occupy Japan. Kowalke had the choice of going to Japan or joining the active reserves stateside. He chose stateside, and home with Roberta.

Kowalke stayed in Amy Air Corps, and later the Air Force, for 28 distinguished years, flying through three wars and earning the Distinguished Flying Cross, four Air Medals and the Purple Heart. He was also awarded the General Foulois Award for flight safety and Air Force Commendation Medal in addition to his many theater ribbons and other honors.

He went into the reserves after the war, but couldn't stay out of the cockpit and so re-applied for active duty in time to serve in the Korean conflict as a B-29 and B-57 pilot and instructor, stationed on Johnson Air Force Base, Japan. He moved his family back to Wisconsin in 1968 and remained in the service through the first years of Viet Nam, where he flew 12 missions with the Snoopy Squadron in DaNang as a flight examiner for the forward air control squadron. Kowalke was promoted to lieutenant colonel and assigned to Air Force Intelligence until his retirement in 1970.

Kowalke, his wife and two children returned to Baraboo where Kowalke continued his dedication to serving his country. This time he served his hometown, quickly accepting a position as the Sauk County Director for the Wisconsin Emergency Management Agency. While there he helped set up the independent emergency ambulance services, establishing them as separate departments like the police and fire departments. In 1984, he was elected state WEMA president and received the Famed Harbor Lighthouse award for duty above and beyond in that post.

He held the post until 1985, when Roberta's health necessitated a move to San Antonio, Texas, for special medical treatment. They returned to Baraboo in 1987 when those treatments failed; Roberta died in 1989.

Over the years, Kowalke has been involved with the Lutheran Church, Red Cross, the Elks, Masons and Optimists and senior services. Kowalke later returned

to San Antonio to be near his sister. He is writing his memoirs not only about his World War II flying days but about his nearly 30 years as a pilot in the armed services, including his experiences flying in the Korea and Viet Nam, and his experiences adopting his two children.

For all his war flying heroics and community service accolades, the adoptions of his children were the greatest moments of his life, Kowalke beams.

"Roberta couldn't have children so we were constantly trying to adopt. Unfortunately, we were in the military and adoption agencies couldn't help. They take way too long.

"It was November, 1954, and I had just transferred from B-29s to learning to fly B-57s at Randolph Air Force Base, Texas. My aunt was secretary to the German professor in Madison. She had received a call from a dear friend in Marburg, Germany, a secretary to the mayor. She knew an orphanage had just received a baby boy who was up for adoption. I told my aunt to tell her to keep him and I would be right over to pick him up. I asked the commander for leave to get the boy and he told me to take all the time I needed. I flew immediately to Marburg.

"The boy was almost three months old and I told the lady at the orphanage that I'd love to have him as my son. I gave her my name and the name of the hotel I was staying at. I met the mayor and his secretary and received his approval to take the boy.

"However, there may have been some confusion in translation because, after I returned to Frankfurt and started the passport paperwork, a nurse came to the hotel with my baby boy. I was an instant "daddy" with this little baby and still working on the paperwork. I named him Kraig Corwin.

"A few days later, there I was flying commercial, a B-4, bag in one hand and a cradle in the other. We were flying at 30,000 feet over Iceland, middle of the night when I heard a small squeak and Kraig squeezed my little finger. I couldn't believe I had a son! Then I got to do something at 30,000 feet I hadn't done in all my years of combat flying — change a diaper.

"It's just miraculous how the Lord blessed us. In 1967, I was stationed at Hickam Air Force Base, Hawaii as an I-Corps operations officer. Roberta and I had kept our names in for adoption. And, that Easter Sunday we received a miracle, a baby girl born in a local hospital to a young mother who wanted to give her up for adoption. We were totally thrilled to learn we were first on the list. We adopted Kimberly Chere' immediately. She turned into a wonderful daughter and now is a mother of two beautiful girls. Her husband is an Air Force major, A-10 pilot with Desert Storm under his belt."

Kowalke's strongest sense of duty was then, and remains, to his family and country. He wittingly sacrificed much for both — a hometown boy fighting for a love to come home to.

SOLDIER BY TRADE
Eugene Skaar
Cottage Grove, Wis.

The Philippines is thousands of miles from Cottage Grove, Wis., where Eugene H. Skaar was born and still lives. But it's as close as his skin by the measure of Skaar's own memory — a memory filled with sweet and bittersweet recollections of the time he served, and those he served with in 1944-45.

Skaar was an older recruit when he was drafted into service in January, 1943, after college, marriage and a job with the Dane County Highway Department. He was activated into basic training at Camp Hulen in Palacios, Texas, as part of the 382nd AA Battalion in the 68th group, 44th Command of the U.S. Army.

After basic training, Skaar was called to enter the 12-week officer preparatory training course. Only 13 of the original 36 made it to the final test. Skaar scored two points shy of passing and was asked to return for another try. He declined.

"My outfit was scheduled to move out and, if I took another session, I'd be reassigned to another. I had no desire at that time to go to West Point, so I chose to stay with my unit."

Since Skaar was in officer prep school when unit assignments were made, he was not assigned to the gun section like others but instead was assigned to battery headquarters as a unit utility maintenance man who drove Army vehicles, did repairs and carpenter work and completed special assignments for the gun section, communications, motor pool, etc.

Instead of sweating out tests at West Point, Skaar soon found himself sweating in the heat of desert fighting training in the Mohave Desert near Death Valley, Calif., at Camp Coxcomb. His unit was preparing to fight the Germans with General Patton in the heat of the African desert, taking in little water and "eatin' sand."

Then, the desert campaign ended and so the 382nd was sent to retrain in jungle fighting at the Marine base in San Diego. They were going to fight the Japanese in the Pacific islands.

Skaar trained in amphibious assault landings and jungle survival, a grueling experience. "We were combat loaded on an LST and made a night landing on Catalina Island, 80 miles off shore from San Diego. I was one of the first to leave the ship to fill sandbags to shore-up the ramp. With full pack and rifle, I missed the land and went down into the sea. I crawled up on shore, wet, cold and almost drowned."

He continued training in San Diego then at Camp Cook near Santa Barbara, Calif., and finally at Vancouver Barracks in Portland, Ore.

NEW GUINEA INGENUITY

With his training behind him and faith to support him Skaar and the 382nd shipped out in February, 1944, bound for further jungle fighting training and preparation, eventually in British New Guinea. They spent a year there on dock patrol and training, marked by longing for home and adapting to the war and jungle environment.

When mail finally caught up to the troops in New Guinea, Skaar learned he would be a father. A rare fur-

lough he had gotten over New Years 1943-44 while at Camp Cook had produced a pleasant surprise, his wife Polly wrote. Their baby was due in October. The knowledge that he would not be home in time for their first child's birth tore at Skaar's heartstrings.

"There were two of us waiting for babies, C.W. Pierce from Esconaba, Mich., and I were both chewing our nails over in New Guinea waiting for news. We figured the Red Cross would contact us right away but instead we found out by v-mail (transmitted from radio to paper but censored) which was fast but still took three to four days. We both had girls.

"I was getting the stage ready for a Christmas Eve 1944 service when I received a letter from Polly that our daughter was born. Polly had a very difficult time and I should have been there. I had applied for a leave to go home but was promptly denied that privilege. However, Polly and my daughter, whom we named Vicki, were both fine, though it would be 14 months before I would see my wife again and see my beautiful daughter for the first time."

Though the pain of loneliness and longing to hold his first born was nearly unbearable, Skaar was kept too busy to focus on it.

New Guinea, while not then an active battle ground, provided many challenges to overcome — the kind of challenges best solved with good old American ingenuity and determination, both of which Skaar had plenty of.

Most importantly, such ingenuity made his unit some of the best shooters around, as Skaar and those in his gun unit were able to make unique modifications to their anti-aircraft gun sights to greatly increase accuracy.

"We were training in a place called Scarlet Beach, so named because the blood from the battle there earlier in 1944 had turned the sand red. In fact, after a storm raged there shortly after our arrival, we saw just why it got its name because sunken war vehicles, bodies and PT boats floated up on the beach. The coconut trees were ragged stumps. It was a horrible first look at the rages and smell of war.

"We trained there because it had the same firing perimeters as Tokyo harbor and found that, with the open area sights we had, we couldn't pick up targets moving across the harbor. So, we rolled brass shell casings and cut circles inside and lifted the web. We worked on it two nights to have it ready by Wednesday afternoon. This made the sights twice the size as normal and we started picking off targets left and right.

"After that, our battalion commander said we were the best shooting outfit in the world!" However, that distinction may not have been such an honor a few months later had the Allied Forces invaded Tokyo. "At a reunion after the war, that commander told us that had the atom bomb not dropped on Japan to end the war, we were such good shooters that we were scheduled to go into Tokyo harbor in the first wave of the invasion. We probably would not have come home."

But not all of Skaar's ingenuity was used on battle readiness. He put it to work to boost morale a bit when he could.

As D Battery's maintenance man of sorts, Skaar found himself doing all sorts of projects to make life a little better. "The guys I was with were miners and lumberjacks and farmers — talk about talent! There was nothing we couldn't do when we put our minds to it."

For example, after Christmas Eve services in 1944 on New Guinea, Mess Sgt. Joe Blume brought a supply of ice cream mix they'd gotten from Deerfield, Wis., back to Skaar's supply tent.

"I made an ice cream freezer out of a 20-gallon insulated container and a 10 gallon container. We used a bomb hoist reduction gearbox from of a wrecked B-17 to turn the dasher, powered by a Briggs and Stratton horse-and-a-half gas-powered engine. I had to solder everything together as there wasn't any electricity.

"We got 300 pounds of ice from the quartermaster by trading them a couple cases of GI beer. We ran the en-

gine from about midnight unil about 10 a.m., when the engine burned a valve and quit. We packed the container with salted down ice.

"So for Christmas Day dinner, we had one extra item on the menu, ice cream which was more like ice soup, but it sure was good. There was enough for every one to have a little scoop and I was the hero for the day."

He was a hero in high demand. "The next day, I tore the engine down and ground the valves so C Battery could borrow the freezer. They had ice cream for New Years."

The troops soon had both electricity and running water as well thanks to American ingenuity. "We did find a way to get some electricity too. I took a Jeep engine and belted two, twin 22-volt generators to the engine. Then we had enough electricity to light up the camp.

"We also didn't have any water but we were near the Guinea River. Joe Truskowski and I hauled water every day and we tried to figure out how to get it to camp an easier way. The corps of engineers had some fire equipment including a pump. One of our guys got formal requisition papers and we got it. We soon had a source of water and enough for showers.

"We had some entertainment come in too and I had to set up a stage but I had to set it up so we'd have lights to see the entertainers but Japs couldn't see us. So I used mattress covers for the backdrop and cover (roof) and even built in dressing rooms."

The result was a working stage well appreciated by the performers, including singing beauty Carol Landis. However, Skaar was so exhausted from spending days and nights building the stage that, when everyone else was watching the entertainment, he was asleep in his tent.

AT WAR
Skaar did not rest long.

In February, 1945, the 382nd loaded onto LST 245 to join the Armada heading for the invasion of Letye Is-

Tech Sgt. Don Vassar was one of many working on everything from engines to ice cream freezers with Gene Skaar in the South Pacific. *(Photo courtesy of Donald M. Vassar.)*

land in the Philippines.

However the 382nd did not see fighting at Letye.

"We missed the fighting there by a day. We started out with everyone — boats as far as you could see — but the next day we were thumping along by ourselves, heading for Leyte Harbor. We were going sideways through the water because one engine went out. So, we missed the heavy fighting. In other words, a lot of

The Hero Next Door

why some survived was just luck."

The unit was ordered to advance into Manila harbor. "As we entered that channel, the Army and Marines were retaking the Bataan and Corregidor (which fell Feb. 26) emplacements that were strongholds of the Japanese forces. Because they were engaged there with ground forces on shore, we entered safely into the harbor. We were the first troops to dock there and thus far, we had not fired a weapon in combat."

D Battery was to take the Lipa Airstrip and maintain and secure it, which they did that first night. In the morning however, they got word that two Japanese were working their way toward the outer camp with automatic weapons and quickly organized a scouting patrol (Skaar included) to intercept them.

"The grass was really high. I was with Leverne LeJune from Chicago and how it worked was one guy would move while the other covered. So I'd advance 20 feet, drop and wave and he'd advance 20 feet and do the same.

"We'd just done that and I was about to get up and move again when Laverne let go. There were Japs right ahead of me about 30 feet and were just waiting for me to move again. I didn't even see them in the high grass. They had leveled their guns and waited for me to get up and move. Fortunately, they hadn't seen Leverne; he opened up and cut them down with his cross fire. He called over and told me to cover him while he moved in. Needless to say, he took them both out.

"You could smell the odor of warm blood and gun powder, a smell you never can forget."

Skaar joined LeJune. "I looked in his eyes with the only thanks I ever gave him. He assured me it was OK for he knew I would do the same for him. In the next 100 days, there were many stories like this.

"For example, we lost Sgt. Chapman by a sniper early in the campaign and my good friend Corporal Steve Hankoski took a slug through a nerve in his neck that

264

The remnants from the U.S. invasion force on Scarlet Beach in New Guinea in Febrary 1944.

came out the back of his helmet. He recovered and spent a useful life back in Chicago, though he was slightly disabled.

"He was leading a patrol around the Lipa Strip, (like the one I'd been on) when a darn Jap machine gun nest let go.

"There was one coconut tree still standing and he jumped behind it. He unhooked a grenade and lobbed it in. He took them out; but, in the fight, that slug went across the back of his neck, another grazed his wrist and another went through his shirt and busted his Ronson lighter. But that tree saved him. The bullets whizzed by and grazed him on the front and back parts not covered by the tree. Fortunately, their rifles didn't have anywhere near the velocity of ours. He was our first wounded to take a hospital flight back to Hawaii."

The worst of those early patrols was Clark Field, on Luzon.

"We got there and had first patrol. There were 22 in a line and you'd move and just hope you weren't next. We knew we'd either come home walking or in a mat-

tress cover. They issued us white mattress covers to sleep on but essentially you carried your own casket. When you became a casualty, that's what they put you in."

The Japanese were dug in every place on the island. They had years to fortify their position and it took days of flame-throwers to clear them out.

Skaar's battalion was assigned certain areas to clear under the direction of Lt. Col. Craig, advancing to form a pincher and drive the Japanese out.

It worked well.

"One time a lone battery, Battery A, was sitting on the 40-mm gun and saw something streaming over the field. When they looked closer it was thousands of Japanese going over a dike. Since it was just them, they didn't open fire as they figured they were certainly outnumbered."

Skaar's battery was assigned to go north from Manila to secure villages like Lucinia, Batangas, Lucican, Bagio, San Fernando and finally Luna.

"There were booby traps everywhere. You checked the trees and ground for wires, wires which you could hardly see when you were looking close but sometimes you didn't have time to look close and just had to hope they weren't there.

"We never ran across any but they booby-trapped bodies of their fallen comrades too. You wouldn't dare turn a dead Jap over. And, it just stunk. I stepped over and over the bodies of Japs that were horribly bloated.

"And, there'd be times you knew the Japanese were close, they were so close you could actually smell them; I don't know if it was something they ate but it was a definite odor."

The battery often had help flushing out the Japanese from the Filipinos themselves, especially two very capable "spies," Rico and Camillo, who offered their assistance as soon as the Americans arrived.

"Rico was pretty jolly but had been in Manila when

they took his sister to be a flower girl (forced concubine). Camillo was just so darn serious but then he had survived a death march and had whips and scars on his head and body," Skaar recollects. "They wanted to help us and spoke enough English. They would also often act as interpreters, helping the soldiers understand many of the islanders' 100 dialects.

"They'd go out into the island and return a day or two later reporting there were two Japanese waiting here for us, etc. I never doubted their information as I never found them to be wrong. They soon became our most trusted scouts. Months later, when we got word that the war had ended, they simply turned around and walked away. We never saw them again."

ON GUARD

In the long months before the war ended, Skaar did more guarding than patrolling.

Standing guard was not that preferred an assignment however, especially when he'd been out patrolling or working all day and then had to take guard shift. It was a huge responsibility, he adds, an assignment that had you on "pins and needles."

"You don't get scared exactly, you just react. Nobody jumps and runs, they do their job; that's your training but I guess you'd say you'd get a little jumpy. Everything that moved could be the enemy, especially at night when it was harder to see. And, those darn banana trees and branches would turn and you'd swear there was someone there.

"There was one night I was standing guard and it was real windy and I bet a dozen times that night I raised my gun ready to open fire."

When he wasn't watching the night shadows, Skaar did most of his guarding work from the passenger seat of a military vehicle, riding "shotgun" mostly on the supply and ration trucks, which kept up with the moving units and brought a hot meal to troops once a day.

The Hero Next Door

Troops cleared a path through the jungle from camp to the docks on New Guinea. (Photo contributed by Donald Vassar.)

Jack Pattison drove the truck with mailman Bob Swanson along for mail call once a week.

"As much as we could, we didn't go the same way, same place, two days in a row because the Japs would lay in wait for us. Jack was uncanny with directions. He could read a map and get us anywhere. I never could because I had to keep such a close eye on the trees and roadside, which is maybe why I still get lost all the time; I'm still watching the trees more than the road."

As a guard Skaar was equipped with a Colt .45, which guards called "Chicago Typewriters," and a Tommy Gun.

"One time on guard, Jack and I came in to where we were headquartered at a village mayor's house with a walk-in basement and outdoor kitchen. We worked it so one would sleep in the basement and the other would stand guard at the basement door. Jack was wide awake and said he'd take first guard; I went back in to sleep.

"After a while, Jack whispered back, 'Skaar, there's something moving out there!'

"'Heck with it,' I said, 'I'm going to sleep.'

"Well, as a driver, Jack had a grease gun, which was so named because that's what it looked like. The barrel was short with a trap door on the side to discharge the brass and a cartridge that was like a Tommy Gun. It wasn't very pretty, but it was practical and had a lot of fire power.

"Jack was sure something was out there so he opened up with that grease gun. The sound in the basement was like a dozen hand grenades going off around you. He sure got my attention and I ran up with my M-1. But there was nothing out there.

"However, between him and what he was shooting at, all the cooks had hung up their pots and utensils to dry for the night. The next morning the cooks came out and there was lead splattered everywhere, but he didn't hit a thing. You could see where the slugs had kicked up dirt but they had gone between every utensil.

"Then Captain Preslock came down from his quarters upstairs and indicated that he too had been been awakened by the commotion. He simply asked: 'So, where's that little guy with the big gun?'"

Dawn's light did not, however, always provide relief from the tensions of his guard experiences. In fact there have not been enough dawns yet to quell the memory of one incident while Skaar was riding guard in the command car with Battery D Captain John Preslock.

"We came upon a gathering of Philippine natives at a newly established tavern-type business, selling drinks of liquor called Bosi. A soldier from Skaar's company was in front of the gathering of Filipinos and soldiers who all seemed in disarray.

"This man was on company restriction since he had gone berserk a week earlier after he had left his gun section with a Tommy Gun and came back to the area of 18 men, told them to take cover and opened up on them with the Tommy.

"Sgt. Don Vassar was the first on that scene and approached him from behind, talking from a distance

269

The Hero Next Door

Skaar and his buddies take a breather from desert training at Camp Young. They trained in the Southwest sand only to end up fighting in the jungles of the South Pacific.

while continuing to move toward him. He gave up his weapon and was taken to our captain who put him on summary court martial and put him back in his unit on restriction.

"So, when we came upon that same man in front of the Bosi tavern, the Captain ordered his driver Ed Wayne to pull over to ask what he was doing there.

"'I think I killed a man,' he replied.

"He had left his section and come into town. A table of soldiers from the 460AA were there. This man noticed one man with a holster and a .45 Texas six shooter. He asked to see the weapon and the soldier handed it to him. Our guy cocked the gun and did not realize the hammer was filed so it would fire when released. It went off entering the base of that soldier's head and killed him instantly. It was a sad happening.

"Captain Preslock ordered me to take the man under arrest and we took him to the 460AA headquarters for court marshaling after which he was sent back to the states and incarcerated at Fort Leavenworth."

"Once again the odor of spent warm blood and gun powder lingered in my mind and always will. This time, it was one of our own who died because of a soldier in my outfit. We can only carry shame because he was not shipped off to concentration when Sgt. Vassar had talked him out of shooting up his own gun section. He was not stable and should never have stayed. This was not one of the proud moments in our campaign in Luzon. I often think still of the family of that soldier back in Texas."

SURVIVE BY FAITH

It was Skaar's desire to see his family back home and his faith in God that carried Skaar through such tragedies and carries him past the memories to this day.

Barely able to speak from emotion when asked how important his faith was then and is now to him, Skaar simply says "VERY important; It carried me through that and gave me a lot of courage."

Some of Skaar's most cherished war time memories are not of battles won or challenges surmounted but of the gratitude of the Philippine people and the moments of religious comfort he found so far away.

"The Filipino kids came to our camp begging for something to eat. At first we would set our mess kits down with our chow and the kids would clean them out, putting the food in cans they had. These kids did not hungrily gobble that food but scurried off to share with their parents or friends. The kids were skinny and pot bellied and some had open sores. But we were soon ordered to stop this since we needed all of our energy to fight."

The Filipinos were very afraid of the military, even the U.S. military at first, he remembers. "We would offer them food and shelter and treated them as we would treat our family back home but they were still not too

271

trusting since an army (the Japanese) had been there once before and had killed and maimed and raped and robbed them."

But they were very grateful to be liberated, though they still often hid when U.S. troops came by, as they did when the Japanese came through before them.

One old Filipino was especially appreciative of the Americans, Skaar fondly remembers.

"In one village we went through on patrol, there were no Filipinos out except one old man. He came running from behind his hut with his arm outstretched carrying what to him was a prized possession, a bottle of Coke. He recognized our soldiers and tears were streaming down his wrinkled face. He cried out: 'The Yanks are here!' He gave the nearest soldier that Coke, as a universal sign of affection.

"That night, back in the bivouac, we opened that Coke. It was genuine but we poured it out. Nobody thought to save the empty."

Moments like that buoyed the troops' cause and determination to win. But nothing buoyed Skaar's own resolve more than his faith.

Especially important to him were the services he attended, in however crude the accommodations, while in the Pacific.

"While we were in Lucican, Father Dillon — the priest assigned to the 382nd — announced he'd hold an ecumenical Easter service in the end of a school house. The early morning sunrise came streaming through what was left of the bombed out roof. Corporal Dan Neason played a portable organ, which Father Dillon and all of us in the field of battle knew was a true luxury.

"Father Dillon and I had first worked together setting up the entertainment stage in New Guineau. I talked with him as a friend and he soon became one. He was Catholic but was there to council and preach to those of all religions from Catholic to Jewish. He did the best he could wherever he served.

"He served his soldier parishioners very well. He was

272

the right person in the right place. There is surely a special place in heaven for Father Dillon."

PRISONER GUARD

After the atomic bombs were dropped and the war ended Aug. 10, 1945, Skaar was in Luna on the north end of Luzon training and packing to make the final assault on Tokyo. With news of the war's end Skaar was more ready than ever to be home with Polly and their baby.

He had 72 points, over the minimum required to be discharged and was confident he'd be in Cottage Grove soon.

"I figured I was going home but instead I watched about a dozen of 382nd men ship out for home. I still remember the last I saw of the 382nd was a barber chair I had made hanging out the back end of the last truck."

Because he was married and a father, Skaar joined the 743rd, which was to ship back to the U.S.

However, plans changed after a couple weeks, and the 743rd was reactivated, with 800 new recruits, for a post-war assignment.

"We were to guard, feed and house 5,000 Japanese prisoners. My duties expanded from battalion supply sergeant to inventorying and supplying those prisoners. Every day I would check with a Jap Mess Sgt., named Yamamoto, and took five prisoners in a 2 ½-ton truck to Manila for rice and fish. Yamamoto would smile and thank me for the rations. He could speak English and I found out that he was a former student at the University of Wisconsin-Madison. How ironic, I thought, that the U.S. would educate him and he would return to Japan to become our enemy.

"Days turned into months and I had never been so busy. It was not until November of 1945, that my wife and family got mail to me. They did not know where I was after the 382nd until I sent mail home. When an uncle died back home, my mother and wife tried to get an emergency leave home for me but it was denied. It was

not until Dec. 8, 1945, that I finally got those orders to go home.

"When I told Yamamoto I would not be there the next day, he asked me to wait and went to his quarters. He came back with an aluminum cigarette case as a token of remembrance. I have it to this day."

HOME TO FARM AND FAMILY

After several impatient days at a replacement center, a Christmas Eve train ride across the U.S. and an eternity of waiting (a few days), Skaar left Camp McCoy, Wis. and boarded the NorthWestern train home to Madison.

"I was wearing my wool olive drab uniform, all rumpled and unpressed, that had been in my duffel bag since I left the U.S. When I arrived in Madison, the bartender across the street at Bailey's Tavern gave me a dime to call home.

"Polly arrived 20 minutes later and we went home. I got my first look at a very beautiful daughter, curly black hair and sound asleep. We did not wake her that night as we wanted to be alone and went to a hotel in Madison.

"The next day I held my little girl, who was well beyond baby stage, for the first time. She was not accustomed to a father, especially one in a rumpled-olive drab uniform. It took us a while to adjust to each other and a while for me to settle back into civilian life. But every year since, she has become more dear to me; maybe my absence her first year was meant to be. I had a lifetime of experiences, but I had missed so much from being gone so long. Three years, three Christmases; you can't get that back."

Second to seeing his family again, Skaar was happy to be back on the farm.

"When I came home, I was just so thankful to be on a tractor because I could be by myself again. I hadn't been alone in three years; there was always someone there except when you were on guard duty but you had to be alert then. Now I could sit on my tractor and feel the land and be alone for a while. It was my recovery."

It didn't take long for Skaar to adjust nor to return to service — this time in service to his community and service he continues to this day.

"The first year I was home, that spring, they put me on the local school board until the one room school integrated with Stoughton around 1960."

In 1955, two friends rapped on Skaar's door and, with a laugh, informed him that they had just put him on the ballot for town board.

"I told them flat out, 'well, now I'll be on there forever!'"

And he nearly was, except for one two-year term when he was voted out of office. In 1965, Skaar became chairman, a post he held until 1999.

"I wanted to keep on farming and as town chair, you could do both. I've been asked to run for county board and assemblyman but it would be hard to do both with those positions."

Still, Skaar has served his fair share of positions, on Associated Milk Producers Inc. Board, the Dane County Towns Association from 1960-87, since 1963 as president of the Dane County Farm Drainage Board, and as a Bryn Mawr Presbyterian Church trustee and elder. He's also an active American Legion member.

He even found himself arguing his and his wife's rights before the United States Supreme Court back in 1971.

"As individual citizens we rattled the state's cage on personal income tax. We fought so Polly could file an income return for her earnings on the farm and the state called us on it. They said marriage wasn't a legal agreement so we weren't financial partners. The state Supreme Court ruled in our favor and the state appealed to the U.S. Supreme Court, which ruled back to the state. The result was they wrote the Marital Property Law to protect married women and allow them to declare personal income."

But most importantly, his wife says, Gene has been

Wisconsin Gov. Tommy Thompson and Eugene Skaar at a dedication ceremony for the state war museum.

home for nearly 55 years serving as a loving and devoted husband, father (to Vicki and two sons), grandfather and friend.

Home indeed but never as far away as years and miles

The War in the Pacific

might suggest from his war-torn memories.

"I served with men who I shall never regret having known and having been with during those trying days," he explains. "They were not only the greatest soldiers in the world, they were some of my greatest friends — friends and comrades I shall never forget. I think each one of them is a better person because of the experiences we shared. I know I am.

To them, Skaar wrote and dedicated this poem — which appeared in a shorter book, *Heroes Everyone*, he wrote on his war experiences:

When the roll is called up yonder
Of those men who won the war
We remember those comrades
Who now have gone before.

The days of danger, patrols and mud,
The duty, detail and forever guard,
As nights are longer yet by day,
We constantly move forward.

From days to months
A landing, another country, another year,
Finally a mail call from loved ones dear,
A letter from home, alone we shed a tear.

Hiroshima, Nagasaki, the atom bomb drops.
The aggressor is conquered; the war stops.
Our dreams of home and a new life,
Our prayers have been answered; we end the strife.

Each of us home, a new life to begin,
But each of us have memories of the war we did win.
Those comrade we knew so well so long,
We remain in touch; those ties are strong.

In these twighlight years our ranks grow thin.

The Hero Next Door

Our maker above has called him in.
From duty, to family and life's new careers,
We earned the privilege from the war-torn years.

Yet none of us knows when we'll answer the final call.
Alone we will stand inspection before our God.
Our families, our comrades will stay to the end,
For each of us proudly will call him our friend.

SOURCES LIST

Author Interviews (all 1999)
Christianson, Tom, public information officer, Wisconsin Veterans Museum. Madison, Wis..
Church, James, Elk River, Minn.
Geach, James, Hurley, Wis.
Hanusa, Glen, Monona, Wis.
Harrison, Richard, archives manager, Wisconsin Veterans Museum, Madison, Wis.
Kinsler, George, Tomahawk, Wis.
Kohloff, Russ, Beloit, Wis.
Kowalke, Garvin, Universal City, Texas
Reilly, Joe D., Janesville, Wis.
Sanderson, Gerald, Elroy, Wis.
Skaar, Eugene, Cottage Grove, Wis.
Stephenson, Clyde, Appleton, Wis.
Topolski, John, Milwaukee, Wis.
Tresch, Ernie, Oregon, Wis.
Van Selus, Carlyle, Highlands Ranch, Colo.

Oral Histories and Memoirs
H.M.S. Seadog Patrol Report, 16 Feb. - 12 March, 1945.
Letters from: Jim Lyons, Anthony Peleckis, Louis Sandrick, Larry Dover.
Reilly, Joe D., told for the Eisenhower Center at the University of New Orleans
Rooney, Bill, interview transcripts with John Topolski, for 40th Bomb Group Association, Wilmette, Ill. 1988.
Sanderson, Archie, written for the Eisenhower Center at the University of New Orleans
Sanderson, Gerald, My History & Life (so far), Elroy,

Wis., 1999

Skaar, Eugene, Heroes Everyone, Cottage Grove, 1995.

Van Selus, Carlyle, told for the Wisconsin Veterans Museum archives.

Periodicals

Beloit Daily News, "Iwo Jima 50th Anniversary"stories, Neal White, Feb. 18, 1995.

Daily Register, Portage, Wis. "Airman Details His French Underground Escape in World War II," Kristin Gilpatrick, July, 24, 1995

Daily Register, Portage, Wis. "Apollo 13 Hits Home for Portage Native" & "Church Recalls Work on Apollo Team," Kristin Gilpatrick, Aug. 24, 1995

Daily Register, Portage, Wis. "North Freedom Flier Played Part in Hiroshima Bombing" Kristin Gilpatrick, Aug. 13, 1995.

Department of the Army Annual Training Guide, Col. Thomas Turner, Ft. Bragg, N.C., May 16, 1995, p. 10.

Elk River Star News, "Veteran Returns to Normandy," Charmaine Barranco, May 25, 1994.

82nd Airborne Hall of Heroes Dedication Ceremony program, May 24, 1994.

Military, Vol. XVI, No. 3, The Press of Freedom, Aug. 1999, p. 14

Milwaukee Journal, "Holy Card a Faded Reminder of Horror at Sea," *JanzAtLarge*, William Janz, 1998.

Paraglide, "Remembering D-Day," 82nd Airborne Division Association, Summer 1994.

Saturday Evening Post, "D-Day," David Howarth, March 14, 1959.

Saturday Evening Post, "Adak: A Woman Behind Every Tree," Eiot Asinof, July 17, 1965.

Soldiers, "Christmas at War: Battle of the Bulge, 1944," Heike Hasenauer, December 1988.

Soldiers, "letters," March 1989.

Super-Fort, "Sharks Attack B-29 Crewmen," April 13, 1945.

The Hero Next Door

VFW, "Time Capsule in the Aleutians, David P. Colley, May 1993, p. 22-28.
VFW, "Komandorskis: Naval Duel in the North Pacific, John Haile Cloe, May 1993, p. 32.

BACKGROUND SOURCES

American Badges & Insignia, Evans E. Kerrigan, Viking Press, 1967.

American Heritage Picture Dictionary of World War II, C.L. Sulzberger, American Heritage Publishing Inc., 1966

Band of Brothers: E Company, 506th Regiment, 101st Airborne: From Normandy to Hitler's Eagles Nest, Stephen Ambrose, Simon & Schuster, 1999.

The Battered Bastards of Bastogne, George E. Koskimaki, 101st Airborne Division Association, 1994.

D-Day, June 6, 1944, Stephen Ambrose, Simon & Schuster, 1994.

Gerald Sanderson: My History & Life (so far), Gerald Sanderson, Elroy, Wis., 1999

Heroes Everyone, Eugene H. Skaar, PFC, Cottage Grove, 1995.

Leyte Gulf: Armada in the Pacific, Donald Macintyre, Ballantine Books, 1969.

Military & Naval Recognition Book, J.W. Bunkley, Rear Admiral, U.S. Navy (Ret.), D. Van Norstrand & Co. Inc., 1943.

The Military History of World War II: Volumes 11-14, Trevor N. Dupuy, Col. U.S. Army, Ret., Franklin Watts, Inc., 1964.

The Random House College Dictionary, Random House, 1975.

The Spearhead: The World War II History of the 5th Marine Division, Infantry Journal Press, first edition.

Unexplained Mysteries of World War II, William B. Breuer, John Wiley & Sons Inc., 1997.

U.S. Department of Defense Dictionary of Military Terms, The Joint Chiefs of Staff, Arco, 1988.

The Victors, Stephen Ambrose, Simon & Schuster, 1998

The Wall Chart of World War II: A Chronological Presentation of the War That Changed the World, Dorset Press, 1991.

World War II, Ivor Matanle, Quadrillion Publishing Ltd., 1989

World War II Strange & Fascinating Facts, Don McCombs and Fred Worth, Greenwich House, 1983

The Writers Guide to Everyday Life From Prohibition through World War II, Marc McCutcheon, Writers Digest Books, 1995.

ABOUT THE AUTHOR

Kristin Gilpatrick Halverson has had a passion for writing since she can remember, scribbling bits of poems and prose on notebooks and napkins since elementary school.

She was born Aug. 26, 1968, in Edgerton, Wis., to educators Robert and Barbara Gilpatrick and lived in Baraboo, Wis. When she was five the family moved to Cedarburg, Wis., where she graduated high school in 1986. She graduated from the University of Wisconsin-Eau Claire in 1990 with a double major in journalism and Spanish, having studied a semester in Valladolid, Spain. Her love telling stories of the "everyday" people who made history has been a passion since college.

She put that passion to paper as a reporter for the *Kewanee Star Courier* daily newspaper and editor of the weekly *Northern Ogle County Tempo,* both in Illinois, before becoming lifestyles editor and columnist for the *Baraboo NewsRepublic* and *Portage Daily Register.* She won nine press association awards. Since February 1997, she's been a magazine editor for the Credit Union Executives Society, Madison, Wis., while free-lancing stories for *The Capital Times,*Madison.

For the past 12 years, she has also been a big sister to two girls in Big Brothers/Big Sisters programs. She married her best friend Steven L. Halverson, an EdwardJones investment representative, on Oct. 25, 1997. They live in Monona, Wis.